To: Jim.
Merry Christmas 1983.
from,
Tom + Paula.

Growing Fruit and Vegetables

Growing Fruit and Vegetables

Edited by Martyn T. Hall

ORBIS PUBLISHING·LONDON

Acknowledgements

A–Z Collection: 42, 83, 88, 90, 94, 106, 119, 140, 145, 149, 153, 154
Bernard Alfieri: 28, 57, 77, 112, 116, 130, 144, 145, 157, 174
Heather Angel: 32, 33, 43, 52
Ardea Photographics: 44, 45, 80,
Ashmer Seeds Ltd: 134
Barnaby's Picture Library: 110
Pat Brindley: 13, 49, 50, 63, 91, 93, 101, 104, 108, 109, 111, 117, 118, 129, 141
Michael Boys: 74, 75
S. Buczacki: 167
R. J. Corbin: 20, 22, 24, 62, 78, 80, 84, 86, 87, 102, 105, 111, 113, 128, 129, 130, 142, 150, 156, 165
John K. B. Cowley: 16, 17, 108, 131
Crown Copyright: 48
Michael Davies: 54
Samuel Dobie & Sons: 69, 79, 124, 126, 142
H. L. Edlin: 52
Derek Fell: 46, 92
Monica Fuller: 47, 69, 107, 124, 126
Brian Furner: 16, 18, 19, 51, 69, 81, 82, 89, 91, 92, 102, 112, 114, 117, 118, 119, 120, 121, 131, 135, 138, 141, 152, 153, 158, 163, 164, 166, 169
J. Hamilton: 173, 174
Iris Hardwick: 6–7, 159
Angela Hormack: 124, 126
G. E. Hyde: 33, 49
IGDA: 12, 15, 21
Leslie Johns: 61, 133
Clay Jones: 146
Michael Leale: 72, 73
Marshall Cavendish: 64, 65, 66
Elsa M. Megson: 51, 143
Tania Midgely: 50
Ken Muir: 36, 37, 40, 45, 59, 60, 61
Murphy Chemicals Ltd: 32, 34, 167, 168, 169, 170, 171,172
National Vegetable Research Station: 67, 71, 163
Nutting & Thodey: 76, 99, 137
Kenneth I. Oldroyd: 70, 76, 95, 99
P B I: 168
Picturepoint: 97
Ray Proctor: 98, 144
Valerie Rose: 120
Shell Photo Service: 156
Donald Smith: 18, 23, 35, 37, 50
Harry Smith: 9, 10, 11, 12, 14, 24, 25, 26, 27, 28, 29, 30, 33, 38, 39, 41, 51, 53, 56, 61, 65, 67, 78, 89, 90, 94, 114, 115, 117, 122, 132, 146, 151, 165
Suttons Seeds: 85, 97, 116, 137, 139
Thompson & Morgan Ltd: 138
W. J. Unwin Ltd: 99, 100, 122
Michael Warren: 42, 43, 44, 82, 91, 103, 121, 123, 162
D. Wildridge: 10, 24

Originally published in 1978 as *Successful Fruit and Vegetable Gardening*
Reprinted in this edition 1982

Printed and bound in Spain
by Graficromo, S.A. — Cordobá

ISBN: 0-85613-459-7

CONTENTS

INTRODUCTION

The publication of a book comprising both fruit and vegetables is of particular value and interest to the gardener for, in the past, it has been customary to deal with these two subjects separately. Possibly this was because a collection of top fruit would normally be planted to form an orchard which would be quite separate to the vegetable garden. Nowadays, except for the plantings of commercial growers, the orchard as such is on its way out. The average garden is not large enough to accommodate this luxury.

This does not mean that interest in top fruit has been squeezed out. It would, I feel sure, be true to say that there has never been a time when the value of fresh fruit and vegetables has been so widely accepted or so much appreciated. Continuing high prices (often with no improvement in quality) have prompted many people to grow at least part of their requirements.

At first sight it would seem that smaller gardens and an increasing awareness of the value of fresh fruit and vegetables pose a difficult problem. Fortunately, the plant breeders have not been idle. The old standard and half-standard trees have largely given way to bush trees where a pair of steps give height enough to gather the crop. More recently, the dwarf and semi-dwarf types, which are small enough for the average garden, have been developed. In choosing these, care should be taken that the varieties will cross-pollinate each other; good nurserymen are always willing to give advice on this point. Cordons and espaliers are two other forms which are eminently suited to the smaller garden. These can be used alongside paths or as a dividing screen between different parts of the garden. All these types are fully described in this book.

House walls should not be forgotten, either. Correctly trained and tended trees grown on house walls yield superb fruit. Some of the more delicate fruits such as apricots, peaches and nectarines will flourish on south-facing walls, while a north or east wall will support a Morello cherry. Another good subject for a house wall, or a cool greenhouse, is the vine. The renewed interest in home wine-making has turned attention to vines, and new cultivars have now appeared which can be expected to set and ripen a reasonable crop. Moreover, we have learnt that grapes can be grown much farther north than was at one time thought possible.

Where soft fruits are concerned it has long been the custom to grow strawberries in the vegetable garden and include them in the vegetable cropping plan. A row of raspberries does not take up too much space if it is sited across one end of the garden or alongside a path. They, too, can be used to make a leafy and productive screen. Gooseberries can be grown as cordons to edge a path, and blackberries and loganberries, trained on wires stretched between posts, also make leafy screens or can be used to clothe boundary fences.

In this connection I would make a special plea for the loganberry – a neglected fruit. Picked fresh from the cane they are tart unless they are *fully* ripe, and this may have turned some people against them, but in pies and flans they are excellent. They also make a splendid jam and a superb jelly.

Most housewives will want a few blackcurrant bushes. This fruit, as many people know, is of particular value because of its high vitamin C content. Nowadays, labour costs of picking are so high it is becoming increasingly difficult to find blackcurrants in the shops, and when they are found they are expensive. Redcurrants and whitecurrants are not so well known, but a handful of redcurrants in a mixed fruit pie gives the whole a delightful, piquant flavour, and they make a fine jelly.

Then, too, for those who like to try something a little more difficult and unusual there are fruits like the Chinese gooseberry and the Cape gooseberry.

With both fruit and vegetables the importance of freshness can never be stressed too much. Most people like strawberries, but this delicious fruit can only be tasted to perfection when a sun-ripened fruit is picked and eaten straight from the plant. The Victoria plum is one of the most popular fruits; perfection here is a ripe fruit freshly picked from a tree on a sunny wall. The limp lettuce so often offered in shops or market stalls has very little in common with a Sugar Cos lettuce, cut and washed only a short time before it is eaten. Nor has the flaccid bundle of leaves which so often passes for spring cabbage much resemblance to a well-hearted spring cabbage, with its own distinctive, 'nutty' flavour. Peas and beans are two other subjects where freshness is so important.

Growing one's own fruit and vegetables allows one to choose those varieties which are of first-rate table quality. The commercial grower, understandably enough, concentrates on the varieties that yield heavily, and pack and travel well. These are not always those of the highest quality.

More and more people to-day are setting aside a part of the garden for a vegetable patch, and more and more people are taking an allotment, or joining the queue in the many areas where the supply of plots does not equal the demand. All the basic vegetables, with their cultivation, will be found within these pages, together with some not so well known.

The increase in Continental travel has awakened interest in vegetables such as courgettes, aubergines and sweet peppers. Courgettes (which are really baby marrows), are not difficult to grow. Aubergines and sweet peppers, although more demanding, should prosper in those areas where outdoor tomatoes do well, and the use of frames or cloches will go far to ensure their success.

Frames and cloches are a great asset in the vegetable garden. Protection to growing crops can be given at both ends of the season, and because of the growing time saved it is often possible to sow or plant an extra crop. A small greenhouse, even without heat, can be used for growing lettuce and raising vegetable seedlings, in addition to its more usual role of producing a crop of tomatoes.

The smaller the plot the more essential it is to get maximum results from it. Intensive cultivation is one of the subjects covered in this book. Another is the correct spacing of vegetables and the latest methods by which space can be saved without crowding the crops. This is a field in which research is still going on.

There is valuable information on the different *types* of vegetables, and the importance of choosing the right *varieties* – subjects of special value to those who are new to vegetable gardening. Recommended varieties are given for all fruits and vegetables. Some of these are old favourites, others are new varieties of merit. Gardeners are often accused of being too conservative in their choice of varieties. New varieties of vegetables are always coming along and, by trying several each season, important discoveries can be made. After all, the established varieties were once new introductions!

Common diseases and pests are listed, together with the measures to be taken against them. Regrettably, such information is necessary, but they should not prove too depressing; no gardener is likely to encounter all the pests and diseases mentioned here. Where fruits and vegetables are grown in good conditions, from tested seeds of healthy stock, disease should not be a problem. Prevention is usually better than cure and is certainly less expensive! Pests will be encountered from time to time, and should be dealt with at the first sign of trouble, *not* when they have gained a firm hold.

Garden terms in common use (which may sometimes puzzle the beginner) are explained in brackets in the text and have been gathered together for easy reference in a useful glossary at the end of the book.

Even with careful planning the supply will sometimes exceed the demand, but the fruit and vegetable gardener of to-day has no need to waste any of his precious crops. A surplus of fruit can be jammed or bottled, or put into the deep freeze. Most vegetables freeze well and can be stored in this way for use in lean periods. There can be no doubt that the advent of the deep freeze has given a boost to fruit and vegetable growing. Another important point is that the gardener who grows his own fruit and vegetables can pick and freeze them when they are in the peak of condition.

Young married couples with growing families, in particular, will be anxious to make the fullest use of their gardens, and this book will help them to do just that. Others, perhaps setting up house for the first time, or planning their first garden, will need advice on what fruit and vegetables they can include. Even the older hands, it is hoped, will find much to interest them and something of use.

Gardening is a relaxing hobby. The stresses and strains of modern living can be soothed away in the garden, and with an added bonus of fresh fruit and vegetables, the therapy is all the more valuable and beneficial.

March, 1978 Martyn T. Hall

TOP FRUIT

APPLES

The apple tree is one of the most adaptable of plants. The main garden types are dwarf and semi-dwarf bushes and cordons. There are also various ornamental forms, but for the gardener who wants to produce a good succession of apples throughout the season by the simplest means, bushes and cordons are the best proposition.

Many of the apple varieties bred over the past few decades do not grow well on their own roots. This means that cuttings rooted may not grow at the required pace or strength. To solve these difficulties, apples are budded (grafted) onto specially developed rootstocks. The rootstocks resemble the original species of *Malus* from which most apple trees are derived. They are usually denoted by numbers and letters which refer to the research stations where they were developed. All apple trees bought from a nursery will be grafted on a selected rootstock.

Always plant bushes and cordons with the graft unions between the rootstock and the chosen variety clear of the soil, and never allow soil to cover them in later years. The union is the swelling at about 15cm (6 in) above the stem base. If the trees are planted to the soil mark on the stem, the unions will be at the correct height above soil level.

Bush trees

The ultimate size of a bush tree depends primarily on the rootstock. Determine the choice of rootstock by the general nature of the soil. The stocks which give dwarf and semi-dwarf trees are M9 and M26 respectively. There is also MM106, which gives trees somewhat bigger than true semi-dwarfs and produces bigger crops, but which is still easily managed from ground level.

Planting and staking

Dwarfs grow well in rich soil, but are often too weak for light, sandy ones. On these soils plant either semi-dwarfs or trees on MM106 stock. On rich soil, dwarfs reach a final overall height of about 1·4m (4½ ft), and at maturity will produce an average annual yield of about 11kg (25 lb) of fruit.

Semi-dwarfs on lighter land will reach about 1·8m (6 ft) at maturity, to give an average of 14kg (30 lb), and trees on MM106 on light land will reach 2·5–3m (8–10 ft) with a cropping range averaging

RECOMMENDED VARIETIES

DESSERT APPLES	WHEN TO EAT
George Cave	early to mid autumn (August–September)
James Grieve	mid autumn (September)
Merton Worcester	mid to late autumn (September–October)
Lord Lambourne	late autumn to early winter (October–November)
Sunset	late autumn to mid winter (October–December)
Chivers Delight	late autumn to late winter (October–January)
Merton Russet	late winter to mid spring (January–March)
Sturmer Pippin	mid spring to early summer (March–May)
CULINARY APPLES	
Arthur Turner	late summer to late autumn (July–October)
Grenadier	mid autumn (September)
George Neal	mid to late autumn (September–October)

All these apples are of excellent quality and are comparatively easy to grow. Although the culinary varieties overlap they are worth planting as a trio, because each has its distinct flavour.
Cox's Orange Pippin is a universal favourite but can be difficult for beginners, so choose Sunset instead.
Some of the listed varieties may be difficult to obtain. Other varieties which are quite good and reasonably easy to grow as dessert apples are:

Discovery	early to mid autumn (August–September)
Ellison's Orange	mid to late autumn (September–October)
Golden Delicious	early to late winter (November–January)
Egremont Russet	late autumn to mid winter (October–December)

16–18kg (35–40 lb). Trees grafted on M26 and MM106 can grow on rich land, when final tree heights will be above those for light soil, and crops therefore bigger.

Bush trees are free-growing. Plant them at minimum distances of 2·5m (8 ft) on M9, 3m (10 ft) on M26 and 3·7m (12 ft) on MM106.

Permanent stakes are needed for dwarfs; semi-dwarfs will need initial staking, but stakes can sometimes be removed later. Trees on MM106 usually do not require stakes.

Shaping bush trees

Except for simple formative pruning, you can leave bush trees for the most part to grow at will. There are some detailed systems of pruning but simple methods give good results, bring the trees into crop at the earliest possible time, and keep them in crop thereafter.

The principle is to have an open, cup-shaped arrangement of four or five main branches (main leaders), each with at least one fork (sub-main leader), to give a final complement of at least eight or ten branches. These provide a more or less permanent basic structure, and should receive little pruning to keep them in shape once the structure has been established. They support the many side shoots (laterals) which carry the fruit.

If you buy a two- or three-year-old tree it should have had the basis of this arrangement already formed in the nursery. However, in the first winter you must tip back each leader to just short of an outward-facing bud, removing 15–25cm (6–9 in) of wood. This will stimulate the growth necessary to build up a rigid framework. You may have to repeat this tipping for the following two or three winters (according to whether the trees were planted as three- or two-year-old specimens). Be sure, also, to cut out any strong inward growths that would cause congestion or compete with leaders. Never allow laterals to rub against leaders. Some young trees may be without sub-main leaders, but these will grow later. When they appear treat them exactly as for the main leaders.

Carry out routine annual pruning of the formed tree in winter. Remove congesting laterals and keep the tree's centre open to air and sunlight. If you do this every year you will find there is not much wood to remove each time.

Top left: James Grieve has an excellent flavour and is frost-resistant. Far left: Merton Russet crops heavily and is crisp and tart. Left: Sturmer Pippin is an excellent early-fruiting variety

Cordons

Cordons are single 'rods' between 1·8m (6 ft) and 2·5m (8 ft) long, clothed throughout most of their length with short fruiting spurs. They are planted 60–90cm (2–3 ft) apart and inclined at 45 degrees, being trained along 2·5m (8 ft) bamboo poles which are fixed to three wires at about 60cm (2 ft), 1·2m (4 ft) and 1·8m (6 ft) from ground level, tightly stretched between strong end posts. These posts should be 2·5m (8 ft) long, buried 60cm (2 ft) and with extra support from wood inside strainers. Long rows need intermediate posts at 4·5m (15 ft) intervals. A typical garden row of cordons takes up no more room than a row of runner beans. Make alleyways 1·8m (6 ft) wide between the rows to allow easy access.

Pruning cordons

On newly-planted trees cut back all laterals longer than 10cm (4 in) to three buds. Good strong rods seldom need cutting, but tip weaker ones back by 15–25cm (6–9 in). Thereafter lateral pruning is done in summer, but any further rod tip stimulation needed is done only in winter.

Above: an apple bough in blossom.

Below: first pruning of dwarf bush. Inset shows graft union 8cm (3 in) above soil

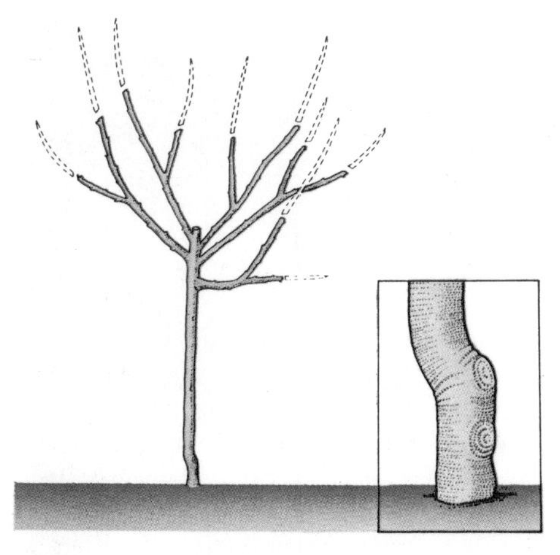

Below: cordon supports. Insets show knot for tying cordon to poles, and graft union

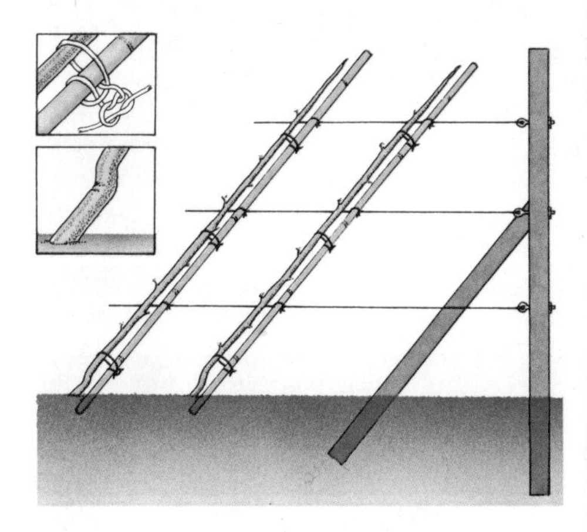

Below: summer pruning of laterals and sub-laterals on cordon apple trees

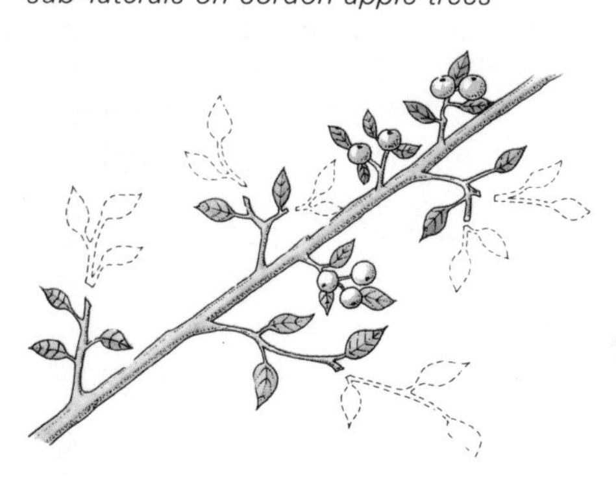

Below: Lord Lambourne flowers early and is a regular and heavy cropper. Below right: Sunset, a good tree for garden cultivation, bearing fine-flavoured apples

Lateral pruning aims at fruit spur formation, and a good rule of thumb is: 'laterals to three leaves, sub-laterals to one leaf'. So cut all laterals growing directly from the rods to the third good leaf from the base, and cut all other shoots (sub-laterals) to one good leaf from the base. Cut only when the shoots are mature along the base portion – that is, when the base is woody, the shoot sturdy, and the leaves fully-formed and a dark green colour. As they do not all mature at once, the cutting process goes on over a period from late summer until early autumn (mid July to mid August) according to the area in which you live. It is absolutely imperative that you don't cut the shoots until they have reached the correct stage of ripeness. Cutting immature wood leads to masses of secondary growth and ruins all attempts to get fruit spurs to form. Even with perfectly-timed pruning some secondary growths may occur from time to time, and these must be removed at their points of origin in mid autumn (September).

Choosing an apple tree

The choice of apple varieties is very wide and it is essential to ensure that the ones you choose will cross-pollinate. Most apples will only produce fully and regularly if their flowers are pollinated by pollen from another variety that blossoms at the same time. There are a few self-pollinating varieties, but even these crop better if cross-pollinated.

If you only have room for one tree, check to see whether any of your neighbours own an apple tree and choose a variety to complement it.

Consider only top quality trees. They cost more than inferior ones, but they will pay over and over again. Cheap trees usually end up on the bonfire. Find a first-class nurseryman, order your trees in good time and take the advice offered in the catalogue.

APRICOTS

The apricot is a truly delicious fruit that deserves a place of honour on a warm wall. It has been grown in Britain for more than 400 years, though not widely until the last century, when not only the great establishments but also the cottage gardens of the countryside had their apricot trees.

There are three primary points to consider in the culture of apricots: the flowers appear early in spring (February) and are therefore susceptible to frost damage; many fruits may fall if the trees are dry at the roots; and fruit set may be sparse unless the flowers are hand-pollinated, because there are few pollinating insects about when the flowers open in early or mid spring (February or March).

Frost protection

Except perhaps during very cold spells apricots grown on south-facing house walls will benefit from some warmth, even if it is only 'domestic' heat from a room that, being south-facing, is probably well lived in. The aim is to conserve this warmth, as far as possible, around the apricot flowers, and also to provide direct protection from frost.

This can be achieved, to a considerable extent, by draping the tree with two or three layers of fish-netting (or net curtaining) each evening when frost is forecast, from the time when the buds first show colour. The material must be clear of the tree, and is best arranged over a temporary frame, that need only be a light construction and can be used again each year. It is a simple matter to attach the upper edge of the netting to a batten forming the top rail of the frame, so that the net can be rolled up and let down as necessary – possibly even until mid summer (June).

Preventing root dryness

Root dryness is a common hazard of wall trees but is easily prevented by watering and mulching. The blossom and fruit-setting period is critical, and so is the time of initial fruit swelling. Throughout these phases, if the weather is dry, water thoroughly till the root area is soaked. As soon as the fruit has set, lay a good mulch over the roots. This will conserve soil moisture for several weeks, thus reducing the need for summer watering.

Right: a fine crop ready for picking

Hand-pollinating and thinning

To effect pollination, touch the flowers lightly with a small, soft brush when the pollen is visible. Do this at midday. If the weather is very dry it is advisable to 'prime' the stigmas by misting the tree with slightly tepid water. Although the pollen grains will be transferred from anthers to stigmas more effectively if the grains are dry, the stigmas may not be fully receptive if they are also dry. Thus the object of misting is to dampen the stigmas so that the pollen grains will adhere more effectively. Mist the tree before noon, and repeat daily for two or three days before the anthers open to shed their pollen. Stop the misting as soon as pollen starts appearing.

Juicy apricots should be the result if the fruit is properly thinned (right)

RECOMMENDED VARIETIES

New Large Early ripens in late summer (mid July).
Large Early ripens from late summer (late July).
Moorpark ripens from late summer to early autumn (mid July to early August).
Croughton ripens from late summer to early autumn (mid July to early August).
Breda ripens from late summer to early autumn (late July to mid August).
Shipley's Blenheim ripens from early autumn (early August).

The fruits should be thinned, at intervals, from when they are nut size until almost full size, so that those left to mature and ripen have about 13cm (5 in) between them.

Choosing and planting trees

Dwarf fan trees are the best for most situations, though even these can reach 2·5m (8 ft) in height and at least 4·5m (15 ft) overall spread. It is extremely important, wherever wall space is limited to an area of about these dimensions, to stipulate the trees on St Julian A rootstock. This is the least vigorous of the stocks commonly used for apricots. Trees on stronger stocks will make far too much growth for garden work, and attempts to keep them within bounds by pruning will almost certainly bring disaster because apricots will not put up with hard pruning.

The best time to plant is late autumn to early winter (October to November). Wall wires will be needed for the training of the main branches. An average spacing for the wires is 25cm (9 in) apart; the final number will depend on the height of the tree. The lowest one starts at about 30cm (12 in) from ground level.

Varieties of apricot

The earliest variety is New Large Early (not to be confused with Large Early) which normally ripens in late summer (mid July). It has large, golden-yellow fruits flushed dark red, with orange-coloured, aromatic flesh and a fine, melting flavour. Large Early matures somewhat later; in spite of its name it does not often ripen before the end of summer (late July). From late summer to early autumn (late July to mid August) there is Breda. This variety is medium-sized and coloured a deep golden-orange with purplish-red spots on the cheek exposed to the sun. The flesh is a rich orange colour, scented, very juicy and sweet flavoured. The kernel is also sweet, unlike that of other varieties.

Another late summer variety, that continues until early autumn is Moorpark. The fruit is medium-large with greenish-yellow skin having dark, reddish markings. The flesh is orange-coloured, scented and very sweet.

One of the finest-flavoured varieties is Shipley's, also called Shipley's Blenheim. This was raised about 150 years ago by Miss Shipley, a daughter of a gardener to the Duke of Marlborough. It blossoms later than the others mentioned. The fruits are yellow-skinned with an orange flush deepened by red. The flesh is very juicy, aromatic and superbly flavoured.

A good variety for jam-making is Croughton. The fruit is small to medium in size, the skin golden-orange with flesh of a similar general colour but deeper. It has a sweet flavour, but is slightly coarse in texture and not very juicy. It should be picked from late summer to early autumn (mid July to early August), with special care being taken to gather the fruits as they ripen, because if they are left beyond the correct stage they may be too dry for fine-quality jam.

You may find some variations between your fruit and the description given here of it. This is because apricot seedlings come nearly true to the parents but with slight differences in skin colour; and among the older varieties at least, seedlings have almost undoubtedly been propagated and sold as the varieties from which they arose, though in strict terms they are not true to these.

Soil requirements

The only fertilizers normally needed are bonemeal at 35–100g per sq m (1–3 oz per sq yd) and sulphate of potash at 25–35g per sq m (¾–1 oz per sq yd), both being applied in autumn, though not necessarily every year. The important thing to avoid is lush growth, which is induced by nitrogen fertilizers. Such growth is unfruitful, and the cutting back necessary to keep it within practical bounds will almost certainly lead to trouble, with dieback of many of the shoots being a strong possibility.

Apricots are by nature quite strong growers, but provided the growth is natural and not forced, it will not be too lush. Some lime may be needed to maintain the pH a little above neutral. Good drainage is imperative. Do not attempt to grow apricots on wet, heavy land; to do so would be a waste of time and money.

Shaping and pruning
Formative pruning follows the standard procedure for fan training (as described in the section on Peaches, page 21).

Existing branches on newly-bought trees are tipped back in early spring (February) by some 15–25cm (6–9 in). The resultant extensions are trained in, fanwise, during summer. One good shoot is selected from the upper side of each of the topmost branches, and these two new ones, which should grow from the basal portions of the parent branches, are trained in. They are tipped back early in the following spring (February) and, again, their extensions are trained in during summer. The centre of the fan is thus filled in by leading more shoots off in this way.

Branch tipping thus proceeds until all the branches have reached the desired lengths. Thereafter pruning with knife or secateurs is replaced by pinching with finger and thumb, which is confined to the sideshoots, or laterals, growing from the branches. Here the object is to induce fruiting spurs to form. When the laterals have made some 8cm (3 in) of growth, which will normally be in early summer (May), pinch out their tips. Secondary growth will then arise. Pinch the tips of these above the first leaf as soon as this leaf has fully expanded. Fruit spurs will then form. Laterals start to appear before the fan has been fully formed. For some time, therefore, branch pruning and lateral pinching proceed together, in their respective seasons.

Some laterals may be more vigorous than others; these should be stopped at a correspondingly greater length, say 10–13cm (4–5 in) with their secondary growths being stopped at one leaf. If strong laterals are stopped initially at 8cm (3 in) and subsequently at one leaf, there might be a further flush from the second stopping. Such a response inhibits fruit spur formation and is an example of the unbalanced growth that it is so important to prevent.

Ripening and picking
Although apricots must have warmth during the growing season, it is natural warmth from the sun that they require, not artificial heat. (The wall warmth mentioned earlier is in a different category, relating to frost prevention.) If you want to grow a greenhouse apricot, the house must be cold. Any artificial heat will cause flower-drop and force out the very type of lush growth that leads to disaster. Even in districts too cold for outdoor apricots this rule still applies.

The fruits must be left to ripen on the tree. The ideal time to pick them is in the early morning when they are literally 'dew fresh', though not many people would be picking and eating apricots at that hour. Nevertheless, that is the time when they are at perfection.

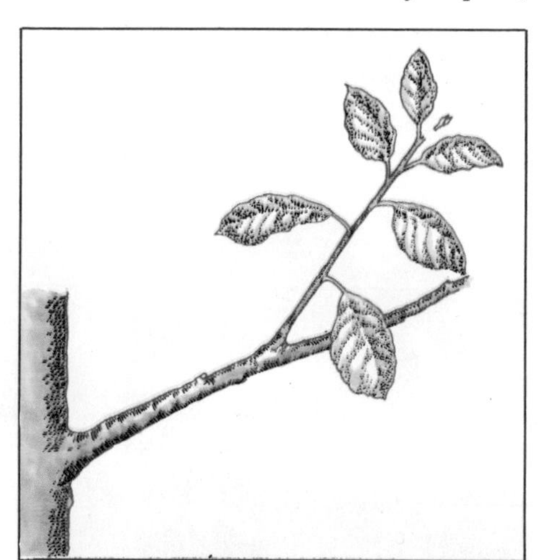

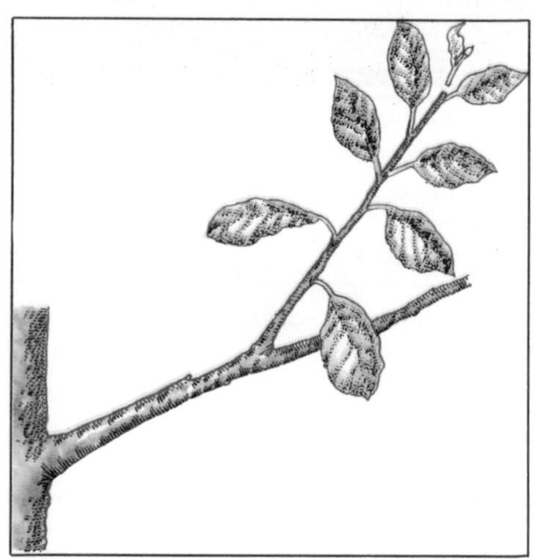

Above left: when laterals are about 8cm (3 in) long, pinch out tips. Above: pinch out tips of secondary growth above first fully-expanded leaf
Left: growing on a south-facing wall that provides warmth gives good results
Below: Moorpark fruits in late summer

Pests and diseases
The most common enemies of apricots are caterpillars, silver leaf disease and a condition known as dieback.

Caterpillars Certain caterpillars attack the leaves of apricot trees but they are easily controlled either by hand picking or by applying a spray of derris or pyrethrum if their numbers warrant it.

Silver leaf Fungus disease that causes the foliage to appear silvery, and infected shoots and branches die back. Cut off infected wood about 15cm (6 in) below the end of the diseased area. Treat large cuts with a protective paint.

Dieback Condition in which large branches and shoots begin to die back. Caused by bad soil conditions or, more commonly, by a fungus that enters through a wound. Cut out and burn infected wood and paint the cut with a protective paint.

GRAPES

There are several fine grape varieties that will succeed on a sunny wall and in an unheated greenhouse, so do not be put off growing a grape vine on the grounds that greenhouse heating is too expensive for 'luxury' fruits. The main points for successful cultivation are good greenhouse hygiene, simple temperature control, correct humidity and ventilation and attention to watering.

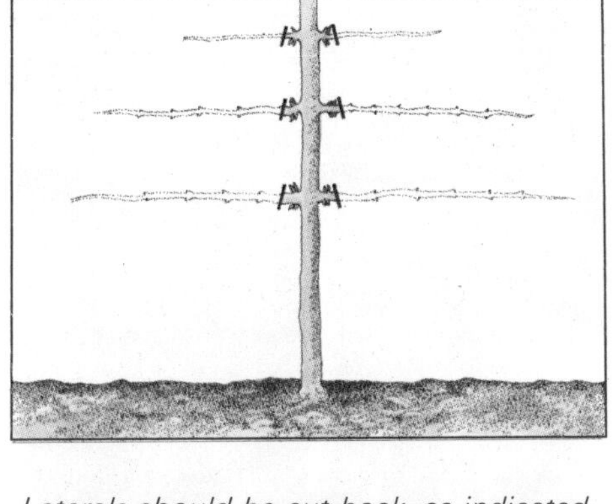

Laterals should be cut back, as indicated, to two buds from the rod

When trusses form, the laterals are cut back to the second leaf beyond each truss

Most old gardening books advise planting preparations for grapes involving the use of chopped turfs and various measures that were all very well in the days of large gardens and plentiful labour, but are hardly applicable nowadays. Neither are they essential, though good ground preparation is necessary.

For greenhouse culture, planting in an indoor border is better than in an outdoor one from which the vine stem is led into the greenhouse (preferably through the foundations). But you may need to use an outdoor border if a large area is to be given over to a vine, for it will then need to produce an extensive root system to promote the required growth. In the small greenhouse, top growth must be more limited, and this means limiting the root area accordingly.

Right: fine-flavoured Black Hamburg
Below: a luxuriant greenhouse crop

Preparing the soil

The essential factor is good drainage. Vines will flourish in a range of soils, even quite heavy ones, so long as their roots are never dry and never waterlogged. If you think drainage needs improving in heavy soil, dig out a border 60cm (24 in) deep and 90–120cm (3–4 ft) wide, line the base with a layer of packed mortar rubble 25–30cm (9–12 in) deep, mix a barrow-load or two of sharp garden sand with the subsoil (which should be kept separate from the topsoil), return this to the trench and then return the topsoil. The border can be as long as you wish, but should not be less than 1.2m (4 ft). This is obviously quite an undertaking, but remember that the vine may be with you for a lifetime so it will pay to make a really good job of improving drainage where necessary. You can spread the workload over many weeks prior to autumn planting. Time will be needed, anyway, for the heaped border to settle.

For general-purpose preparation, where the soil is well drained and needs no special measures, dig thoroughly over the area that the roots will gradually occupy during the first few years. Mix in some old mortar rubble, a half-dozen or so shovels of bonfire ash, and bonemeal at about 100g per sq m (3 oz per sq yd). There is not much point, at this stage, in applying bonemeal over more than the immediate area into which the roots will grow. To start with a length of 1.8m (6 ft) – 90cm on either side of the planting spot – will suffice. So a 90cm (3 ft) wide border will have an initial area for bonemeal of 1.5 sq m (2 sq yd).

Planting and training

Vines are best planted in the autumn. If your plant arrives in a pot, take it out, spread out its roots and place it in the hole to the depth indicated by the soil mark on the stem. Fill the hole with fine soil, firming in carefully as you go. Water thoroughly (using a rose on the can) and apply a mulch of well-rotted compost.

There are several ways of training vines. You can stretch wires across the roof area of the greenhouse at about 30–38cm (12–15 in) apart – or along one wall. The simplest method, and almost certainly the best for beginners, is to grow the plant as a single rod (stem) from which laterals grow out right and left to be trained along the wires. The main rod is allowed to reach the top wire, which should be 30–38cm (12–15 in) below the roof ridge, so that the vine leaves are not pressed against the glass. Although the length of the laterals is more or less determined each season by the pruning, there may be circumstances (such as when growing outdoors or in a large greenhouse or conservatory) when they can be left uncut. They will then reach their full natural length which can be 1.2–1.8m (4–6 ft), giving an overall spread of 2.5–3.8m (8–12 ft). Make provision for this by planting the vine at the centre point of the greenhouse or the wall, rather than squeezing it in at one end in order to save space. Planting at, or near, one end of the house or wall is possible, but you will have to keep the laterals on that side of the rod short, or even suppressed. This may result in loss of crop, because the yield from the other side of the rod will not necessarily be increased.

Pruning a vine

After planting the vine, cut it back to four buds. The top bud will normally send out an extension in due course. Train this in vertically, to form the rod, and rub out any shoots breaking from the other three buds. If the top bud fails, use the best growth from one of the remaining buds. While the rod is being formed, allow no more than about 60cm (24 in) of each season's extension to remain at the season's end. If much more than 60cm (24 in) is made, cut off the portion above that length (as soon as the leaves have fallen) to ensure a strong rod capable of producing fruiting laterals annually for many years. Thus it will take five summers to form a 3m (10 ft) rod: this is about the average size for the amateur's greenhouse.

The buds on the rod will produce lateral shoots. From each bud, two or more laterals will start into growth in spring. Remove all but the strongest one when they are 2–5cm (1–2 in) long, and train the retained ones along the wires. It is unlikely that flowers will appear at this early stage, but if any do, cut them off. It is imperative to prevent both premature and excessive cropping. Allow no fruit to form until the third season, and then only one bunch. In the fourth season three bunches will be ample, and in the fifth, six will be enough. Thereafter one bunch per 30cm (12 in) of rod is a useful guide, giving ten bunches from a 2.5m (10 ft) rod, though a well-established vine in good health can safely produce more.

For the first two years, leave the laterals to grow freely during the growing season. As soon as possible after leaf fall, cut them all back to one or two buds close to the rod, and cut the rod back to 60cm (24 in) as already described. Some of the lighter laterals will automatically be removed by cutting back the rod. Thereafter, the laterals must be cut on a routine spring and summer basis.

In spring reduce the buds to one per lateral. Then allow laterals to grow. Subsequently stop all laterals that have made flower trusses at two leaves beyond the trusses, and all flowerless ones at approximately 75cm (2½ ft). Stop secondary growths (arising from the stoppings) at one leaf.

When the rod has reached the full required height, cut back its tip each autumn to well-ripened wood. This will mean removing only a few centimetres in seasons of good ripening weather unless the vine is extremely vigorous and makes long tip growth. In this case, however, it is better to check its growth in summer when you are doing the lateral cutting. Cut back all laterals again in the autumn. This summer and autumn treatment is given every year.

Left: a good wine grape and a generous cropper, Seyve-Villard; right: Noir Hâtif de Marseilles, an early black variety that does well in the open; below: use vine scissors for thinning and harvesting

Care of growing plants

The year's routine maintenance programme begins after harvesting and pruning. Start by giving the greenhouse a thorough clean, including both sides of the glass. Remove the top few centimetres of soil and replace with a fresh layer mixed with well-rotted compost and bonemeal. If necessary treat the plants for mealy bugs (see Pests and diseases section). Maintain full ventilation from now until early spring (February), the object being to keep the vine dormant during the winter. In early spring adjust the ventilation lights to give about 10°C (50°F) and damp down in sunny weather.

Reduce the young shoots to one bud and train in resulting new growth. Take precautions against powdery mildew if necessary (see Pests and diseases section).

By early summer (May) growth will be rapid. Tie in as necessary, keeping leaves clear of the glass. Hand pollinate the flowers by first tapping the rod smartly to expel the flower caps; then enclose the trusses in your hand and run it lightly downwards. Pollination should be done about midday. The pollen must be dry, so at this period avoid damping down and overhead sprinkling. Close side lights to conserve heat.

Tending fruiting plants

After pollinating, damp the greenhouse down and water the border thoroughly. When the grapes have set, remove any poor bunches and, a little later, remove any of the surplus in accordance with the number to be retained in relation to rod length. Use vine scissors to thin the grapes. You will have to learn by experience how many to remove, but as a general guide one-third of the total per bunch is removed, always taking off lateral fruits and the inward ones on each strig (fruit stem) and leaving the tip ones. If outward grapes are removed, the shape of the bunch at maturity will be spoilt, and this applies particularly to the fruits at the top or 'shoulder' of each bunch.

From now on keep the temperature at around 10°C (50°F) and the atmosphere fairly moist, but never at the expense of ventilation, and never let the vine be 'cooked' on hot days or scorched by fierce sunlight. If the weather is very hot, apply a light limewash (or Coolglass) to the outside of the glass.

After thinning the bunches, apply a standard vine fertilizer (according to maker's instructions), soak the border and mulch with compost. Stop secondary growths from routine pruning.

In late summer (July) the grapes swell visibly and then cease for two or three weeks. This is the stoning period (when the pips swell) after which the grapes will resume growth. When they do, you can apply a second dressing of fertilizer if past experience has shown that one dressing is not enough; but if growth is good and the fruits normally finish well, a second dose of fertilizer will not be needed.

From late summer through early autumn (July to late August) open the lights early in the morning and close them in late afternoon (after damping down thoroughly) but leave a roof light open all night. Ensure that the soil is always moist, but do not flood the border. In early to mid autumn (late August) reduce the humidity by decreasing the amount of damping down. The grapes will nearly be ready for harvesting. Examine them frequently for any that are rotting and remove these immediately. Use vine scissors for harvesting and do not handle the grapes; hold each bunch by its stalk.

Wall-grown grapes

Except for measures obviously referring to a greenhouse, the year's programme outlined here applies equally well to a wall-grown vine outside. Perhaps the main point for special attention with wall culture is watering. Wall plants always dry out at the roots much more quickly than others do because the wall absorbs moisture along its base.

Pests and diseases

Vines in a greenhouse may be afflicted by mealy bugs and powdery mildew. Grape splitting can also be a problem.

Mealy bugs This small, whitish, bug-like creature is often troublesome in the greenhouse. It sucks the sap from the stems and leaves of vines (and other plants), thus greatly weakening them. If you have had trouble from them in the past, then after harvesting and pruning remove loose bark (under which they hide) from the rod and spray with tar oil at 500cc to 10 lit (1 pt to 2½ gal) water.

Powdery mildew Produces greyish-white powdery patches on stems, leaves and grapes. If the vine was seriously affected the previous year, then spray with dinocap when the shoots are 5–8cm (2–3 in long). This is not a routine treatment but a special measure. Follow it with another spray before flowering, when the laterals are 30–38cm (12–15 in) long. Apply a third spray just before flowering and a final one after fruit set.

If mildew was previously troublesome but not severe, then apply only three sprays, omitting the very early one.

Thinning out non-flowering laterals, to give better air circulation, can also help to reduce the incidence of mildew.

Grape splitting A condition arising when the grapes are 'overcharged' with sap. In this event, leave about one-third of the flowering laterals unstopped in the following year, to absorb sap that would otherwise have gone to the grapes.

RECOMMENDED VARIETIES

Black Hamburg For cold or heated greenhouses and warm walls in mild areas; produces fine-flavoured grapes.
Royal Muscadine For cold or heated greenhouses and warm walls in mild areas; has pale amber-skinned fruit.
Muscat du Samur Fine-flavoured, very early-fruiting variety suitable for wall culture.
Brant Late-fruiting variety; produces heavy crops of small black grapes and beautiful autumn foliage; can be grown outdoors in mild areas.
Noir Hâtif de Marseilles Bears an early crop of black, muscat-flavoured fruit.
Seyve-Villard Excellent white grape for wine-making; crops and ripens well.

PEACHES AND NECTARINES

The melting quality of peaches and nectarines, allied with their delicate skins, gives the impression that these fruits are tender subjects on which infinite care must be lavished. In fact, although they are often grown in heated or unheated greenhouses, fine specimens come from trees growing outdoors in temperate regions.

The nectarine is a smooth-skinned form of the peach. Technically it is a mutation, or bud sport, which arose more than 2,000 years ago. Many people prefer nectarines to peaches, finding they have a more delicate flavour.

As a bush tree, the nectarine has not proved as popular as the peach in northern Europe, and it is said to be somewhat less hardy. It is, however, a fine subject for fan training.

Follow the advice given for the culture of peaches. Pests and diseases that affect peaches also apply to nectarines.

Choosing the site

Far from being tender subjects, peaches are hardy enough to succeed in the open almost anywhere except really cold regions such as northern Britain, provided the trees are sheltered from spring frosts and cold winds. Peach flowers open early, sometimes in a period of sharp frost, so never plant a tree in a hollow or in low-lying land that terminates in a wall, building or dense hedge. These form barriers to the flow of air, and such positions are frost traps.

Shelter from frost really means exposure to air flow; the hollow may look like a well-protected site, but it will be lethal to peach flowers. There is, however, a difference between air flow and blasting winds. These can do as much damage to blossoms as can frost. The ideal site is open and sunny but not windswept.

Soil requirements

Peaches do not need any special soil requirements, but the soil must be up to normal garden fertility, adequately drained but moisture-retentive. The best aid to moisture conservation is a generous mulch of compost laid over the root area each spring.

A tree on a lawn is very attractive, though not everyone likes the idea of a mulched tree in this position. If the soil is rich, the tree may well succeed without a mulch, but on lighter land the competition for water with the lawn may be too much for an unmulched tree. The fruits will be small and lacking in juice.

A peach without juice is a certain sign of insufficient soil moisture. Peach trees need large quantities of 'free water'; this is the term given to water which is present in the root zone of trees and which they can draw on when they need it during the growing season.

Training and pruning bushes

The initial framework of a bush tree comprises five or six main leaders (main branches) which soon produce fruiting laterals (sideshoots). After planting, tip back the main leaders by about 30cm (12 in) to just above a growth bud to encourage further extensions. Repeat this treatment annually for a year or two until the tree head has reached the desired size. Fruit is borne only on two-year-old

RECOMMENDED VARIETIES

FRUIT	TIME OF RIPENING
PEACHES	
Bush	
Peregrine	early autumn (August)
Rochester	early autumn (August)
Fan-trained	
Hale's Early	late summer (July)
Peregrine	early autumn (August)
Rochester	early autumn (August)
Bellegrade	mid-autumn (September)
NECTARINES	
Early Rivers	late summer (July)
Lord Napier	early autumn (August)
Elruge	early autumn (August)

Below: nectarine Lord Napier. Right: two peaches – Peregrine (above) and J. H. Hale

wood, thus when laterals have carried a crop they are cut out to make way for maiden (one-year-old) ones. Cut these out when they, in turn, have cropped the following year.

The entire pruning can be compressed into five words: cut out the fruited shoots. Nothing could be simpler.

The only other point needing explanation is that the tree's framework may need modifying from time to time when the main leaders, or parts of them, cease to send out laterals. When this happens, cut the leader back flush with a strong outward-going sideshoot; this sideshoot then becomes a replacement leader. If there is no suitable growth present, remove the old leader completely at its point of origin. On a well-growing bush peach tree there is always an ample supply of maiden laterals to take over from the fruited ones, and always enough strong shoots to replace old leaders. Indeed, there is often too much growth; in this case the surplus, which will congest the tree if left, must be cut as early as possible in summer. From time to time there may be shoots with dead tips. This is nothing to worry about unduly; simply remove the tips in spring, cutting to two buds or so below the dead portions.

Training and pruning fans

The other tree form is the fan which is grown on southerly-facing walls and fences. Buy trees already partly formed, because fan forming is skilled work. The tree will have foundation branches growing out left and right from a short stem. The centre will be open, but will fill up as the fan becomes established.

The tree should be planted about 25cm (9 in) away from the wall. Erect a supporting system of parallel wires, about 15cm (6 in) apart, tightly strained, and firmly held by wall nails. Autumn is the best time to plant. Tip back the foundation branches by about 25cm (9 in) to stimulate further growth. Repeat the tipping as necessary each year, until the branches have covered their allotted wall space. Shoots will grow out from the basal portions of the upper sides of the foundation branches. Train in one from each of the two highest foundation branches, thus adding to the original complement. Tip back the two new extensions by about 25cm (9 in) in winter. These additional two branches may be enough to complete the basic form, but if more are wanted, repeat the process annually as appropriate, until the fan's centre has been filled in.

Make all these cuts for stimulating new shoot and branch growth down to small,

Below: cut back fruiting laterals after harvest, as indicated. Bottom: Worn-out old leader cut out in favour of new one

Below: basic shape of 3-year-old fan, and right, wall wires fixed with vine eyes

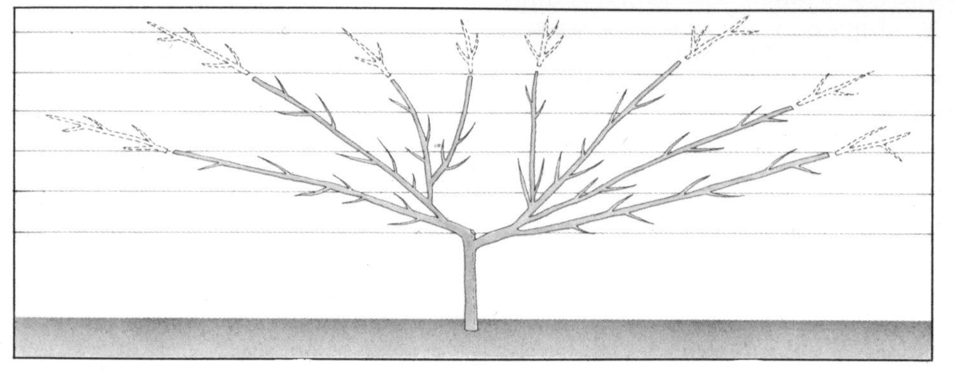

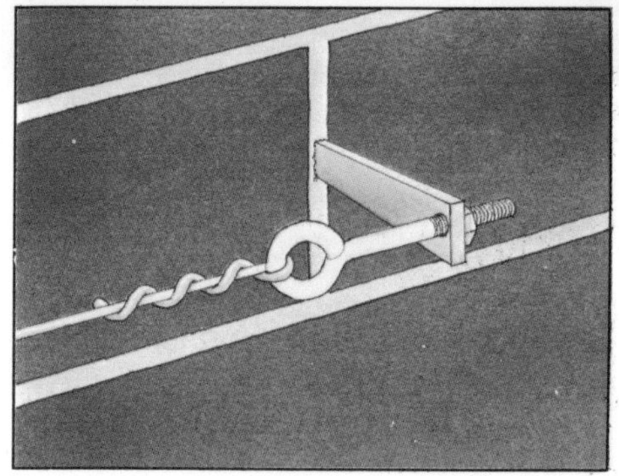

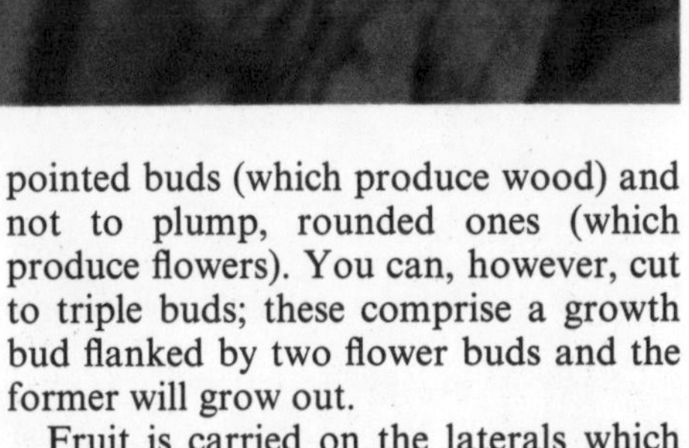

pointed buds (which produce wood) and not to plump, rounded ones (which produce flowers). You can, however, cut to triple buds; these comprise a growth bud flanked by two flower buds and the former will grow out.

Fruit is carried on the laterals which grow from the foundation branches. As with the bush tree the guiding principle is to cut out the fruited shoots after harvest. There will be plenty of maiden ones for the next year's crop. Tie these in neatly from time to time during the season. They grow out from both the upper and lower side of branches, and sometimes may be excessive in number, causing congestion. In this event thin them to some 15cm (6 in) apart, either by removing the surplus ones or by cutting them back to two or three leaves.

Ideally, you should not tie the young foundation branches directly to the wires, but train them along thin bamboos. When the branches have become well established, remove the canes and then tie the branches to the wires with soft string.

Left: peach Rochester. Above: tree form of Peregrine on Brompton root stock

Thinning the fruit

The peach tree usually sets an enormous number of fruits. Quite a lot will fall naturally within a fortnight, but the number remaining will frequently be far too many. If they are left they will not reach anything like the full size, and quality will be poor. When they have reached the size of small walnuts they must be thinned to about 25cm (9 in) apart. This may seem a shocking waste, but it is absolutely essential if you are to achieve a crop of good-quality fruit instead of dry little specimens.

Pests and diseases

Bush peach trees are not usually attacked by pests to a degree that warrants spraying, but the fungus disease peach leaf curl must be prevented. Fan-trained trees are vulnerable to greenfly and red spider mite.

Peach leaf curl An extremely destructive fungus disease that causes the leaves to become red and distorted. The fungus takes up residence on the tree, over-wintering in the bud scales and breaking out again in spring when some of the unfolding leaves may already be red along their edges. Affected foliage is swollen and fleshy, and symptoms are unmistakable. To prevent peach leaf curl, spray in early spring (February) just before the buds burst, using lime sulphur, liquid copper fungicide or captan. Repeat the treatment a fortnight later and once again at leaf fall.

Greenfly These aphides can be serious pests of peaches grown as fans on walls. They curl the leaves, stunt the growth and greatly depress yields. Apply a tar oil wash in mid winter (December) to kill the overwintering eggs. Alternatively, spray in spring using either a systemic insecticide, or liquid derris or malathion, to check greenfly that have hatched.

You must apply spring sprays before the greenfly have curled the leaves. Keep a close watch for early damage and for the appearance of greenfly. There are two main species found on peaches; one is green, the other is blackish-brown. Bush trees are rarely attacked by greenfly.

Red spider mite Causes the leaves to become mottled and bronzed, though not curled. The leaves fall prematurely, and trees can be severely checked. Spray with derris, malathion or a systemic insecticide just before the flowers open and again at petal fall. The timing of these applications is critical; adhere to it strictly, otherwise control will not be effective. Red spider mites are much less of a menace on bush trees than on fan trees.

PEARS

The finest-quality pears are not only delicious fruits, but are one of the supreme tests of the gardener's skill. Yet they are by no means difficult to bring to the picking stage. The secret of perfection lies in picking at the right time, and in good storage of the 'keeping' varieties.

To grow well, pears need a soil that is warm, fairly rich, moisture retentive and well drained. Use a good-quality compost, dug in to a spade's depth when planting and also as a spring mulch. Give new trees a good start by picking off any flowers appearing in the first spring after planting, but leave on all the surrounding leaves. Do this at white bud stage when the blossoms are easily handled.

There are several tree forms you can grow. Pears are ideally suited to the trained systems, which are very attractive, and the normal forms of these are fans, cordons and espaliers.

Pruning bush trees

Bush trees, the easiest form to grow, are planted 3–3·5m (10–12 ft) apart. Their shape is virtually the same as that of the bush apple. They have an open centre and a cup-shaped arrangement of main and sub-main leaders.

The formative pruning work is the same as for apples: cut back the leaders of the newly-planted tree by about 15–25cm (6–9 in) to stimulate further extension growth and repeat the process in subsequent winters until the tree has made a sturdy framework.

Most pears are free flowering. This means that the laterals growing from the main and sub-main leaders (the branches and their forks) will form many fruit-bearing spurs – the fat-looking buds that are seen in winter. On some varieties multiple spurs (or spur clusters) develop from the original buds. The pears will hang from these in bunches. If you cut the laterals too much they will not make fruit spurs, but will make growth instead. So keep lateral pruning on bush trees to the essential minimum to ensure good crops.

You must, however, remove congesting laterals; cut back fruited ones that are past their prime (and are producing poorly or not at all) to growth buds near the base, so that fresh laterals will grow out for future cropping.

One of the signs of a neglected tree is a vast conglomeration of old, unproductive fruit spurs, with few or no young laterals. This condition need never arise if you cut back laterals in winter when they begin to show symptoms of decline.

Some varieties (such as Doyenné du Comice) droop noticeably. This is a natural habit, and it would be wrong to try to prevent it by excessive cutting. Nevertheless, some corrective work may

be needed. Where a badly drooping leader has a strong shoot growing near the bend, cut off the drooping part flush with the point of origin of the upright shoot. The latter will then become a replacement leader. If there is no shoot present, cut back the drooping part to a fruit spur just behind the bend.

It cannot be emphasized too strongly that you must not prune bush pear trees hard or haphazardly. Prune lightly, with a definite purpose for every cut. If you are in doubt, wait until the summer before doing any corrective pruning.

Pruning trained pears

With trained forms the pruning system is entirely different. Whether you are growing fans, cordons or espaliers, comparatively hard summer pruning is essential. The underlying reason is that trained forms are kept to the right shape and size, and encouraged to bear heavy crops by a combination of root and top restriction. This can be achieved only by summer pruning, since this automatically checks growth and stimulates fruit bud formation. Winter pruning has the completely opposite effect.

Prune as for cordon apples, by cutting all laterals growing directly from the cordon rods (or from the main branches of fans and espaliers) to the third good leaf from the base; cut all other sideshoots to the first good leaf from the base.

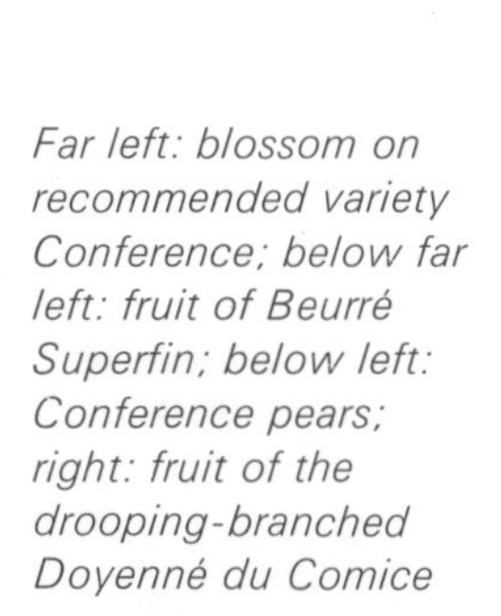

Far left: blossom on recommended variety Conference; below far left: fruit of Beurré Superfin; below left: Conference pears; right: fruit of the drooping-branched Doyenné du Comice

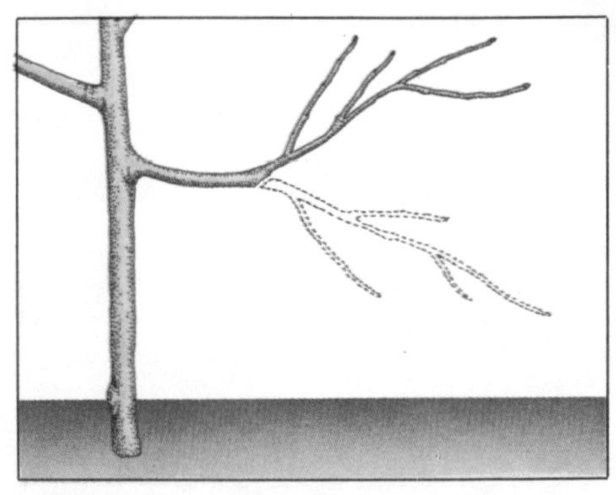

Above: cut back a drooping leader to an upper shoot, which then becomes the replacement leader.
Below: upright cordon showing graft

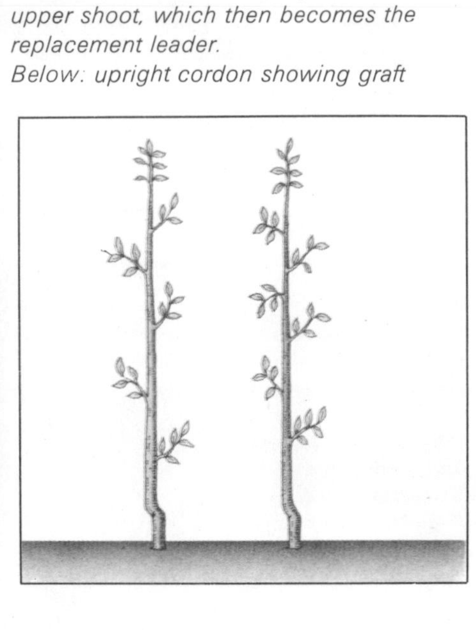

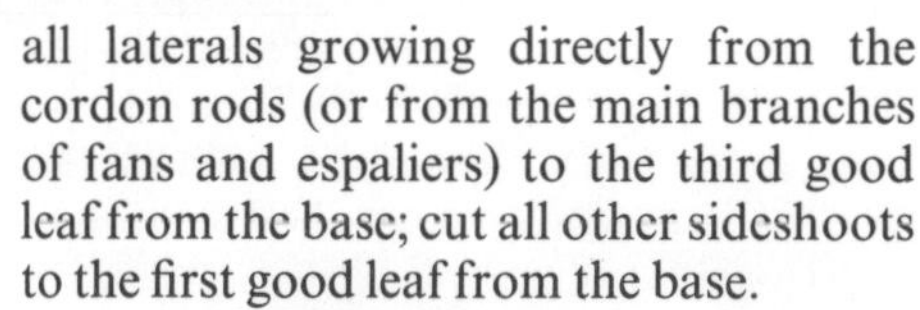

As with apple trees, do not prune pear shoots until they are ripe along their basal portion – that is, when they are clothed in dark green leaves along that portion and resistant to bending. This stage is reached earlier than with apples, occurring throughout early to mid summer (mid June to mid July). In autumn remove any secondary shoots arising from the cuts at their points of origin.

Training cordons

You can grow cordon pears either at an angle or vertically. The latter way is excellent for training up pergolas or arches. Plant the trees 75cm (2½ ft) apart and train them up the two sides of the pergola. Then lead the trees over the top so that each tree meets its opposite number to form a covered arch.

Upright pear cordons are ideal for a sunny wall, especially if it is high and narrow. Bear in mind the balance between the size and shape of your wall and the dimensions of the tree you wish to grow. A wide wall is suited to fans and espaliers, a narrow one to vertical cordons. Do not make the mistake of cramming a fan or espalier onto a short wall as you would need to chop the trees hard in order to make them fit the space.

Training espaliers

Espaliers are horizontal cordons arranged in parallel tiers left and right of a central stem. Several nurseries supply partly-formed specimens, usually of three tiers, that are just right for small or medium-sized gardens. Tip back the branches or 'arms' of the newly-planted espalier by 15–25cm (6–9 in) to encourage further extensions. When they have grown to the length you require, remove the tip growths in early spring (February) to form lateral buds; in due course, these will become the fruiting spurs. Continue winter tipping for two to three seasons.

Espaliers can be grown against walls or fences, either as path edgings or as divisions between different parts of the garden. The overall length at maturity varies somewhat according to type, but on average is about 3·6m (12 ft), that is 1·8m (6 ft) on both sides of the stem. Thus you should estimate 3·6m (12 ft) as the minimum planting distance where more than one tree is wanted. Initially, you will need a supporting system of posts and wires. Train the branches along the wires – the supports can often be removed later once the tree has established its shape. Do not train the trees directly against the wall, as free air circulation behind the trees is imperative; instead, use a temporary structure of light posts.

Training fan trees

Fan pear trees are basically the same shape as the peach fans (see page 21) and are also supplied partly formed. Tip back the leaders or 'ribs' in winter for extension growth; the fruit is carried on short spurs along these. All trained pear trees are, in effect, multiple cordons until they reach their desired length.

Picking and storing

The seasons given under Recommended Varieties are for edibility and not necessarily for picking. It is extremely important to pick at the right time and store properly. Skin colour is not a guide to picking and pears must never be left to ripen on the tree. Instead, use the 'lifting' test; it is not infallible, but it is the safest guide to follow. Lift each pear to a horizontal position; if it parts readily from the spur, then it is ready for picking. If they fall into the hand at a touch, then this usually means they have been left too long; if they fall off untouched then they are definitely past the picking stage, and may go mealy or 'sleepy' in store. If they leave the spur with a snap, then you are probably picking too early, and the pears will shrivel up in storage.

Right: the variety William's Bon Chrétien will cross-pollinate with both Buerré Superfin and Conference
Below: three-tiered espalier, showing the branches trained along the wires

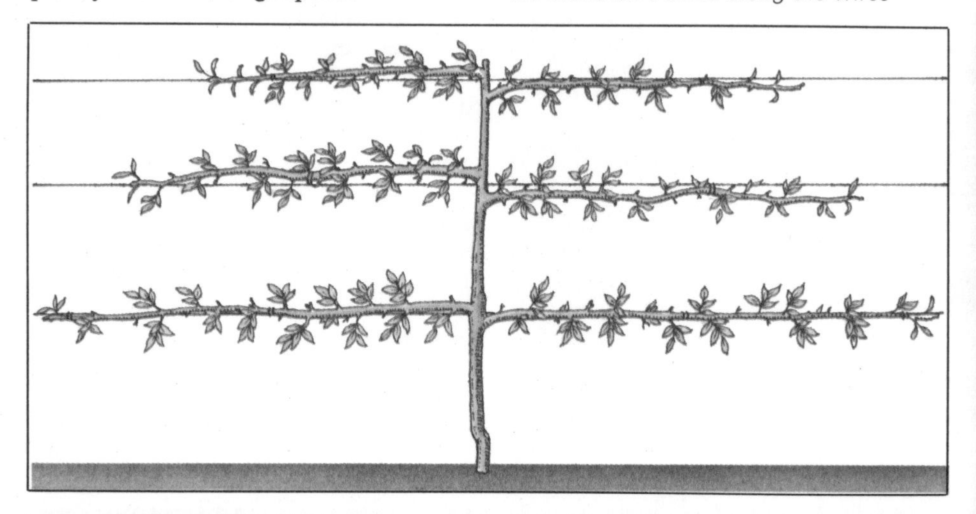

RECOMMENDED VARIETIES

TYPE	WHEN TO EAT
Doyenné du Comice	early winter (November)
William's Bon Chrétien	mid autumn (September)
Conference	late autumn to early winter (October–November)
Buerré Superfin	mid autumn (October)
Marie Louise	late autumn to early winter (October–November)
Winter Nelis	early to late winter (November–January)

Of course, they will not all reach picking stage together, so you can pick them over a period and allow them to ripen over a similar period.

At the correct stage for harvesting, very few varieties will have their full skin colour; some may have a flush or tinge of colour, others may still be green. The full colour will come later. Most storage pears attain perfection over a period, but once attained it lasts for only a short time – though only the connoisseur would detect a deterioration of quality early on.

Keep storing pears in a fairly dry atmosphere at 4–7°C (40–45°F) and lay them out on shelves or trays. Storage cabinets with pull-out slatted trays are ideal. If you are storing the pears in a shed keep it free from strong smells; oil, fertilizer, paint, binder twine and creosote tend to destroy the flavour and aroma of pears. When the stalk ends yield to very slight pressure, bring the pears into a temperature of about 15°C (60°F). They will then complete their ripening process quite soon.

Choosing for cross-pollination

Provide for cross-pollination by choosing a succession of pears. Choose varieties whose flowering periods overlap sufficiently, but avoid grouping certain varieties that will not cross-pollinate, even though their blossoms do coincide. Almost the only pear that is fully self-fertile is Fertility Improved, but it is not one of outstanding quality. The variety Conference produces some fruits from its own pollen in some seasons, but many of them are seedless and misshapen.

The queen of pears is probably Doyenné du Comice which is in season in early winter (November). Of the many available varieties, any of the others listed under Recommended Varieties would be suitable to go with it. If you only want two trees (the minimum for cross-pollination) select them from Conference, William's Bon Chrétien and Buerré Superfin, or from Doyenné du Comice, Marie Louise and Winter Nelis. William's Bon Chrétien is a dual-purpose variety, being a splendid dessert pear *and* excellent for cooking.

If you only have space for one bush tree, buy the Family Tree which comprises three varieties on one rootstock. Varieties are selected by the nursery for quality, effective cross-pollination and seasonal succession. Naturally, the yield of each type is only one-third of the total, but can still average about 30kg (15 lb) from a well-grown tree. One excellent combination offered is William's Bon Chrétien, Doyenné du Comice and Conference.

PLUMS AND CHERRIES

Plums (including gages) and cherries are both popular fruit and most larger gardens have room for at least one or two of each, especially if there is a suitable large wall for them to be trained against. Some of the finest varieties of plums are self-pollinating and will produce without pollinating partners, though all cherries will require a second pollinating variety.

One of the great advantages of plums is that varieties grown on St Julian rootstock are semi-dwarf, suitable for growing in the open or as fans on walls. In addition, many of them are self-fertile – a useful point if you only have room for one tree. A single bush tree of Victoria plums can give around 18kg (40 lb) annually, from the sixth to the fifteenth year from planting, and often much more in later years. A fully-grown fan tree of a size suitable for the average garden should give about 9kg (20 lb) annually. Many garden trees, however, are under-nourished and so fail to reach these yields.

Soil requirements

Plum trees are fairly high nitrogen users, and they also need potash and phosphates. A routine feeding programme for well-cropping bush trees should be 20–35g nitro chalk or sulphate of ammonia per square metre ($\frac{1}{2}$–1 oz per sq yd) of root area in mid spring (March), 20g ($\frac{1}{2}$ oz) sulphate of potash similarly in late winter (January), and 100–140g ($1\frac{1}{2}$–2 oz) superphosphate during every second or third autumn.

The fan uses less nutrients than the bush, though roughly in the same proportions; adjust the application rates to not less than half of the above figures.

Plums prefer either a neutral or a slightly alkaline soil; if acidity is suspected, test the soil and, if necessary, apply lime (according to the instructions) to bring the pH up to 7 or a little above. Most soils will eventually be depleted by heavily-cropping trees, so you must maintain the balance in the 'soil bank'.

Planting the trees

Plant bush trees 3·5m (12 ft) apart, and fans 4·5m (15 ft) apart. For each bush tree, dig a circle approximately 1m (3 ft) in diameter and add half a barrow-load of well-rotted compost. Mulch this area in spring for the first few years. For fans, dig a hole about 1·20m (4 ft) long, and up to 60cm (2 ft) out from the wall. Plant the tree 20cm (9 in) from the wall, allowing 60cm (2 ft) each side of the stem.

Right: the favourite variety Victoria, a self-fertile plum and a good cropper
Below: the ideal sour cherry, Morello

Pruning the trees
Winter formative pruning for plum trees is the same as for the other fruit trees we have mentioned so far (see pages 11, 20 and 24). Because of the risk of silver leaf disease, routine pruning is done only in summer. Silver leaf rarely attacks the thin wood cut during winter formative work, but could infect the thicker wood removed in routine pruning. Prune preferably in early mid summer (early June), otherwise defer it until early autumn (late August).

Plums fruit on both old and new wood, but do not leave the old wood until it has become worn out. As the best quality fruit is carried on young shoots and twigs, try to have as much new wood as possible on the tree.

Routine pruning
Routine pruning consists of eliminating congestion each year, taking out older wood and retaining the young. This will often mean sacrificing a few plums, but the results will be beneficial at harvest time. Prune systematically, retaining the basic shape of the tree, and (as far as possible) leaving the main leaders uncut. On some varieties, notably Victoria, the leaders may droop. In this event cut back as appropriate, removing the badly drooping portions, or cut back to upward-growing laterals if these are present.

Caring for fans
When pruning fans, train in the laterals and remove any that are growing into the wall or straight out. In late summer (July) tip back laterals at the fifth to seventh leaf from the base. Remove the older fruited shoots when the crop is finished, retaining the younger ones, and shorten earlier tipped laterals by half.

As the fan settles down to production, establish and maintain a clear pattern of pruning. There will be laterals that have cropped for two years or so, others just starting into crop, and maiden ones not yet in fruit. Keep this rhythm going, but avoid having masses of surplus shoots. Some maiden shoots may have to be suppressed for a year by cutting them back to one or two buds, while others may have to be removed altogether.

Pests and diseases
The main enemies of plums are silver leaf and two types of aphid.
Silver leaf The commonest disease of plums, particularly Victoria, is silver leaf, a fungus infection that invades newly-damaged wood. In its early stages, when only a few leaves are silvered, it can often

be controlled by cutting away all the silvered shoots down to clean, unstained wood. A heavily-silvered tree, however, will rarely survive. The silvered leaves are not infectious, but in time the wood bearing them dies, and fungal infections appear on it. These discharge masses of spores that endanger not only plums but other fruit in the garden as well. In the final stage of silvering the leaves are very torn, with brown edges and brown-edged holes.

Branch breakage under heavy crops is a frequent cause of silver leaf. To prevent this, thin the small plums in mid summer (June) to one per cluster. Excessive crops will not produce high-quality fruit, so thinning is often needed anyway. Where branches remain heavily laden even after thinning, prop them up with stout forked sticks, with a pad in the fork to prevent chafing. Never let wall ties bite into the wood of fans, and always allow sufficient room for shoot and branch expansion.

If any branches get damaged, remove them at once and paint the wounds immediately with grafting wax or horticultural bitumen paint. It is useless to take these protective measures long after the damage has occurred; if silver leaf is going to infect it will do so at the time of the damage or very soon afterwards. If treatment is left until too late and the wood is already infected, the disease will be sealed in.

Aphides Two types of aphid can seriously debilitate the trees. One type causes severe leaf curling, particularly of Wyedale. The other infests the undersides of leaves, secreting honeydew on which black, sooty-looking mould forms. Regular attacks of aphides can cause failure with garden plums. A tar oil wash thoroughly applied in mid winter (December) will kill most of the eggs, but if this presents difficulties apply malathion at bud burst (just before the flowers open) and repeat two weeks later.

Damsons

Do not forget damsons, which make lovely pies and jams, and are useful for bottling. They are grown and cared for in the same way as plums.

Cherries

Cultivation of cherries is similar to that of plums, although the sweet varieties do present problems.

The two biggest difficulties of sweet cherries are that, except for a variety now on trial, all sweet cherries must be cross-pollinated (which means that at least two trees are needed to give correct partners), and all varieties produce standard trees that grow too large for the average garden. They take some years to start bearing fruit, and when they do fruit many cherries are ruined by birds. Those that escape the birds are usually out of reach unless you use long ladders.

These problems may be reduced by a new semi-dwarfing rootstock now on trial and giving good results. However, it will probably be some time before such trees are available to the home gardener. The alternative to this problem of size is to grow sweet cherries as fans against a wall.

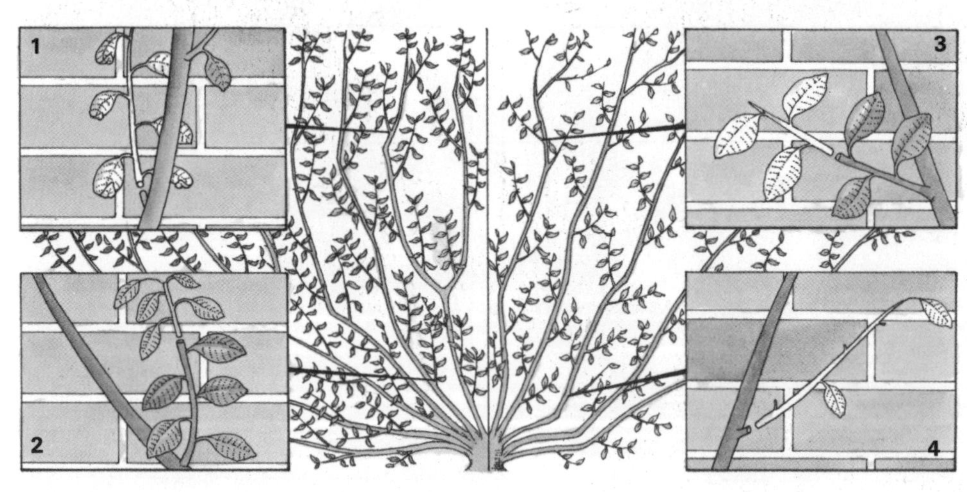

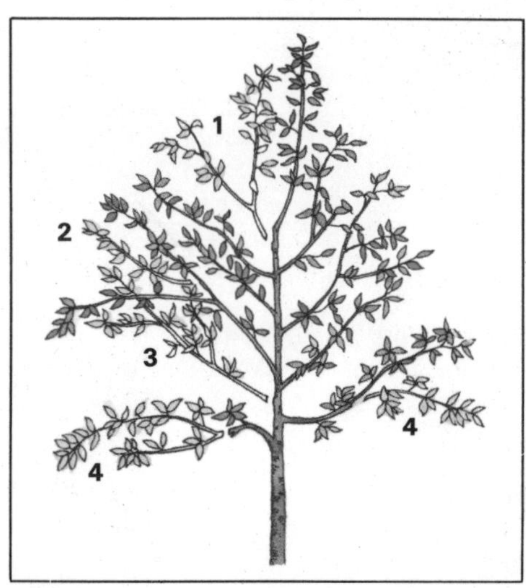

Fan trees

A wall space of about 10·5m (35 ft) and 2·5m (8 ft) high is necessary for fan trees. Plant two trees about 5·25m (18 ft) apart. Fan cherries are built up in the same way as fan plums. The routine pruning

Below: self-fertile gage, Denniston's Superb, ideal for use as dessert fruit

To prune a fan-trained plum tree
Above left: before fruiting, **1** *cut back laterals growing into wall, and* **2** *tip back laterals at fifth to seventh leaf from the base in late summer (July); after fruiting,* **3** *shorten earlier tipped laterals by half, and* **4** *remove older fruiting laterals*

For routine plum pruning
Left: **1** *cut back lateral competing with main leader;* **2** *cut back long laterals running alongside sub-leaders;* **3** *cut out old sub-leaders; and* **4** *cut out drooping leaders back to an upward-growing lateral or downward-growing bud*
Above: support heavily-laden branches of plum tree with a forked stick, placing a protective pad in the fork to avoid rubbing of branches

comprises stopping the laterals at the fifth or sixth leaf. In early autumn (late August) shorten these shoots to about three leaves. The object is to get the tree to bear fruit on fairly short spurs close to the main branches. Pruning is virtually the same as for plums, as fruits are produced on old and new wood. Mulch with well-rotted compost at fruit set, with about 20g of sulphate of potash per sq m of root area ($\frac{1}{2}$ oz per sq yd), and 90g ($2\frac{1}{2}$ oz) superphosphate similarly every second or third year. After a heavy crop give 25–35g per sq m ($\frac{3}{4}$–1 oz per sq yd) of nitro chalk or sulphate of ammonia in late winter (January), but generally 20g ($\frac{1}{2}$ oz) will be enough.

Pests

The great scourge of sweet cherries is blackfly, which cripples the tip leaves and generally makes a mess. Winter tar oil kills most of the eggs, or the alternative measures given for aphides affecting plums can be taken. To protect against birds, drape the fan with lightweight netting while the fruit is ripening.

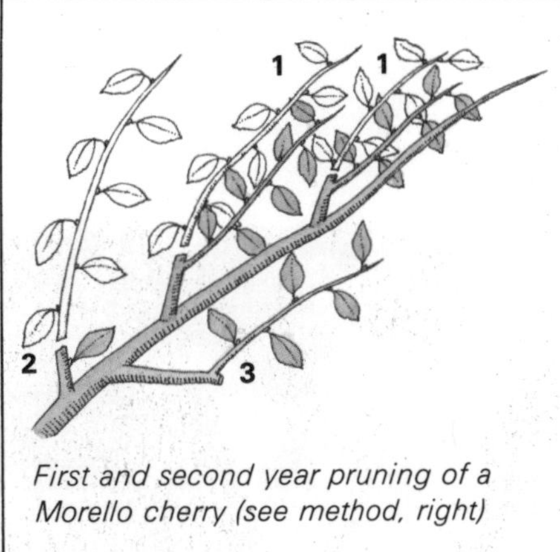

First and second year pruning of a Morello cherry (see method, right)

Morello cherries

Morello cherries are classed as sour and are not dessert fruit, but they are splendid for cooking and jam-making. Bush trees are fairly small and easily managed, as are fans. Fans of sour cherries thrive on any wall aspect and can be planted in positions that would be too cold for most other fruits.

Allow a wall space of about 4·5m (15 ft) for fans with the stem in the centre. Build up the fan from its nursery stage exactly as for plums. Thereafter train in laterals and remove fruited ones or cut them back to basal buds as appropriate when the crop is over. This *must* be done every year, for if neglected the system will break down. It is equally important to prune bush trees each year. With both forms the annual pattern to maintain is two-year shoots in crop and one-year shoots for the next year's crop.

Fruit is carried only on two-year wood, so when routine pruning is done either in mid summer (June) or just after harvest, you should remove the fruited shoots and retain those of the current season, **1**. Many of the fruiting shoots send out new ones from basal growth buds. If there are too few new shoots in the tree, cut the fruited ones back to the basal buds instead of removing them, **2**. If **2** was carried out in the previous year, it will look like **3** now (see left).

Pests and diseases

The main enemies of cherries are blackfly, blossom wilt infection and birds.

Blackfly As for sweet cherries, you can use winter tar oil to combat blackfly, or take the alternative measures given for aphides affecting plums. However, it should be made clear that Morello cherries can – and often do – survive and, indeed, flourish for many years without ever becoming infested.

Blossom wilt infection which causes shoots to die back is almost endemic on Morellos in some areas. Cut out all affected twigs as soon as they appear. However, it is far better to prevent severe infection by spraying with Bordeaux Mixture or liquid copper fungicide just pre-flower.

Birds The best protection for Morello cherries while they are still ripening is afforded by lightweight netting.

RECOMMENDED VARIETIES

PLUMS AND GAGES

Coe's Golden Drop Grows well on sunny walls. Has superbly-flavoured golden or amber fruits and is pollinated by Denniston's Superb or Victoria.

Denniston's Superb Self-fertile gage that provides fine dessert fruit.

Jefferson's Gage Must be pollinated by Denniston's Superb; also produces dessert fruit, golden yellow with red spots.

Laxton's Delicious Bright red dessert plum of good quality that can be planted with Wyedale.

Quetsche Richest-flavoured stewing plum; self-fertile. From specialist fruit nurseries.

Victoria The favourite variety and ideal choice if only one tree desired. Self-fertile, the fruit is ideal for dessert, cooking and jam.

Wyedale Excellent English jam-making plum, pollinated by Laxton's Delicious.

DAMSONS

Merryweather Heavy cropper, with large fruits excellent for bottling.

Shropshire Prune The finest damson, with fruit that makes lovely pies and jam. Like Merryweather, is self-fertile.

SWEET CHERRIES

Merton Favourite Fruits mid to late summer (June to July), producing richly-flavoured black cherries. Cross-pollinates with **Bigarreau Napoleon,** a variety producing red or yellow fruits in late summer.

SOUR CHERRIES

Morello The ideal sour cherry, splendid for cooking and jam. Trees are self-fertile, so only one tree is needed.

PESTS AND DISEASES
of stone fruit

Peaches, cherries, plums and damsons – and the infestations that can affect them – are our subject here. As well as describing the symptoms to look out for, we also advise on what remedial action should be taken.

Stone fruit suffer from only a limited number of pests and diseases. Consequently, effective control is achieved with the minimum of spray treatments.

Plum pests

The following pests also affect damsons, but whether it be damsons or plums, the steps outlined for the control of these pests are the same.

Aphides Three species of aphid attack plums and damsons, and all overwinter as eggs on the bark. These eggs hatch out at bud-burst, and the young greenfly move on to the new growth. All three species interfere with extension growth, the leaf-curling aphid particularly so.

Caterpillars Winter moth and other caterpillars feed on developing foliage.

Red spider mite Damsons, and some varieties of plum – Czar, for example – are prone to attack by this pest. Red spiders pass the winter as bright red eggs on the bark, and hatch out in early summer (May). The small, reddish-coloured mites feed on the undersides of the leaves, causing them to become speckled and sometimes bronzed. In certain cases, the leaves may fall prematurely.

Plum fruit moth Adult moths lay their eggs at the base of the fruit stalk from late summer to early autumn (mid July to early August). The developing caterpillars eat their way to the fruit stone, where they mature, and then – in early to mid autumn (late August) – they depart to complete their development. When mature the caterpillars are reddish in colour, hence their name of red plum maggots.

Plum sawfly The adults lay eggs on the flowers during blossoming, and the creamy white caterpillars then live on the fruits till they are mature, when they drop to the ground to pupate.

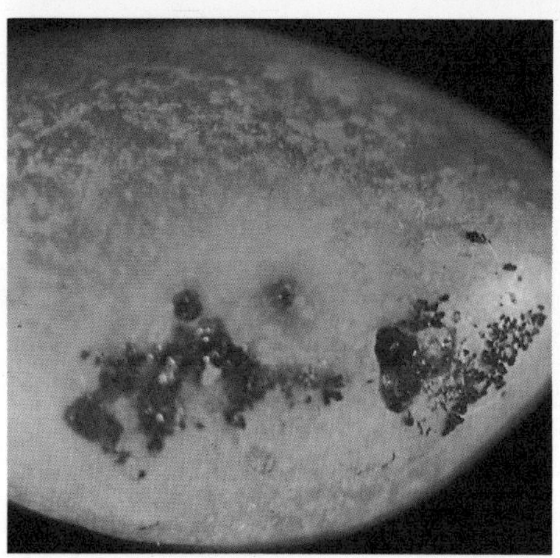

Prominent among plum pests are aphides, that swarm over new foliage (top) and caterpillars, that burrow through to the fruit stone (above)
Right: spotted underside to plum leaves points to infestation of rust disease
Pests affecting peaches include red spider mite (centre right) and aphides, that cause leaves to curl (far right)
Above right: blackfly on cherry leaf

Control of plum pests

Winter washes are some help against aphides and red spider mite, but a simpler, easier approach is to rely on spring and summer sprays. Normally all that is needed for the effective control of

aphides and caterpillars is a routine spray at white-bud stage with a good garden insecticide such as malathion, fenitrothion or dimethoate. Ideally, the spray should show some systemic activity in order to control leaf-curling aphides.

If plum sawfly is a problem, then you will have to give a second spray at petal fall, but in most cases this will be enough. However, if red spider mite appears, it will also be necessary to spray in mid summer (early June), and again two or three weeks later.

Finally, an attack by plum fruit moth will mean further sprays in late summer and again in early autumn (late July and mid August).

Plum diseases
The following diseases also affect damsons; treatment is the same as for plums.
Blossom wilt and brown rot This overwinters in cankers and in mummified fruits. These infection centres then produce spores in spring that infect the blossoms, causing them to wilt. The same disease is responsible, later in the season, for a brown rot of the fruits.
Plum rust Small brown spots on the underside of the leaves and a speckling of the upper leaf surfaces are the indications of this disease. Severely-infected leaves fall prematurely.
Silver leaf A fungus enters the wood through a wound, causing a silvering of the leaves and die-back of the shoots.

Control of plum diseases
Cutting out cankered wood – painting the wounds with a sealing paint – and collecting and burning mummified fruits is the best way to deal with blossom wilt and brown rot. Should plum rust develop, however, protective sprays with thiram or zineb should be applied to reduce the spread of the disease.

In the case of silver leaf, cut out infected shoots and burn them, and paint the wounds with protective paint.

Cherry pests
Most people think of birds as being the main pests of cherries, but the following insects can also be a great nuisance.
Aphides Cherry blackfly, that overwinters in the egg stage and hatches at about the time of bud-burst, can be very damaging to cherry trees. Infected leaves curl up and the new growth is severely checked.
Caterpillars Winter moth and related caterpillars sometimes attack cherries as the flower-buds open.
Cherry fruit moth The caterpillars of this moth bore into the flower-buds and feed on the flowers and young fruitlets.

Control of cherry pests

As with plums and damsons, winter washes give some control of the main pests, but it is easier to rely on a general insecticide, such as malathion, fenitrothion or dimethoate, applied at white-bud stage. Ideally, the selected product should have some systemic activity to control the leaf-curling cherry blackfly.

Cherry diseases

Always cut out diseased wood of the cherry in the summer, thus lessening any risk of further infection.

Bacterial canker This bacterial disease can be very damaging, as it kills whole branches and can lead to the complete die-back of the tree. Infection occurs during autumn, and the disease then progresses during the winter months. Leaves on infected branches turn yellow and brown.

Control of cherry diseases

The recommended method of control for bacterial blight is to give three applications of a copper fungicide – Bordeaux mixture, for example – at two-week intervals, starting in early to mid autumn (end of August). It is also desirable to cut away any badly infected branches.

Peach pests

The following pests also affect nectarines and apricots, when the controls are the same as for peaches.

Aphides Several species of greenfly and blackfly attack peach trees at bud-burst or shortly after, causing severe leaf curl.

Red spider mite These small, reddish mites feed on the undersides of the leaves, causing a speckling of the foliage. In severe cases, the leaves may fall early.

Control of peach pests

Since winter washes are liable to damage some varieties, it is better to rely on spring and summer sprays. A routine spray with a systemic greenfly killer such as malathion, dimethoate or fenitrothion should therefore be applied at the end of the blossom period to deal with greenfly and blackfly. If red spider mite is present, spray against it before flowers open.

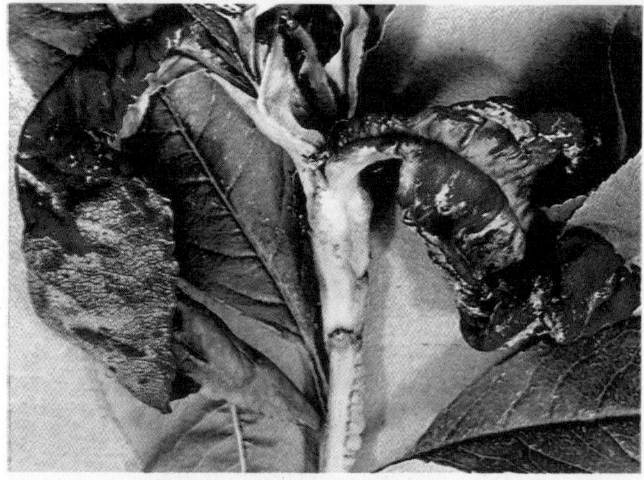

Above: powdery growth on skin of peaches indicates presence of powdery mildew
Left: leaf curl causes peach leaves to swell and distort, and also to redden

Peach diseases

The following diseases also affect nectarines and apricots, and the same controls apply as for peaches.

Leaf curl This extremely widespread and common disease causes the leaves to thicken and become distorted. Infected leaves also fall prematurely, so the disease has serious effects on the cropping and general vigour of the trees.

Powdery mildew This overwinters in the buds, causing them to produce stunted growth covered with a thick coating of powdery spores that are capable of infecting healthy leaves.

Control of peach diseases

The standard recommendation for the control of leaf curl is to spray the trees in early spring (end of February) with either a copper fungicide or lime sulphur. A second spray should be applied in autumn just before. leaf fall. An alternative approach is to spray with thiram at fortnightly intervals, starting when the first diseased leaves appear.

Thiram sprays will also help to control powdery mildew, as will a series of sulphur sprays, applied every 14 days, starting when the disease is first noticed.

SOFT FRUIT

BLACKBERRIES AND HYBRIDS

Blackberries are a versatile fruit. They can be used for making a variety of desserts, jams and wine, and they also keep well in the freezer. A certain amount of training and some pruning is necessary for a good crop, but otherwise the plants are easy to cultivate.

BLACKBERRIES

One of the earliest articles on cultivated blackberries appeared in 'The Gardeners' Assistant' in 1859, when ten types were listed under the name bramble. This fruit belongs to the genus *Rubus* and was originally given the name *Rubus fructicosus*. Botanists later recognized much variation in wild blackberries and they were divided into more than 150 species.

Everyone who has picked the wild fruits will know that some are large, juicy and well flavoured, while others are small, woody and poorly flavoured. Seasonal conditions play a part, but the main reason for the difference in quality is the difference in species. Added to this is the fact that seedlings arise, of which some may be superior or inferior to the species from which they sprang.

Cultivated varieties

The best of the wild types have been selected for cultivation or used in breeding programmes for raising improved forms, and the list has now been reduced in the last thirty years from sixteen or so to about half a dozen. The most widely-known is probably Himalaya Giant, that was introduced to this country at the end of the last century by a Hamburg nurseryman, Theodor Reimers, who gave it his own name in Germany. It was known as Himalaya in Great Britain because it was thought that it arose from seed collected from the Himalayas but it is now known to be a species, probably a form of *R. procerus*, which grows throughout much of western Europe.

Himalaya is very vigorous, producing canes up to 3m (10 ft) long, which are heavily thorned. The jet-black berries are large (hence the 'Giant' part of the name), juicy and impressive looking, but can be disappointing in some seasons, with little discernible 'bramble' flavour, though this does come out well when the berries are used with apples to make jam. The variety is a prodigious cropper, sometimes giving 14kg (30 lb) per plant, and it rarely fails. It is in season from mid to late autumn (mid August to October). Its main drawback is the difficulty of handling the canes.

The earliest variety, starting to crop at the end of the summer and continuing for about a month (late July to late August) is Bedford Giant. This is said to be a seedling of the Veitchberry, which is a raspberry-blackberry hybrid. Bedford Giant is another vigorous, prickly grower producing abundant crops of large berries. The flavour is sweet and superior to that of the Himalaya. Bedford Giant is rather susceptible to the bacterial infection crown gall; galls, that can be quite

Above: early-fruiting Bedford Giant
Right: popular Oregon Thornless

large, appear on the canes – sometimes at the crown and sometimes farther up. These are unsightly but, as far as research work has established, they do not unduly affect growth and cropping. Occasionally, however, a gall may completely girdle a cane; and then the cane will die above that point.

A fine variety for early to mid autumn (August to September) is John Innes, raised at the John Innes Horticultural Institution in England. This is juicy, sweetly-flavoured and crops heavily from canes up to 2·6m (8 ft) long.

Thornless varieties

However good the thorned varieties are there is little doubt that the thornless ones are preferable for the garden. Oregon Thornless, one of the most popular varieties, tends to be a lighter cropper than the thorned varieties, but it can yield well in a good year. It is a wild plant, native to Oregon, and was taken up there for domestic culture around the first quarter of the century, but it was introduced into Britain only recently. Growth is moderate, with canes reaching some 1·8m (6 ft). The berries are fairly large, sweet and with a good 'bramble' flavour. The parsley-leaved foliage is attractive, lending the plant a decorative aspect, and making it an ideal subject for a dividing screen between the flower and vegetable gardens. It crops from mid to late autumn (September to October).

Another excellent thornless type from the United States is Smoothstem, – resulting from a cross between Merton Thornless and the American variety Eldorado. It is in crop from the end of early autumn until late autumn (late August to October), producing very heavy yields of large berries.

HYBRIDS

The list of blackberry hybrids has shrunk considerably over the last four decades, perhaps because there was not a great deal to choose between most of them. The three main types now offered are those with deep red berries, represented primarily by the loganberry (described on page 56), those with purplish-black berries of which the chief example is the boysenberry, and the raspberry-blackberry hybrid – the Veitchberry.

Boysenberry This originated in California, and the first type seen in Britain was thorned. This type is still available but is likely to become superseded by the thornless variety now on sale. The berries are large, have a fine flavour, and ripen from late summer to early autumn (July to August). A yield of approximately 3·5–4·5kg (8–10 lb) is given per plant. The canes are up to 2–4m (8 ft) long. The berries make delicious jam. A useful feature of boysenberries is that they are good drought-resisters and will thrive on soils that might normally be too light for maximum production of blackberries.

Veitchberry This is a cross between the

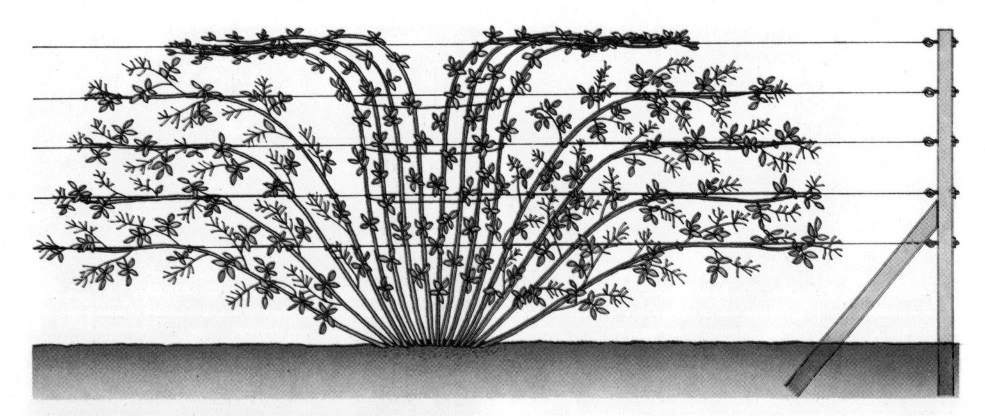

Above: plants can be trained by modified open fan method (as used for loganberries)
Left: thornless boysenberry, good for jam

raspberry, November Abundance, and a large-fruited blackberry. It fills the gap between the summer-fruiting raspberries and the blackberries. The berries are borne on vigorous canes and are finely-flavoured. This hybrid was raised at the famous English nursery of James Veitch.

Planting blackberries and hybrids

In practice any reasonably good soil will suit blackberries and their hybrids. They will always benefit from organic treatment, with compost being dug in before planting, at the usual rate for soft fruit of one barrowload per 10sq m (12 sq yd) or so, and thereafter used as a spring mulch over the root area. Plants given a good start and then well tended, will crop for ten to fifteen years, often longer; a planting distance of 2·5m (8 ft) apart is about right for John Innes, Oregon and Smoothstem; the others will need about 3–3·6m (10–12 ft).

Training the plants

Support the plants with posts and wires; ideally you should have four wires spaced at 90cm, 1·2m, 1·5m and 1·8m (3 ft, 4 ft, 5 ft and 6 ft) from ground level. The end posts should be 2·5m (8 ft) long, buried to 60cm (2 ft). Treat the bottom 75cm (2½ ft) with a standard preservative. Provide additional support by using inside strainer posts or outside wire struts, firmly anchored. Struts do, of course, take up extra room and can be effective trip wires for people not watching their step, or for children in a hurry.

The same training systems are used as for loganberries (see page 56). Thus you can train the canes on the open fan principle, with fruiting ones spread out fanwise left and right of centre along the first three wires, with a gap in the centre up which the current season's canes are led to a temporary position on the top wire. Alternatively, the fruiting canes can be led off along the wires in one direction, and the current season's ones in the opposite direction (the rope or arch method). These are arranged each year to ensure that where there are two or more plants, the fruiting canes of one plant meet the fruiting canes of its neighbour, while non-fruiting (i.e. current season's) meet similar ones.

Autumn and winter pruning

Prune all fruited wood as soon as possible after harvest. If you are using the open fan system, release the new season's canes from the top wire and tie them fanwise ready for fruiting the following year. With the rope or arch method the new canes are already in position. Remove the fruited ones; the space they occupy will, in due course, be taken over by the current growths of the following year.

With John Innes and Himalaya some once-fruited canes can be left for a further season if desired, since these varieties will make a second year's flush of fruiting laterals from the previous season's canes, thus boosting the crop. In these cases, cut back (in winter) all laterals to basal buds on any canes to be left; new ones will grow out and fruit in the next summer. Often, however, there are enough new canes, especially with Himalaya, to fill the allotted space without worrying about retaining any of the fruited ones, and in any case it is a mistake to retain wood for two seasons if this means congestion.

Pests and diseases

Blackberries and their hybrids are fairly sturdy plants but are prone to one or two ailments.

Blackberry mite A condition that frequently mystifies gardeners, particularly when the season is ideal for ripening, is failure of the berries to ripen fully. Many of the drupels (the small globules of which the berries are composed, and that contain the seeds) remain red. Himalaya is probably the most widely affected. This trouble is caused by the blackberry mite, sometimes called red berry mite, a microscopic species that feeds on the berries, preventing the drupels from ripening, and often causing distortion. Complete control is difficult to achieve but the mites can be substantially reduced by burning canes carrying infested berries immediately after harvest, and following this up next season with a spray of lime sulphur in early summer (mid May) at 500ml to 10 litres (1 pt to 2½ gal) water; or a solution of wettable sulphur in water at 50g to 10 litres (2 oz per 2½ gal) water just before flowering. Lime sulphur may cause some leaf scorch, but this is not usually enough to do serious damage. Wettable sulphur is not the same as sulphur dust; the latter is not formulated for use as a spray.

Virus diseases (such as stunt) affect blackberries and hybrid berries. They are spread by leaf hoppers and aphides. Burn affected plants, and only propagate from healthy specimens.

RECOMMENDED VARIETIES

BLACKBERRIES

Himalaya Giant	fruiting in early to late autumn (mid August to October)
Bedford Giant	fruiting in late summer to mid autumn (late July to late August)
John Innes	fruiting in early to mid autumn (August to September)
Oregon Thornless	fruiting in mid to late autumn (September to October)
Smoothstem	fruiting in mid to late autumn (late August to October)

HYBRIDS

Boysenberry	fruiting in late summer to early autumn (July)
Veitchberry	fruiting in late summer (July)

BLACKCURRANTS

Blackcurrants are the richest source of vitamin C of all the garden fruits. Here we give full details on how to plant and care for your bushes, so that they crop regularly and heavily, and also explain how you can raise new plants from cuttings.

Blackcurrants thrive in organically rich soil. They can hardly have too much good quality, well-rotted compost. Dig it in before planting, at the rate of one full barrowload per 8–10 sq m (10–12 sq yd), and use it as a mulch every spring just after fruit set. If there is enough compost, cover the pathways as well as the plant rows. Use a depth of 8cm (3 in) if it can be spared. This will not only cut out hoeing, thereby leaving the near-surface root mass undisturbed, but it will ensure the greatest possible degree of summer moisture retention, and encourage each bush to make a really large root system. Abundant roots mean abundant top growth; the fruits are borne on shoots made the previous year, so the more two-year shoots, the bigger the crop.

Compost alone often will not boost growth and crops to the maximum. It may have to be supplemented with a proprietary fertilizer high in nitrogen in early or mid spring (February or March) at 25–35g per sq m (¾–1 oz per sq yd).

Planting the bushes

It is imperative to get the plot really clean before planting. If such weeds as couch grass, bindweed and creeping buttercup are left, it will be almost impossible to eradicate them later from around the bushes without disturbing the roots.

Planting holes must be wide enough to take the roots comfortably and, more important, deep enough to ensure that the crotch of the bush is about 10cm (4 in) below soil level. New shoots are needed not only above ground but also below. The latter are 'stool' shoots, and can provide a significant portion of the crop.

Plant the bushes a minimum of 1·5m (5 ft) apart. Cut back newly-planted bushes to buds just above soil level. Do not crop them in their first summer as they must be given every chance to build up strongly. They will then crop well in the second summer and onward.

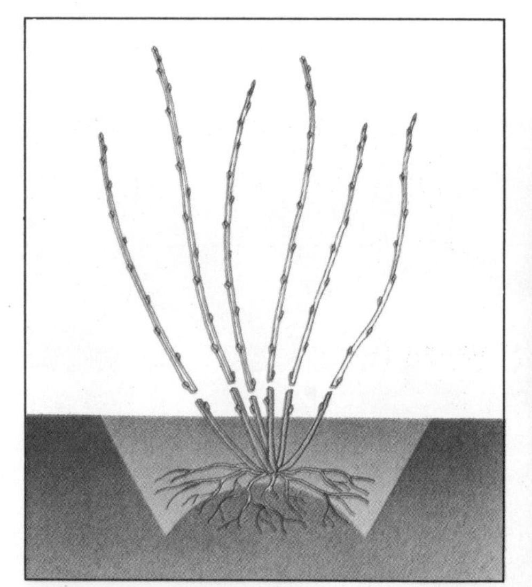

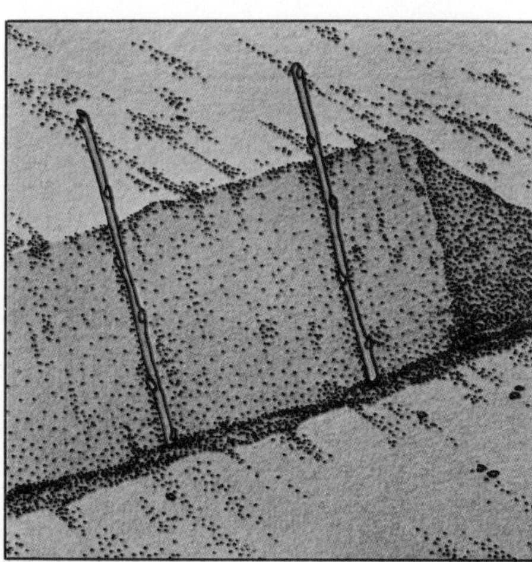

Below left: plant bush in 10cm (4 in) deep hole and cut back shoots; below: plant cut-off shoots 15cm (6 in) apart

Raising from shoots

Use some of the cut-off shoots to raise more bushes. Trim them to 20–23cm (8–9 in), removing tip portions. Plant them 15cm (6 in) deep and 15cm (6 in) apart, with all buds intact, into a well-prepared nursery strip. The maiden bushes will be ready for planting out during the following winter.

Caring for growing bushes

Blackcurrant bushes have no permanent framework, but they send out many shoots from old wood. The aim in pruning is to have good supplies of maiden shoots each year for cropping the following year. Fruited shoots can be cut out when the fruit is picked, and this is often sufficient pruning. The other time to prune is in winter, leaving maiden branches, but cutting out fruited shoots. The two are easily distinguished; cropped shoots are darker than maiden ones, and carry the dried remains of the fruit strings.

Many fruited shoots will have maiden ones growing from them, and maiden tip extensions. Where a fruited shoot is supporting a maiden one, cut off the upper fruited part at the junction with the new shoot, and leave the latter intact. The

Below left: juicy fruits ripening and picked ready to eat (above)

basal portion of the old piece will then become a temporary support.

Where fruited shoots have no maiden side growths but do have good maiden extensions, leave them in. Such extensions can produce useful fruiting trusses. But where the extensions are very short and puny, cut out the shoots at the base. Cut out entirely any fruited shoots bare of maiden side growths and tip extensions.

Below: cut out fruited shoots at harvest time and, if necessary, in the winter

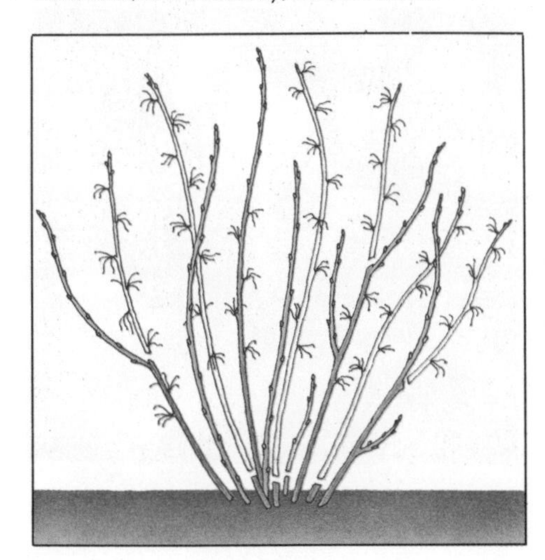

There may be weak maiden shoots deep within the centre of the bush. Their poor growth is due to lack of sunlight. Remove them as they are useless for cropping.

Protection from the wind

One of the commonest causes of crop failure is 'running off', when the flowers either shrivel or set fruit that falls soon after. This is the result of imperfect pollination due to strong, cold winds at blossom time. The winds not only damage the flowers but discourage pollinating insects, without whose help pollination is rarely satisfactory. If the garden is windswept, plant the bushes in the lee of any existing shelter from the east round to the north-west. The best shelter is an evergreen hedge. A temporary screen of sacking stitched to strong hazel rods is not as effective as the windbreak hedge, because it shelters only the bushes and not the surrounding area. If the area remains windblown, it will not attract pollinating insects.

Pests and diseases

The main pests infesting blackcurrants are aphides and gall mites ('big bud' mites).

Aphides These insects can do great damage to the leaves by sucking the sap and distorting them. The familiar sooty mould forms after an attack of aphides, often on the berries. The most practical control is a winter tar oil spray, thoroughly applied to kill the eggs. Alternatively, spray with derris, malathion, or a systemic in the spring as soon as aphides are seen on the undersurface of the leaves.

Gall mites These live and breed inside the buds, causing them to swell to several times the normal winter size. The buds are killed by the mites, which then infect new buds in the spring. The mites also transmit a virus disease called reversion, which does not kill but renders the bushes incapable of fruiting. Never use cuttings from infested bushes for propagation.

A limited measure of control may be achieved by picking off and burning swollen buds. The standard control is a spray of lime sulphur according to the maker's recommendation at the grape stage: that is, when the unopened flower buds hang like bunches of tiny grapes.

Some buds infested with gall mites may become detached from the plant and carried by the wind to nearby bushes, causing 'big buds' to appear on previously clean bushes. The mites may also be transported by various flying insects (particularly aphides) to which they cling. It is therefore a sound policy to spray with lime sulphur every year as an insurance against infection from any blackcurrant bushes in the vicinity.

The only variety of blackcurrant in present cultivation that has some degree of immunity to gall mites is Seabrook's Black. It is not completely immune, but may go for several years without an infestation.

RECOMMENDED VARIETIES

Tor Cross Early season variety fruiting mid to late summer (late June–mid July)

Laxton's Giant Early season variety fruiting mid to late summer (late June–early July). Good alternative to Tor Cross. Crops heavily, with very large, sweet fruit.

Seabrook's Black Early–mid season variety fruiting mid to late summer (late June–mid July). Only variety resistant to gall mite. Good crops of large fruit.

Wellington XXX Mid season variety fruiting late summer (July). Very heavy cropper, producing large fruits on long, spreading branches.

Baldwin Mid to late season variety fruiting late summer to early autumn (mid July–August). Produces heavy crops of well-flavoured fruit very rich in vitamin C.

Amos Black Very late season variety fruiting early to mid autumn (August–September). Flowers late enough in most areas to miss frosts.

DECORATIVE BERRIES
from blueberries to wineberries

There are several bush fruits that are edible and also sufficiently attractive to warrant a place in the garden as ornamental shrubs. We shall now look at several of these dual-purpose plants.

BLUEBERRIES

These berries grow in wild and cultivated forms in Canada and the northern regions of the United States of America. The British wild type *Vaccinium myrtillus* (known as whortleberry, whinberry, bilberry and blaeberry) is related to them. It grows on acid moorlands and produces small fruits that, although palatable, are inferior to garden forms.

The fruiting season for cultivated varieties is from late summer to late autumn (mid July to early October).

Species of cultivated blueberry

The species most grown for its fruits is *Vaccinium corymbosum*, known as the highbush blueberry; this has also been a recognized ornamental garden plant for a considerable time. Several named varieties with improved fruits have been raised from it.

The general habit of the species is dense, rounded and twiggy with a height of 1·5–2·2m (5–7 ft) according to variety. The leaves vary in size from about 2–9cm (1–3½ in) long. They are bright green in summer, turning gradually to red in the autumn. Clusters of six or more small, white or pale pink flowers appear in early summer (May) before the leaves are fully expanded. The black, blue-bloomed berries also appear in clusters and ripen during early and mid autumn (August and September). They make delicious pies and other desserts, and are sweet enough for eating fresh.

The other main type is the lowbush blueberry *V. angustifolium*, a compact, dwarf shrub with leaves that become richly coloured in autumn. The flowers and berries are very similar to those of the highbush. Another dwarf species, *V. deliciosum*, produces solitary flowers and sweet black berries.

An evergreen, red-berried form is *V. floribundum*. As its name implies, this produces an abundance of flowers. The densely-clustered, rosy-tinted flowers appear in mid summer (June) and the fruit follows in early autumn (August). This is a most attractive species; the young shoots are red, and the leaves change from purplish-red to dark green. It is probably not sufficiently winter-hardy for cooler regions (since it is tropical in origin) but it will thrive in mild areas.

Soil requirements

Blueberries need an acid soil with a pH of 4·5. If your soil grows good azaleas or rhododendrons it will usually suit blueberries. They also require a good supply of moisture. The native British blueberries grow not only on moorland in high rainfall areas, but also on sandy heathlands where rainfall is much higher, and the species *V. corymbosum* is known in North America as the swamp blueberry, a name that clearly indicates its need for abundant moisture.

Blueberries will not grow in chalk or limestone soils so in these conditions you will have to prepare special beds or planting holes for them. One way is to dig holes 30cm (12 in) deep and 45cm (18 in) square, and to fill them with a mixture of moist peat and 25 per cent sharp sand. The sand is included to improve drainage; blueberries need plenty of moisture but they will not stand being waterlogged. Peat and sand do not, of course, provide the plants with much nourishment; so apply sulphate of ammonia at 35g per sq m (1 oz per sq yd) in early spring (March), and sulphate of potash at 17g per sq m (½ oz per sq yd) in winter. Alternatively, apply a general NPK (nitrogen, phosphate and potash) fertilizer in spring.

Another way of cultivating the plants

Two varieties of the highbush blueberry – Blue Ray (top) and Jersey (above)

where the soil is alkaline is to grow a bush in a tub, using the peat and sand mixture.

Planting and tending

In the garden, set the plants 1·2–1·8m (4–6 ft) apart, with the crowns about 10cm (4 in) below soil level to encourage the growth of new shoots from the base. Give them a good mulch of peat or compost annually to help conserve moisture.

Adequate summer moisture is essential and, since watering may become prohibited in some regions if drought sets in, this is all the more reason why soil water must be conserved. If the plants establish themselves quickly they should make some 30–45cm (12–18 in) of growth during the first season.

Don't prune newly-planted bushes and confine routine pruning to the removal of some of the old shoots from time to time.

Pests and diseases are practically non-existent, so no routine spraying is required, but netting is advisable to protect the fruit from birds.

CRANBERRIES

Vaccinium oxycoccus, the small cranberries, are natives of the northern hemisphere. They are very small evergreens with a spreading habit, bearing red, somewhat acid berries that make delicious tarts, pies and jellies. The leaves are small and silvery on the underside, and the tiny delicate flowers are pink-petalled. There is an American form, *V. macrocarpum*, with much larger oval berries, but it is not very readily available in Britain.

Planting and tending

The cultivation and soil requirement of cranberries are very similar to those of blueberries except that the bushes, being smaller, may be planted close together; 60–90cm (2–3 ft) apart is suitable. Birds can soon eat up much of a cranberry harvest so, as with blueberries, you would be wise to protect the berries with netting.

Above: small cranberry in fruit; top: the Worcesterberry, a gooseberry hybrid

WORCESTERBERRIES

Confusion over the history of Worcesterberries has existed for many years. The myth that the berry arose as a blackcurrant-gooseberry hybrid has been around for over half a century. Some versions even gave its parents as Boskoop Giant blackcurrant and Whinham's Industry gooseberry. Hybrids between currants and gooseberries have long been known but they are completely sterile and also thornless, whereas Worcesterberries are very fertile and thorned.

Science, however, has established that it is a hybrid between two gooseberry species; technically it is an inter-specific gooseberry hybrid, known as *Ribes divaricatum*, this being the name of one of the two species from which it is thought to have arisen. It is sometimes listed as an American wild gooseberry.

The reddish-purple berries are roughly midway in size between blackcurrants and gooseberries. They have a pleasant flavour when eaten fresh, and may be used for jam and in cooked dishes.

Planting and tending

The Worcesterberry makes a hardy, free-growing bush with strong branches reaching about 1·2–1·5m (4–5 ft) in height and arching over at the tips.

To accommodate the arching habit, and to see it at its best, bushes should be planted 1·8m (6 ft) apart – if more than one bush is wanted.

The soil should be well-drained and loamy, with a good organic content, and the bushes will always benefit from mulching. Although gooseberries in general need fairly heavy supplies of potash (without which they are liable to show marginal leaf scorch) Worcesterberries do not seem so prone to potash deficiency. If leaf scorch does appear, apply sulphate of potash at 17–25g per sq m ($\frac{1}{2}$–$\frac{3}{4}$ oz per sq yd) of root area in autumn.

Pruning is much the same as for blueberries. In addition, keep the growths thinned out enough to make picking among the thorns less hazardous.

RECOMMENDED VARIETIES

BLUEBERRIES
Early Blue (or Earliblue) Early season.
Pemberton Early season.
Burlington Early to mid season.
Rubel Early to mid season.
Grover Mid season.
Goldtraube Mid season.
Jersey Late season.

CRANBERRIES
Vaccinium macrocarpum **Early Black.**
Vaccinium oxycoccus (red cranberry) No named varieties.

WORCESTERBERRIES
Ribes divaricatum No named varieties.

Many members of the bramble family are ornamental as well as producing fine-flavoured fruit. These include the Chinese raspberry, the Japanese wineberry and one with no common name, *Rubus leucodermis*.
Two other unusual fruits are Cape gooseberry and Chinese gooseberry – neither of which is related to the gooseberry family, or to each other.

CAPE GOOSEBERRY

Salads made from fruit as well as vegetables are a pleasant change from the conventional lettuce and cucumber mixture, and one of the best fruits to add is the Cape gooseberry. This fruit, *Physalis (edulis) peruviana*, originated in South America. It can be eaten fresh and is also excellent for making preserves, or stewed.

Many gardeners will know its decorative relation, *P. alkekengi* (Chinese lantern plant). This has rounded, veined, downward-hanging husks containing the fruit. The berries are of indifferent dessert quality and so are used mainly for other culinary purposes.

The fruit of *P. peruviana* is a deep golden colour and roughly cherry sized. The flavour is very good and the fruit has a high vitamin value. It will keep in first-class condition within the husk for several months if dried carefully before storage and kept in a cool dry and airy place. The husks are considerably larger than the fruits; they are very attractive (as are the small, pale yellow 'starry' flowers) but are partially hidden by the large leaves.

Right and below: Physalis alkekengi *(Chinese lantern plant)*
Bottom: Physalis peruviana *(Cape gooseberry)*

How and where to plant

Grow the plants in the open garden, under glass or in pots. For outdoor culture they require no special soil, and should not be given rich treatment. They will make good growth in any normal garden soil without additional feeding provided they are kept sufficiently watered. Give them a mulch (such as peat) to conserve water but do not use a growth-promoting type like animal manure.

Set the plants 60–90cm (2–3 ft) apart in mid spring (March) and keep them under cloches or in frames to protect them from late frosts or cold, drying winds. Such winds can check the plants severely, or even shrivel them up. If you cannot supply this protection put the plants temporarily in small pots and keep them indoors in a sunny position until early to mid summer (late May). Then transfer them to 25cm (9 in) pots for outdoor cultivation.

In colder regions pot culture is preferable anyway, because the plants can be brought indoors to avoid the autumn frosts and will then ripen their fruits in safety. Use medium-sized pots and J.I. No 3 or a peat-based compost.

Actinidia chinensis *(Chinese gooseberry)*

Providing support

The growth habit is not unlike that of tomatoes, and so the plants need to be supported by canes. They reach a height of about 60cm (24 in) on average, but can exceed 90cm (3 ft). If you want to restrict the plants to a certain height, simply pinch out the stem at the highest sideshoot. If sideshoots are growing at the expense of stem height, stop some of them when about 30cm (12 in) or so long, and pinch out new ones as they arise. Do not, however, adopt any form of regular stopping and pinching; as long as growth is within the required limits, let it proceed.

After fruiting

The fruits are ready for gathering in the autumn when the husks part easily. Make sure that the husks are perfectly dry if you are going to store them. Apart from that no special storing measures are necessary.

When the fruit has been gathered, cut the plants back to soil level and, with outdoor culture, give the stools winter protection under straw or a thick layer of garden litter.

Pests and diseases

Inspect the plants weekly for aphides, especially the tips of the shoots and at the stalk ends of the 'lanterns'. If you find any, spray with derris or malathion.

CHINESE GOOSEBERRY

Another ornamental and edible fruit is the Chinese gooseberry *Actinidia chinensis*. It is believed to have come to the West in the 19th century. 'The London Journal of Botany', in 1847, described specimens sent to the Royal Horticultural Society by the famous plant hunter Robert Fortune. The plant was also found in Japan by another of the Society's plant hunters who wrote about it in 'The Garden' in 1882.

It is a hardy climber with very large, handsome leaves, and clusters of bright yellow flowers 2–4cm (1–1½ in) across, bearing many stamens. The fruit is about the size of a walnut. It is covered with gooseberry-like hairs, and also tastes rather like a ripe gooseberry. It may be eaten fresh or stewed.

How and where to plant

This plant is a rapid grower suitable for covering walls, fences and trellises in sunny positions in mild areas. It grows to a considerable length, and the recommended minimum planting distance is 5·5m (18 ft). You will need at least one male and one female plant for pollination; it is said that one male will pollinate eight females.

No special soil is needed for outdoor growing, but good supplies of organic matter should be dug in, and mulching will always help. Garden soil of good fertility will suffice for pot culture, together with a feed of liquid manure at regular intervals during summer. For greenhouse cultivation, artificial heating is not necessary.

Providing support

Chinese gooseberries, being climbers, need a support structure of canes or wires. You can also grow the plants individually in 30cm (12 in) pots; train them up bamboo canes and stop them according to the vertical space available. A good method for pot culture is to stand the plants in a greenhouse with their lower stem portions trained up bamboos, and the higher portions supported by wires.

Pollination and pruning
Hand pollination of the flowers is advisable for greenhouse culture; this is a simple matter of transferring the pollen from the anthers of the male flowers to the stigmas of the female, using a pollinating (camel hair) brush.

Routine pruning consists of cutting off, in mid to late winter (December to January), the stem above the last bud that bore fruit during the preceding year. In spring a new branch will grow and bear a number of grown fruits.

CHINESE RASPBERRY

The Chinese raspberry is an ornamental bramble with yellow, edible fruits. There are some related forms, one of which is probably better than the type species since it bears more heavily (though it does not seem to be so easy to come by). The type species is *Rubus biflorus*, and the heavier-cropping form is *R. biflorus quinqueflorus* which crops more heavily because it produces more flowers.

The Chinese raspberry is not widely grown and you may have difficulty in obtaining it from nurseries or garden centres. But you may well find some canes growing in a friend's or neighbour's garden and be able to take a cutting.

This raspberry has strong, spiny stems completely covered in a coating of white wax. These 'whitewashed' canes are most striking, particularly in winter. The leaves are composed of three to five leaflets, dark green above and white beneath. The habit of *R. biflorus* is semi-erect, giving a strong, medium-sized shrub; that of *R. b. quinqueflorus* is erect or semi-erect with a definite arching over of the canes. In this form the canes can reach 3m (10 ft) and will touch the ground and tip root if allowed to do so. For propagating purposes this is very useful; the newly-grown canes can be dug up in autumn or winter and planted out. But, unless you want new canes for propagation, discourage tip rooting as the new canes produced in this way will be in addition to those growing seasonally from the stools, and you will soon have a miniature forest.

Another point worth noting is that the growth habit of *R. b. quinqueflorus* is far from orderly. So if you want more erect, more manageable (though not so productive) plants you would do better with *R. biflorus*.

Planting and tending
Allow 60cm (24 in) or so between canes when planting and dig in a good quantity of compost. The object is not only to get fruit but also to encourage stout canes, because the stouter they are, the whiter is the waxy covering. After the crop is gathered, cut out the fruited canes in exactly the same way as for summer fruiting raspberries.

Rubus phoenicolasius *(Japanese wineberry) is a particularly decorative plant, as well as having delicious berries*

JAPANESE WINEBERRY

Perhaps the most ornamental of all the decorative berries is the Japanese wineberry *Rubus phoenicolasius*. This was discovered growing wild in the mountains of Japan, and is recorded as having been introduced to British gardens in 1876.

The canes are vigorous, semi-erect and can reach 1·8m (6 ft) in good soil. They are covered in soft, red bristles, and the leaves are large, pale green above and covered with a whitish down underneath. The berries are golden-yellow (or sometimes bright orange) and are enclosed in an attractive hairy calyx. They are rather small but very pleasantly flavoured, and may be eaten fresh or used for cooking. Each spray ripens its berries evenly.

Planting and pruning
Any good soil will suit this fruit. Plant 1·2m (4 ft) apart to give the bush-like growth enough room to flourish. Prune out the fruited canes at soil level as soon as the crop is finished for the year. No training system is required.

RUBUS LEUCODERMIS

A distinctive variation on the theme of ornamental brambles is provided by the blue-bloomed stems and purplish-black fruits of *Rubus leucodermis*. It was introduced into Britain nearly 150 years ago. Partly erect and partly spreading in habit, it fruits in mid summer (June).

Its leaves have three to five coarsely-toothed leaflets and a white, felt-textured underside.

GOOSEBERRIES

In Britain, the traditional time for the first gooseberries is Whit Sunday, which usually falls towards mid summer (June). An early-fruiting variety will certainly give enough small green berries by this time to make a pie. And if you have planned your gooseberry bed, it will herald the start of a three-month season of this versatile fruit that is equally good whether eaten raw, cooked in pies or turned into jam.

For an early crop of gooseberries, try a variety such as Keepsake, whose berries make rapid growth from the time the fruits set to maturity. The main crop comes in mid season and is heavy, with medium-sized, pale green, slightly hairy berries.

Another good variety for an early pick, followed by a mid season main crop, is Careless. When fully ripe the berries are large, milky-white and practically hairless, with a transparent or semi-transparent skin. But avoid this variety if your soil is on the poor side, because it will not make much headway and the berries will be small. Improve the soil first and plant Careless later, when conditions are better. Good soil is necessary for all gooseberries but Keepsake is a more vigorous grower than Careless, and is a better choice if your soil is below par.

A fine mid season, deep red berry with a rich flavour is Lancashire Lad, which makes delicious jam. You can also pick it while still green, for cooking. The queen of the yellow-green varieties is the large-fruited Leveller, which also ripens in mid season and is ideal for showing. But, like all the highest-quality fruit, it does need the best conditions. On light soils that drain too freely it will be stunted, often with the greyish, brittle leaf margins that denote potash deficiency. And you will get the same results on heavy soils with impeded drainage.

If your soil is heavy but nevertheless well drained, a good choice would be the mid season, dark red Whinham's Industry. This is one of the best flavoured of all. The sweetest-flavoured mid to late season green variety is probably Lancer, which has translucent, thin-skinned, pale green berries tinged with yellow.

There are several other varieties available, but those given here will provide first-rate fruits for cooking and dessert.

Preparation and cultivation

Gooseberries need a fertile, well-prepared soil, but not one that is too rich or overcharged with nitrogen; excessive richness will help to encourage American gooseberry mildew. Whatever your soil type, dig in thoroughly plenty of well-rotted compost before planting. A free root run and adequate drainage combined with a summer moisture reserve are the essentials for a good crop. The only fertilizer likely to be needed on any sort of routine basis, provided you maintain a good organic content, is sulphate of potash. The standard dressing is 25g per sq m ($\frac{3}{4}$ oz per sq yd) in early spring (February). However, if the leaves are a healthy green and show no signs of marginal scorch, not even this is necessary. But it must be applied if signs of potash deficiency appear.

Gooseberries detest the hoe. They make a massive, absorbing root system in the top few centimetres of soil, and like these roots to be left in peace. Annual mulching in spring (March–April) just after the fruits set will suppress weeds, maintain a moisture reserve and eliminate hoeing. If you cannot manage this every year, then as far as possible get the weeds out by hand in the root area of the bushes, and restrict the hoe to a narrow strip along the centre of the alleyways.

In any event there will not be many weeds from the mulched area, even if you treat it on a two-year basis, provided the compost is properly made and free of weed seeds. Remember that although hoeing cleans the soil initially, it stirs up the weed seeds that otherwise might have died, remained dormant, or had their new growth smothered by a mulch.

Gooseberries can be grown as cordons 30cm (12 in) apart, or as bushes 1·2–1·5m (4–5 ft) apart. Bushes must be grown on a short stem, while cordons should be free of suckers from below soil level, so plant

Left: top-quality large-fruited Leveller

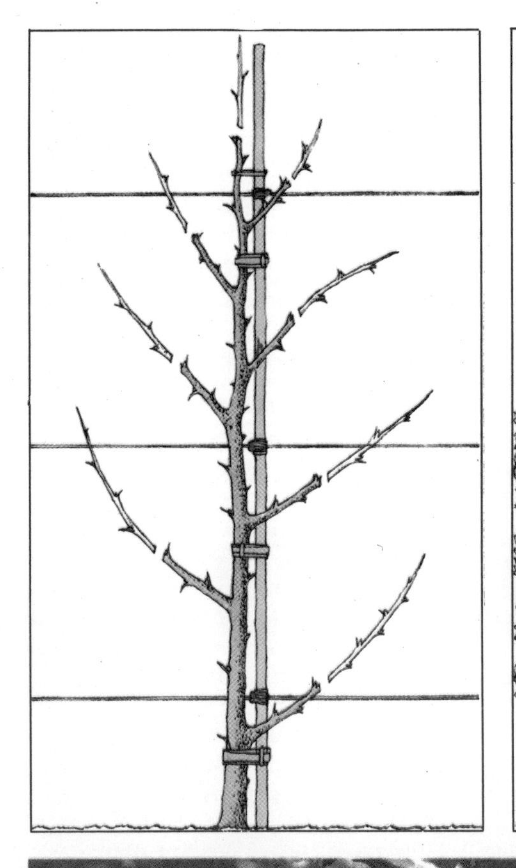

both types no deeper than the soil mark on the newly-purchased plant. Spread the roots out to their fullest extent, cover them with friable soil, then tread in lightly. Add more soil and tread in firmly. Finish off with an untrodden surface. You do not want depressions round the stems collecting pools of winter rain.

Training cordons

Cordons are usually grown vertically, though you can train them obliquely if you prefer. Using light end posts, 1·2m (4 ft) long and sunk to a depth of 30cm (12 in) or 45cm (18 in) to be on the safe side, strain three wires between them at 30cm (12 in) intervals. Then fix bamboo canes about 1 m (3 ft) long to the wires, allowing one cane for each plant.

Cordons make neat path edgings, but remember in this case to allow the stems about 30–38cm (12–15 in) of soil width on each side so that the roots can forage well, and mulch this strip each spring. One of the objects of the system is to get quality berries, and an organic root covering is a definite aid to this.

Tip back the newly-planted cordons by some 15cm (6 in) and repeat in subsequent winters if necessary. Some varieties will reach the top wire with little tipping. At the same time, cut back sideshoots to three buds. Thereafter cut back all sideshoots to the fifth leaf from the base in mid to late summer (late June or early July) and to three buds each winter. The result will be fine berries growing from induced fruiting spurs along the cordons.

Pruning bushes

You can prune bushes in exactly the same way. In this case each branch is really a cordon, the only difference being that it grows naturally from the bush and is not trained. Tip back each branch of a newly-planted bush by half, and repeat the operation in subsequent winters as it becomes necessary.

Some varieties droop considerably. If this habit becomes too pronounced, prune back in winter to an upward bud just below the bend. Remove any weak or congesting shoots to maintain an airy atmosphere in the bushes.

Light pruning method

The method described above is the conventional one that has been used for

Top, far left: prune a cordon by cutting back sideshoots to three buds.
Top left: on a bush, cut back sideshoots to five leaves in summer.
Left: dark red Whinham's Industry

many years, but light pruning (which was advocated by William Forsyth, gardener to King George III) can give just as good results and brings the bushes into crop earlier. In trials with Careless and Leveller, planted in mid spring (March) of one year and pruned lightly, they produced some 2kg (4 lb) of fruit per bush the following year.

With light pruning, the branches are not built up over successive winters and there is no sideshoot cutting. All the growths are left, except for poor or congesting shoots. Berries soon form on the uncut ones, usually in singles or perhaps doubles, from individual buds rather than in spur clusters. Each growth is cropped for a year or two, and is then removed in favour of a new one. Not all fruiting growths are removed in any one year; a pattern evolves in which there are always some shoots still in fruit and some maiden ones ready to fruit in their second summer. The only danger is overcrowding, so to prevent this, work on a basis of allowing at least one full hand's span between all adjacent growths. Be very strict over this.

Pests and diseases

There is one serious disease liable to attack your gooseberries and at least three fairly common pests.

American gooseberry mildew This shows first as thick, white, powdery patches on leaves and fruit while in the final phase there is a brownish, felty covering on the berries. It is essential to stop this fungus early, as soon as you see the first white patches on the young leaves and shoots. Apply a systemic fungicide at once and repeat at 10–14 day intervals if necessary.

Sawfly caterpillar These green caterpillars with black spots are very common pests on young bushes. They can strip a bush of every leaf. There are three generations annually, so if the first is not controlled there will be trouble at intervals throughout the season. The first batch of eggs is laid in late spring and early summer (April and May) on the undersides of leaves in the centre of the bush near ground level. They hatch about 2–3 weeks later. Look for the tiny, newly-hatched caterpillars and give them a few squirts of derris while they are still bunched in the centre of the bush. At this stage they are a sitting target and easily killed.

Magpie moth caterpillar These pests also eat the leaves, and are frequently confused with sawfly caterpillars. The magpie moth caterpillars are 'loopers', drawing themselves into a loop each time they move forward, and have black and white markings with a yellow stripe along each side. They start feeding before flowering time, but often go undetected at this stage. A derris spray immediately before flowering will kill them, but if you miss this out, then apply derris after the fruits have set as soon as the caterpillars are seen.

Aphides These are the other main pests, curling the leaves and distorting young shoots. One species, the lettuce aphid, flies from gooseberries to lettuces, so there is a double reason for controlling it. The second sort flies to certain types of willow herb. Both overwinter on gooseberries in the egg stage, and can be eradicated with a tar oil spray. The alternative is a spray of malathion or a systemic insecticide just before, or immediately after, the flowering period.

Top: immature aphides on the underside of a gooseberry leaf; these pests overwinter on the plant in the egg stage

Above left: early-cropping variety Keepsake is a vigorous grower. Above: later-fruiting dessert variety Lancer

RECOMMENDED VARIETIES

EARLY AND MID SEASON	
Keepsake	pale green
Careless	milky-white
MID SEASON	
Lancashire Lad	deep red
Leveller	yellow-green
Whinham's Industry	dark red
MID AND LATE SEASON	
Lancer	pale green

MEDLARS, QUINCES AND MULBERRIES

Medlars, quinces and mulberries make attractive trees and produce fruits that have many culinary uses – particularly for jellies and jams. Many people also enjoy mulberries and medlars as fresh fruit.

Medlars and quinces both belong to the rose family but mulberries are unrelated. All share a liking for moist loam, and the quince nearly always does best by the side of water, though such a site is by no means essential. On light, freely-drained soil, however, quince trees will not make a great deal of headway unless the root area receives generous amounts of well-rotted compost – initially before planting and thereafter as an annual mulch.

MEDLARS

Medlar trees (*Mespilus germanica*) reach on average about 4·5m (15 ft) in height, and their habit (form of growth) is spreading. The leaves are long (oblong-lanceolate, in botanical terms) and downy, with dark green on the upper surface and lighter green on the lower. In autumn they become russet coloured. The young twigs are also downy, and eventually turn black. The bark of the stem and branches tends to peel. The flowers are borne singly and have white- or pink-tinted petals, and are up to 4cm ($1\frac{1}{2}$ in) across. The fruits are mainly round with a reddish-brown, rather leathery and rough skin. At the top the fruit is indented and retains a hairy calyx and leaf-like segments. The trees are virtually free of pests and disease.

Medlars are an unusual fruit to include in your harvest, while their trees make an attractive addition to the garden. Top right: the single flowers. Right: autumn tints of the leaves. Below: recommended variety Dutch, almost ready for picking

Shaping and pruning

The trees appear to have a rather mazy branch system that, particularly in winter, may look untidy or congested at first sight; but this is actually a distinctive feature of its growth and you should not try to correct it by too much branch pruning, though any laterals that are cluttering up the tree should be removed. The regular cutting away of worn-out shoots and fruit spurs is, however, very important. Although medlar trees will crop year after year without being pruned, they will become heavily congested if not kept tidy, and a major thinning operation will then be necessary. It is much better to remove potential congestion when the shoots are young, and to do this annually between mid winter and mid spring (November and March).

Picking and storing

Medlars are not edible in their raw state until the flesh has become very soft. Pick them from late autumn to early winter (October to early November), preferably after a sharp frost, and store them in a single layer, eye downwards. You can store them on a shelf in a cool shed, but the best method is to lay them on a bed of silver sand. Let them become thoroughly ripe ('bletted'); this is the stage at which they are ready for eating, and is normally reached within two or three weeks.

Medlars are normally free of pests and diseases but the stored fruit is rather susceptible to a mould that starts on the stalks. If you dip the stalks in a cup of water into which two tablespoons of salt have been thoroughly mixed, this will usually give protection.

How to use

Medlar jelly is very good, and beautifully coloured. Some recipes use fruits taken straight from the trees, still firm and only just ripe. But there are old recipes that recommend using the ripe fruit, and some of these, especially those that include apples, make very fine jelly.

QUINCES

Quince trees do not often reach more than about 4·5m (15 ft) in height as standards, and are only about shrub size in bush form. They are a lovely sight when the pale green, downy leaves are expanding in spring against the dark-coloured wood. The habit is rather drooping. The flowers are sweet-smelling and very beautiful, with five large, pinkish petals of delicate hue. The autumn leaf-colour is a rich yellow. The common quince *Cydonia oblonga*, the type with edible fruits, is quite distinct from the ornamental Japanese ones. The ornamental types have fruits of varying shapc and sizc, and flowers of different shades of red, white and orange. They have been known by various botanical names, *Cydonia japonica* being one, but are now classed separately from the common quince in the genus Chaenomeles.

Training and pruning

The tree habit of the common quince is very twisted, though the branches are relatively thin. Do not attempt corrective pruning; just let the tree grow at will, but remove obvious congestion in winter. This removal is important; without it you will find, fairly soon, a considerable mass of thicket-like growth in the tree. This will inhibit free air circulation and sunlight penetration, so increasing the likelihood of leaf blight. The growth habit of the tree is not suitcd to wall training.

Picking and storing

The fruit is pear-shaped, has a golden-yellow, slightly downy skin, and is aromatic. It remains hard long after picking time, which is probably a reason why it can be stored for a considerable period. Unlike medlars, quinces do not benefit from frost, and although the end of autumn (late October) is often given as the harvest time, it sometimes happens that a frost has struck by then. The fruits will usually come away from the spurs in late autumn (mid October). Pick them when they are quite dry and store them in a cool, frost-proof shed away from apples and pears. The aroma during storage is strong, and can spoil other stored fruit. The quinces are ready for use after two or three months.

How to use

Slices of quince are excellent for adding a touch of extra flavour to stewed apples – they are much more subtle as a flavouring than cloves. Quince jelly is very pleasant, and a lovely amber colour. The jam is ruby coloured and slightly sharp with a rather odd smell.

Pests and diseases

Quince trees may suffer from leaf blight. This causes reddish-brown spots on the foliage, often resulting in severe leaf drop, and the fruits can be affected. Prevent it by spraying with liquid-copper fungicide just after blossom and, in winter, by cutting out and burning any twigs and fruit spurs showing reddish-brown, mainly circular, areas with dark margins.

Left and below left: Cydonia oblonga, *the edible common quince. Below: the purely ornamental Japanese quince*

MULBERRIES

The habit of mulberry trees is rather similar to that of medlars, but unless your garden is spacious enough to take a standard tree, a bush is better since standards can reach 9m (30 ft) or more at maturity (though it will be quite a long time before this height is attained). They can also be grown on walls, and a fan on a southerly wall is usually advised for colder regions.

The roots, though fleshy, are brittle, and if you damage them at planting time (or if you cut them) they bleed. To avoid this, make sure your planting holes are large enough to take uncut roots.

RECOMMENDED VARIETIES

MEDLARS	
Nottingham	Small, richly-flavoured, russet-brown fruits; erect habit.
Dutch	Large, russet-brown fruits, spreading habit.
QUINCES	
Bereczki	Heavy cropper with large, fine-flavoured, pear-shaped fruits; sometimes listed as Vranja – an almost identical variety.
Meech's Prolific	Very large flowers; starts to crop at an early age; fruits are pear shaped and medium sized.
Champion	Large, apple-shaped fruits with golden-yellow flesh.
MULBERRIES	
Morus nigra	Reddish-black fruits with a pleasant, rather acid flavour.
M. alba	Lighter red, sweetish fruits.
M. australis	Dark red, sweet fruits; shrub-sized tree.
M. cathayana	Fruits vary in colour from light red to black; shrub-sized tree.

Edible species

Two main types of mulberry are grown for their fruit: the black *Morus nigra* and the white *M. alba. M. nigra* has heart-shaped leaves that are rough on the upper surface and downy on the lower. The fruits are blackish-red at maturity, and look much like loganberries. They have a pleasant, somewhat acid taste. The leaves of the white mulberry are smooth on the upper surface and downy below. The fruits are a much lighter red at maturity, sweetish and about half the size of the black type. The flowers of both species are small, borne on spikes, and not a very decorative feature.

Of several less common forms, *M. australis* and *M. cathayana* are valuable fruiting species for small gardens, as they make trees of little more than shrub size. The fruits of *M. australis* are dark red but sweet. Those of *M. cathayana* are variable in colour from black to light red. For wine, tarts and jam, mulberries are among the choicest of fruits, particularly those of the black species.

Training and pruning

Mulberries can be grown as pyramid-shaped trees. It is generally recommended that laterals be cut to six leaves from the base in late summer (July), but that leaders be left uncut unless they are too vigorous, in which case their tops should be cut back.

With wall trees, train in the main leaders fan-wise at some 38cm (15 in) apart; they usually cover the wall space without having to be stimulated by pruning. Train sideshoots of wall trees to six leaves from the base in late summer (July). Free-growing trees require little pruning other than the winter removal of congestion, but if the spur formation is sparse, cut back some maiden laterals to four or five buds.

When to pick

Fruit for eating fresh comes off at a touch when fully ripe, or can be left to fall – preferably onto closely-shaven grass, which is the best setting for a mulberry tree. For culinary use the fruits are best gathered when slightly under-ripe.

Pests and diseases

Mulberry trees are virtually disease-free, but they do occasionally suffer from twig canker. Affected shoots, carrying brownish waxy pustules, should be cut out and burnt as soon as you spot them.

Mulberries are best grown in bush form. Below: the flowers, and below right, the fruit, of the black Morus nigra

RASPBERRIES AND LOGANBERRIES

Raspberries and loganberries are most rewarding soft fruits and are comparatively easy to grow. Many people, however, are unfamiliar with loganberries. These are larger than raspberries and their colour, when fully ripe, is a deep wine-red.

Raspberries and loganberries thrive on most garden soils which retain summer moisture but do not become waterlogged in winter. The only basic soil type on which they will usually fail is the highly alkaline. If their roots are in chalk or limestone where the pH is above 7, iron deficiency will be a problem. The higher the alkalinity, the greater this problem will be. In theory you can overcome it by adding a proprietary iron compound, but this method can be expensive and might have to be adopted annually.

Some acidity, however, is safe; cane fruits will be happy in a soil with a pH of 6, which is slightly acid, or in one of 7, which is neutral, and they will tolerate acidity down to a pH of 5, but not below. You can always check acidity with a soil-testing kit, and apply lime as appropriate. The amount recommended by the manufacturers should be scattered evenly and forked in, preferably a few weeks before planting.

Preparing the ground

The best foundation is good quality compost dug deeply into the top 30cm (12 in) of soil at the rate of about a bucket – 9 litre (2 gallon) size – to a trench 60cm (2 ft) wide and 1·5m (5 ft) long, following the complete removal of all perennial weeds and their roots.

Prepare the ground in late summer or early autumn (July or August), ready for planting either when plants become available from the nurseries – usually from late autumn (October) onwards – or in the spring. Do not skimp on the compost at this stage because the plants will rapidly produce masses of shallow roots, making it impossible to dig in compost later without damaging them.

This base dressing of compost can be supplemented by laying a mulch each spring along the raspberry rows in a continuous strip some 45cm (18 in) wide and 2–5cm (1–2 in) deep, and – if you have enough to spare – round the root area of loganberry plants as a circular mat about 45cm (18 in) in diameter. To be fully effective as a conserver of soil moisture and to suppress weeds, which are two of the prime functions of a mulch, the material must be generously applied. Some perennial weeds, like dock, may still appear, but the roots are easily pulled out by hand from the friable soil which results from efficient mulching.

Choosing the site

The main factor in choiee of site is shelter from cold winds. At blossom time these can ruin the flowers, and at any period in the growing season they may cause leaf damage, sometimes to a severe degree. Every effort should be made to plant in a spot sheltered from northerly and easterly winds.

Westerly winds, on the other hand, cause little or no leaf scorch. However, if you have no choice but to plant in the path of any prevailing wind – and this is sometimes the case in country gardens – be sure the rows run along the wind rather than across it. Rows planted broadside could be badly blown about.

Spring frosts are seldom damaging because cane fruits come into flower when the frost hazard has passed.

How to plant raspberries

Plant your raspberries 45–60cm (18–24 in) apart, the latter distance being advisable for varieties making many canes (main stems), leaving a gap of 1·75–2m (6–6½ ft) between the rows. The roots should be covered to a depth of 7–8cm (3 in).

The simplest way is to take out a wedge of soil to the required depth and about a spade's width, and then, with someone holding the cane in position, replace the soil. Firm planting is essential; press home the soil (by treading it down) and then finish off the surface lightly. After planting, cut back the canes to 25–30cm (9–12 in) above soil level, so that the plants do not fruit the following summer, but spend the first year building strong roots and canes.

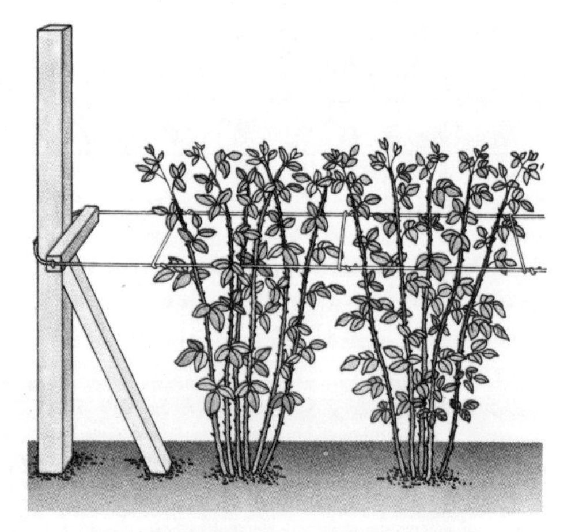

Training raspberries by the box system

The best method of training raspberries is the box system. With a post at each end of the row, firmly staple two parallel wires at about 60cm (24 in) above ground level to each one and fit with cross wires twisted around them to separate the canes of each stool (the root or stump from which the stems grow) from those of its neighbour. If necessary the wiring can be repeated at about 1·25m (4 ft) above the ground to accommodate the tall-growing varieties. To hold the parallel wires at the right distance apart, nail or screw 15cm (6 in) distance pieces (battens) to the end posts, and to intermediate posts where the rows are long. The battens, which should be about 4cm (1½ in) in

Malling Promise, a strong and upright variety producing heavy crops of firm fruit, provided the stock from which the excellent Malling Exploit was derived

diameter, can be grooved to take the wires, or the wires can be stapled to ungrooved surfaces. You don't have to tie in the canes, and the cross wires are easily adjustable to accommodate new ones. In this way every stool with its canes is enclosed within its own 'box', which greatly facilitates the pruning out of old canes, and allows a good air flow between the canes. This is an important point: adequate air movement to dry the canes, leaves and berries quickly after rain is a necessary factor in the prevention of fungus diseases.

End posts need not be particularly heavy, since they take little strain, serving mainly to hold the wires taut: 5–6cm (2 in) in diameter and 2m (6 ft) long is usually adequate. Sink them 45cm (18 in) and strengthen them with wood strainers. The bottom 60cm (24 in) should be thoroughly treated with a standard proprietary preservative. Creosote in this case is not suitable because it gives surface protection only and can be harmful to plants.

Pruning the canes

Routine pruning (for all except autumn fruiting varieties) consists of removing all fruited canes after harvest, and all weak new ones, leaving about 6–8 of the best per stool. Tip back (cut the tops off) new canes in early spring (February) at 1·5m (5 ft) or so (or just below the point where they have bent over) to encourage fruiting. Autumn-fruiting raspberries are left unpruned until early spring (February) when old canes are cut back to just above ground level.

Pests and virus diseases

Although there may be occasional outbreaks of pests and diseases, routine detailed spraying will not be necessary. The virus diseases are, in principle, the only really severe threat, but the Malling raspberries recommended here are tolerant of virus infection in varying degrees. This means that if they do become infected they will not suffer to any marked extent, and often no leaf symptoms will appear.

The Glen Clova variety is, however, showing itself to be intolerant, and susceptible to cross-infection, so it would be unwise to plant it with a tolerant variety. For example, if Malling Jewel and Glen Clova were neighbours, the former might become infected (without showing any symptoms of the disease) and pass the infection to Glen Clova, which could then suffer. Planted on its own, however, Glen Clova has so far shown virtually no virus infection.

Virus diseases are transmitted by certain greenfly species. The most common form of virus is probably mosaic. If the virus-transmitting greenfly feed on an infected plant and then (within 24 hours) feed on an uninfected one, they will transmit mosaic to the latter. It is almost impossible to keep down greenfly completely, but if you are growing a virus-intolerant raspberry it pays to apply an annual winter wash of tar oil against the over-wintering greenfly eggs.

The nastiest pest is the grub of the raspberry beetle. A spray with a derris pesticide after full bloom and again 10 days later is the answer.

Deficiency diseases

The chief nutritional element which may be lacking from time to time is potash; deficiency in this will show as greyish or brownish leaf margins which become dead and brittle. To correct this, apply 15–25g per sq m ($\frac{1}{2}$–$\frac{3}{4}$ oz per sq yd) of sulphate of potash in the autumn.

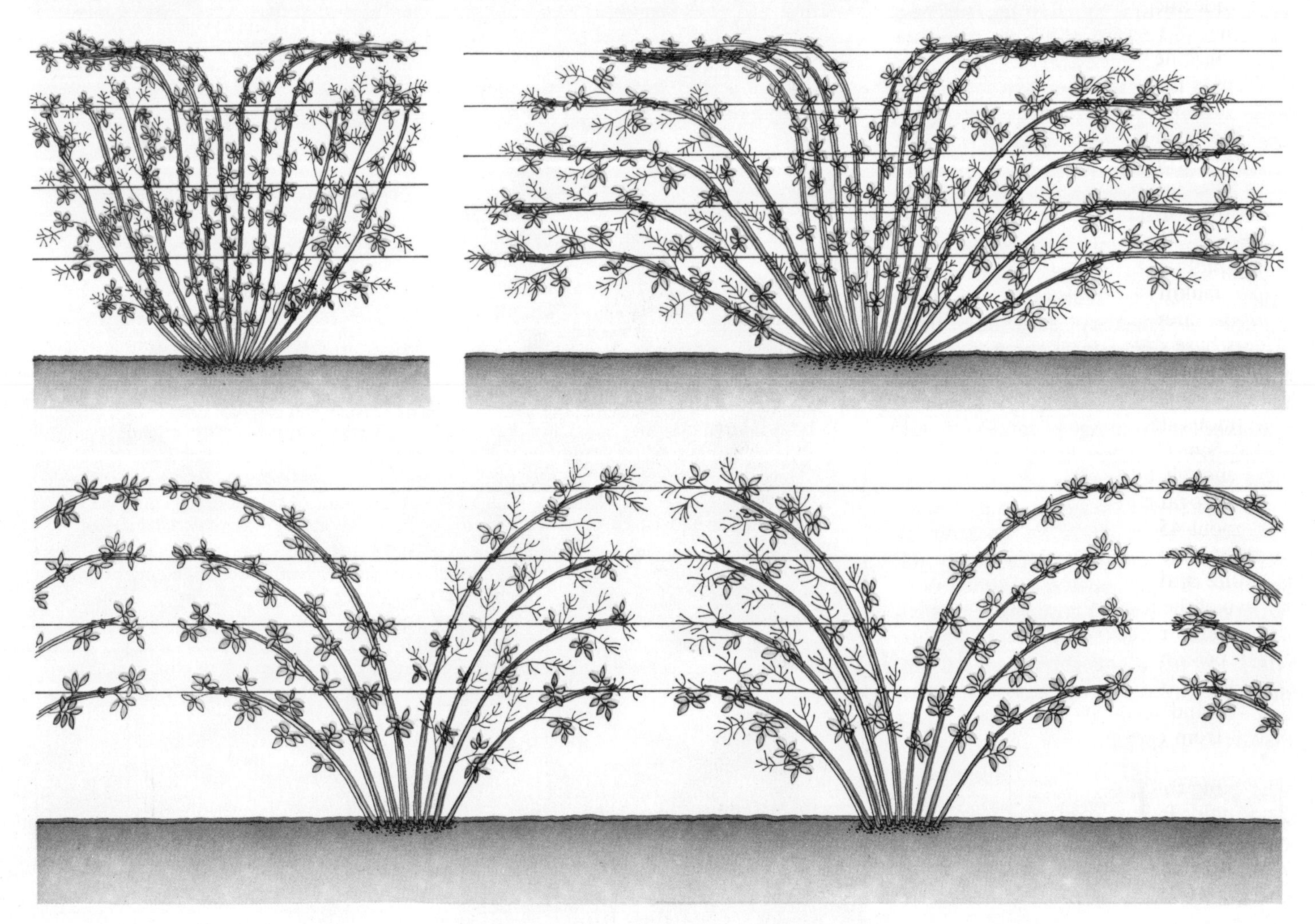

LOGANBERRIES

Loganberries are usually planted about 3·75m (12 ft) apart and are cut back as for raspberries. The main training systems are the open fan, the 'modified open fan' and the 'rope' or 'arch' method. The two latter systems make use of practically all cane growth whereas half of this may have to be sacrificed with the open fan – resulting in much crop loss. But the open fan method is more convenient where space is limited, as the plants can be put in much nearer together only 2·5–3m (8–10 ft) apart.

Open fan Fix wires at about 60cm (2 ft), 1m (3½ ft), 1·5m (5 ft) and 2m (6 ft) from ground level to stout end and middle posts 2·5m (8 ft) long, which have been sunk 60cm (2 ft) into the ground. Arrange the fruiting canes fan-wise on the first wires, with a gap in the centre. Lead the new canes up through this gap and tie temporarily to the top wire. After harvesting cut the fruited canes right out at the base and tie the new ones in to replace them.

Modified open fan Fix wires at 60cm (2 ft), 90cm (3 ft), 1·25m (4 ft), 1·5m (5 ft) and 2m (6 ft) from ground level. Train the fruiting canes to more or less their full length, left and right of centre along the first four wires, while the top wire again takes the new ones.

Rope or arch Train all fruiting canes in one direction, and all new ones in the opposite direction. When more than one stool is planted, arrange the training so that the fruiting canes of one stool always meet the fruiting canes of its neighbour.

Separation of fruiting from non-fruiting wood makes picking and pruning much easier and reduces the risk of cane spot fungus, the spores of which are washed from old to new canes. (All methods of training provide for this separation.) Other pests and virus diseases are covered opposite.

Modern loganberry plants can produce a dozen or more canes each season, all of which you can tie in practically full length with the rope and modified open fan systems, thereby ensuring the maximum crop – which may be 4·5–5kg (10–12 lb) per plant when the plants are fully established. In all cases you need to sink stout posts 2·5m (8 ft) long, to a depth of 60cm (2 ft).

Above right: ripe loganberries
Previous page: systems of loganberry training .Open fan, for use in limited space (far left, above), modified open fan (above left) and rope or arch (left)

RECOMMENDED VARIETIES

Skilful selection from among the modern varieties of raspberries and loganberries means that the gardener can enjoy the benefits of an extended picking season.

RASPBERRIES

The modern range of raspberries in Britain is composed chiefly of those raised at the East Malling Research station in Kent. In order of ripening the following are the best of those available.

Malling Exploit Early season variety fruiting in late summer (July). Canes abundant and vigorous; fruit large, bright red, firm and well-flavoured. Crops heavily and picks easily. Generally acknowledged to be superior to the earlier-raised Malling Promise from which it was derived.

Malling Jewel Early to mid season variety fruiting in late summer to early autumn (July–August). Cane growth strong but not abundant; fruit fairly large, medium to dark red, good flavour; picks easily and berries do not crumble. A reliable variety cropping well and regularly.

Malling Enterprise Mid to late season variety fruiting in early to late autumn (August–October). Canes strong but not usually abundant; fruit very large, medium red, firm, with excellent flavour; picks easily and does not crumble. Crops well, and tolerates heavier soil than other varieties provided drainage is adequate.

There are several more East Malling varieties, such as **Orion, Admiral** and **Delight,** on trial or being tested. Some are extremely heavy croppers producing fine quality berries, and will no doubt be released for general culture in due course. Two more outstanding varieties now available are **Glen Clova** from Scotland and **Zeva** from Switzerland. The former is an exceptionally heavy producer of top quality berries which are first-rate for eating and processing. The canes give a heavy mid season (early autumn) crop and a small mid autumn pick. Zeva starts to fruit in late summer and continues until mid to late autumn, though the summer crop is not abundant, and autumn is the period of heaviest cropping. The berries can be huge, sometimes 2–3cm (1 in or more) long, and the flavour is very fine. A distinct advantage of Zeva is that it needs no supporting system. It makes bush-like growth and can be grown as a single bush (where space is too limited for raspberry rows) even in a large tub or container. Finally, the autumn fruiting variety **September** is a splendid choice for those who want mid to late autumn raspberries, and the old favourite **Lloyd George** is still a winner if the improved New Zealand strain is bought. This latter is stocked by most leading fruit nurseries.

LOGANBERRIES

The best loganberry is the **Thornless**; it arose as a mutant or bud 'sport' of the thorned type which means it is identical to the original loganberry in all respects – except for having no thorns. Any natural plant variation is called a 'sport'.

REDCURRANTS AND WHITECURRANTS

Redcurrants eaten straight from the bush are among the most refreshing of soft fruit and are a delicious addition to fruit salads. They also make fine jelly and mix well with other fruit (especially raspberries) in jams, juices and desserts. Whitecurrants are sweeter and are usually eaten as fresh dessert fruit.

Although redcurrants and whitecurrants will grow on a wide range of soils, they prefer a medium loam that is well drained but able to hold summer moisture, and is slightly acid or neutral (though they will stand some degree of alkalinity).

They do, however, react adversely to waterlogged roots and lack of potash. These often go together for, although potash is not necessarily absent in such soils, waterlogged roots cannot use it. Dry roots cannot make use of potash either, so if the soil is too light it will need good supplies of well-rotted organic matter to build up a moisture-conserving medium, and if it is too heavy it will need the same treatment to open up the soil and improve its drainage.

Above: Jonkheer van Tets – one of the best varieties for garden culture, it produces fine crops early in the season

Below: Red Lake is an American variety
Overleaf: White Versailles has sweet berries in very long bunches

Bushes, cordons and espaliers

Both redcurrants and whitecurrants can be grown in bush form or as cordons and espaliers, and you can plant them in partial shade or in full sun. Redcurrant cordons can be trained against a north-facing wall if necessary, where they will do quite well, though their ripening period will be somewhat delayed. If possible choose a fairly sheltered spot for planting, to avoid wind damage.

The planting distances are 1·5m (5 ft) apart for bushes, 38cm (15 in) for cordons and 1·2–1·5m (4–5 ft) for espaliers.

You may want no more than one heavy-cropping bush. The variety called Earliest of Fourlands, for example, can produce about 5kg (11 lb) of redcurrants per bush in its fourth summer from planting, though average yields of all varieties could be some way below those of bumper years.

Bushes have a short stem from which the branches grow out to give an open centre bush. Plant to the soil mark at the base of the stem.

Each bush should have about eight cropping branches. Since the pruning of cordons and espaliers is the same as for bushes, a single cordon can be expected to produce one eighth of a bush crop, and a three-tier espalier (which would have six horizontal branches) would give about three-quarters of a bush crop.

Summer and winter pruning

Newly-bought bushes will not usually have eight branches, but they may have four, and these can easily be doubled by pruning.

After planting, cut back each branch by about half to an outward-pointing bud. During the next year extensions will grow, and generally each branch will send out a strong shoot from just below the extension, thus doubling the original number of branches. Tip these secondary shoots back by about half in the following winter and tip the leading extensions back by about one-third. Repeat as necessary in future winters, cutting all extensions back by one-third until the branches have reached the desired length. Some varieties grow strongly and quickly; with these, two (or at most three) winter cuttings are often enough.

Fruit is borne in clusters from short spurs along the branches; these are induced by summer and winter pruning. Summer pruning is done when the side shoots are mature along their basal portion, a stage that normally coincides with an increase in colour of the berries, about mid to late summer (late June). Cut the shoots back to within about 10cm (4 in), of the fourth or fifth leaf from the base. The branches are not cut. In winter cut the sideshoots again, to one or two buds from the base, leaving them as short spurs 13–20mm ($\frac{1}{2}$–$\frac{3}{4}$ in) long.

From time to time remove older branches to make way for new ones, maintaining a total of about eight branches.

The sideshoots of cordons and espaliers are treated in the same way, and the cordon rods and espalier branches are tipped as necessary in winter to stimulate extensions.

Feeding the plants

Red and whitecurrants do not need a great deal of feeding, but remember that heavy crops take their toll of soil foods. So keep the plants steadily supplied with moderate dressings of a combined organic fertilizer – applied annually or biennially as you think fit. Generally the lowest rate given in the maker's instructions will suffice; if they recommend, say, 70–100g per sq m (2–3 oz per sq yd), then use 70g (2 oz). Look out, however, for early stages of marginal leaf scorch, denoting potash deficiency. If this appears do not step up the routine dressing of combined fertilizer, but apply a separate dressing of sulphate of potash in autumn at about 17g per sq m ($\frac{1}{2}$ oz per sq yd). Do not use muriate of potash on currant bushes. Mulching, either in autumn or directly after fruit set, will help to conserve soil moisture.

Pest control

Aphides are the only serious pests. These can cause severe leaf damage. Distorted foliage with red blisters is a common sight on unsprayed bushes. Use a winter wash of tar oil to destroy the eggs. Alternatively you can spray the young aphides in spring with insecticides (such as derris or one of the systemics), but you must apply them as soon as the pests appear. As hatching occurs over a period, it may be necessary to apply two sprays (especially of derris). With tar oil, however, only one application is needed.

Choosing varieties

Some varieties have a lax habit; the form of the bush is loose and droopy, and shoots can easily be broken by the wind. Avoid varieties that grow in this way and also those that make 'blind' buds – ones that fail to grow. The recommended varieties given here are all strong, heavy-cropping bushes with no blind buds and little or no tendency to loose, open growth. All of them will give good-sized, high-quality currants.

RECOMMENDED VARIETIES

REDCURRANTS

Jonkheer van Tets Very early season variety ripening in mid summer (mid to late June); vigorous, upright growth; good cropper producing large fruit.

Earliest of Fourlands Early season variety ripening in mid to late summer (late June to early July); large bushes of erect habit producing firm, bright red fruit.

Laxton's No 1 Early season variety ripening in mid to late summer (late June to early July); produces heavy crops of good-sized fruit.

Red Lake Mid to late season variety ripening in late summer (mid July); an American variety producing long trusses of large, fine-flavoured fruit.

Wilson's Long Bunch Late season variety ripening in late summer (late July): produces large crops of medium-sized, light red fruit on very long branches.

WHITECURRANTS

White Versailles Mid season variety ripening in late summer (early July): strong-growing, fertile bushes producing large, pale yellow, richly-flavoured currants.

STRAWBERRIES

Strawberries will flourish in the open garden, under frames, cloches or polythene tunnels, in the greenhouse and in practically any properly-drained container – from an old wooden wheelbarrow to the modern, highly ornamental tower pots. If you give them the right soil conditions and are careful about watering, they will grow in hanging baskets, and be decorative as well as productive.

The main requirement of strawberries is a well-drained, moisture-retentive soil enriched with organic matter. The modern varieties are largely free of pests and diseases and produce crops of finely-flavoured, brightly-coloured berries, varying in size from medium to very large.

Summer fruiters and perpetuals
There are two types of strawberries: the summer fruiters, that produce berries from mid to late summer (June to July), and the perpetuals that fruit in relays from mid summer to mid or late autumn (June to September or October) – if the plants are kept under cloches during the summer.

The summer fruiters will generally crop for three seasons, though the third season's yield will usually be light. The perpetuals are more or less finished after one season, except for the variety Gento that can give quite a good yield in its second year.

Although the total crop from perpetuals is heavy, the number of berries gathered at each picking is often small. One variety may give a total of 500g (1 lb) per plant, but from perhaps 15 or more pickings spread over eight or nine weeks. Other varieties, of which Gento is an example, can produce some huge berries. So if you want the weight to be made up in berry numbers as well as in size, you must buy an appropriate number of plants, say a dozen for a family of four, to give each person a worthwhile share of the pickings.

Soil requirements
Strawberries are essentially a rotation crop. The summer fruiters occupy their plot for two or three seasons, and new plants are put in elsewhere. The perpetuals remain for one season, or at the most two seasons, and again a fresh site is chosen for new plants. If you are growing plants in containers, use fresh soil for each new planting. Never plant into soil if the crop previously occupying it was infected with verticillium wilt – a fungus infection which affects strawberries. Potatoes and tomatoes are susceptible to this disease, and so are the weeds groundsel, thistles and plantains.

Rotate strawberries with crops needing and receiving good organic manuring – like peas and beans. These have nitrogen-fixing nodules on their roots, so cut off the spent tops and leave the roots behind to supply nitrogen to the strawberries. Additional nitrogen-supplying fertilizers are not often required; an excess leads to leaf growth at the expense of berries, and this in turn hinders air circulation and sunlight penetration. These conditions invite grey mould (botrytis) that thrives in cool, damp conditions.

Strawberries like acidity, so do not add any lime to the strawberry bed. However, should you have limed the vegetable garden for a previous crop, this will not usually cause any trouble. One variety, Gento, does not appear to mind a limy soil, which makes it a good perpetual to choose for chalky districts.

On soils rich in humus you can achieve excellent results without using any fertilizers, but on less fertile land apply a general fertilizer (according to maker's instructions), that includes strawberries among plants for which it is formulated.

When to plant
Early autumn (August) is the best time to plant summer fruiters. You can then allow the plants to crop freely in the following summer. If you plant summer fruiters in the spring, remove all blossoms that appear, allowing the plants to build up strength for cropping the following year. Whether you plant in autumn or spring, remove the flowers appearing in early summer (May), but leave subsequent ones. Thereafter (with perpetuals that fruit again in the second year) leave all flowers intact.

How to plant
To prepare the soil, trench to about 15cm (6 in) to facilitate the placing of compost in the root zone. One barrowload per 8–10 sq m (10–12 sq yd) is a satisfactory dressing. A standard spacing is 45cm (18 in) between plants and 60–90cm (2–3 ft) between rows (depending on varieties). The summer fruiting variety Elista, however, can be planted with only 25cm (9 in) between plants. Plants must be set with their crowns level with the soil surface. If they are too high the new roots, that spring from the crown bases, will fail to contact the soil quickly enough and will perish; if too deep the crowns may rot, especially in wet summers.

Many nurseries sell pot-grown plants. These may arrive either in composition-type pots that are planted directly into the soil, when they soon rot to provide free root growth, or else with their roots enclosed in a fibrous net (that also rots). In both instances the tops of the containers should be at soil level. Make sure,

when buying plants, that they are certified as being from virus-free stock; most reputable nurseries now supply these.

Propagation by runners
Summer fruiters should have their runners removed in the first summer. These grow out from the parent plants and in due course form 'runner plants' that root on contact with the soil. In the second season you can leave them to grow on and use them to provide new plants for setting out in early autumn (August). They will then crop the following summer, thus giving you a continuation of summer harvests, and save the expense of buying new stock every third year.

Propagation is simple. Separate the plants from their parents by cutting the runners. Avoid cutting too close to the plantlet. Then lift them carefully and plant them out. Runners normally root readily in friable soil (or in a pot sunk in the soil). To make certain of rooting, however, peg the runners down with stones when the first leaves have appeared.

Allow no more than three runner plants (and preferably only two) to grow from each parent plant, using only the first to form on each runner. Never propagate from plants that are doing poorly; runner stock from poor parents will rarely succeed, and may well harbour disease.

Alternatively, keep two or so healthy plants just for runner production. Plant them away from the main strawberry bed and keep them 'de-blossomed'. If you choose this method, then remove and destroy runners from fruiting plants.

Some perpetuals do not make runners. Leave the runners on those that do, since the plantlets produce fruit in addition to that on the parents, thus increasing the total crop by up to about 25 per cent.

Mud and frost protection
When the first fruits have started to weigh down the stems, the plants can have a mat of straw laid round them to protect the berries from being splashed by mud. Another method is to lay strips of polythene sheeting, anchored by stones, along the rows. See that the soil is moist before laying down sheeting and that plants sit on a slight mound so that water does not collect around them. Black polythene sheeting is often recommended because it suppresses weeds. However, clear sheeting has been shown to give bigger crops in recent experiments.

Far left, above left and left: Tamella, Pantagruella and Baron Solemacher
Below: for best flavour, pick and eat strawberries when they are 'dew fresh'

Tunnel and cloche cultivation
Polythene sheeting tunnels are the latest means of getting an early pick from the summer fruiters. This is useful if you want early strawberries for a special occasion; otherwise you may not find the extra attention they need worth the end results. There are various patterns of tunnel. The best is the type which has a bar running along the length of its ridge. The sides can then be rolled up and fixed to this bar at flowering time to allow pollinating insects free play. Without their help many flowers may fail to set or may produce small or malformed berries.

An advantage of tunnels is that they reduce the need for watering. Loss of water by evaporation through the leaves is greatly reduced – but, of course, the water must be there in the first place. This means giving the plants a thorough watering just before the tunnels are fitted, usually in early to mid spring (late February to mid March) for a first pick in early summer (the third week of May) in the south of England. After a wet winter, however, there will probably be enough moisture in the ground to make this initial watering unnecessary. Roll up the tunnels in any unseasonably hot weather. If you are using cloches or Dutch lights, take off alternate cloches at flowering time, and open Dutch lights fully. With all types of culture the coverings must be in position overnight for early berries. If frost is forecast it is wise to cover Dutch lights, cloches and tunnels with light sacking or something similar, removing this the following morning.

Protect plants in the open from frost in flowering time – early summer (May) – by covering them with newspaper or straw at night; remove it in the morning. Never put down a straw mulch under the plants until the frost has gone, the mulch can worsen frost damage to blossoms by insulating them from ground warmth.

Pests on strawberries

Strawberries fall prey to many pests, but most of them are easily controlled.

Slugs Mostly a problem on soils with a high content of organic matter. Put down metaldehyde pellets at fruiting time.

Red spider mite Mostly found on plants grown under cloches or polythene tunnels. It causes a mottling of the foliage, and plant growth is weakened. Spray with malathion before flowering, or make several applications of derris.

Aphides These pests cause a curling of the foliage, and sap the strength of the plant. More seriously they are carriers of virus disease. The variety Royal Sovereign is particularly susceptible to aphides. Spray well into the centre of the plant with derris, malathion or pyrethrum.

Squirrels and birds Both these animals are fond of strawberries. The best protection is netting.

Virus diseases

There are several types of virus diseases that attack strawberries. The superficial symptoms of these diseases are very similar – stunting of the plant and discoloration of the leaves.

Green petal, arabis mosaic, yellow edge and crinkle These are spread by eelworms in the soil and by aphides and leaf hoppers. To help control the spread of the diseases, spray with derris or malathion. Remove all weak and unhealthy plants and burn them. Buy certificated stock plants, and propagate only from healthy plants – and from these only for four or five years.

Fungus diseases

Leaf spot, red core, mildew and grey mould (botrytis) are fungus diseases which may attack strawberries.

Leaf spot Pick off and burn any leaves with greyish-red spots.

Red core This is only likely to occur in areas where drainage is poor. Gradually all plants infected will appear stunted and die. If you cut into the roots, they will appear red in the centre. Spores of the fungus can live in the soil for twelve years or more. See that the ground is properly drained (by correct soil preparation) before planting. If plants become infected, burn them; strawberries should not be planted on the infected land again.

Mildew A dry-weather disease which shows as a white powdery mould. To control it, spray with dinocap, benomyl or wettable sulphur. Royal Sovereign is particularly prone to mildew. Although this variety is a fine summer fruiter it is much more prone to disease than the modern types, and therefore not recommended for beginners.

Grey mould (botrytis) This attacks mainly in wet summers. The fungus first appears in early summer (May), though it is invisible then, because only the spores are present. To defeat it at the outset, apply an appropriate fungicide. Several are available to gardeners, and are either protective formulations based on captan or thiram (don't spray during the three weeks before picking because of taint), or systemics based on benomyl. They are sold under brand names, complete with full instructions.

Tending the plants

The main jobs are weeding (best done with a hoe), removing or attending to the runners and watering in dry weather – especially important from first flower until just before harvesting. If you are using strips of polythene sheeting these will conserve root moisture and reduce watering, but they will prevent the penetration of rain. So, as with tunnels, a thorough watering must be given before the strips are laid.

As soon as the final harvest has been gathered, the old leaves should be cut off plants that are to be left for a further year. Old foliage produces substances that inhibit the maximum development of flower-buds for the next season. The simplest way is to clip over with shears, taking great care not to cut the crowns or any young leaves surrounding them. The cut-off foliage is then gathered up and burnt. Prick over the surrounding ground lightly with a fork, and lay a light dressing of compost.

The exception to this treatment is Cambridge Favourite. With this variety, the removal of the leaves would result in a reduced crop the following year.

Straw protects berries from mud; as shown here with Cambridge Favourite variety

RECOMMENDED VARIETIES

SUMMER FRUITING	**In season from mid to late summer (June to July)**
Pantagruella	Early season; acid-sweet in flavour.
Cambridge Rival	Early to second early; medium to medium-large berries; shiny, darkish crimson at maturity; flesh pinkish, sweet and rich; moderate cropper.
Cambridge Vigour	Mid season; first berries medium-large, then smaller; scarlet at maturity; heavy yielder in maiden year.
Domanil	Mid to late; high proportion of large berries; heavy cropper.
Grandee	Mid season; produces some giant berries; heavy second-year cropper; a show bench variety.
Tamella	Mid to late; very heavy cropper; an outstanding strawberry for all purposes – highly recommended.
PERPETUALS	**In season from mid summer to mid autumn (June to September)**
Gento	The supreme variety to date; crops heavily on parent plants and runners; gives some very large, shining, scarlet berries.
Trelissa	Medium to large berries in abundance on parents and runners; can be trained against trellis work for decoration.
Baron Solemacher	A fine old favourite of the alpine type, producing masses of small berries of the best quality for making jam; does not make runners; a fine decorative plant for shady borders.

BRASSICAS

BROCCOLI

The term broccoli – a plural form of the Italian 'broccolo', or cabbage-top – covers two types of vegetables – the heading broccoli, which is closely akin to the cauliflower, and the sprouting broccoli. The latter, instead of producing a large curd, forms many leafy shoots each of which bears its own curd. There are both white and purple varieties and, in addition, a green kind that is known as calabrese or Italian sprouting broccoli.

Above: shoot of white sprouting broccoli

Nowadays it is customary to find the heading varieties of broccoli listed in the catalogues as 'winter cauliflower'. This is reasonable enough, but it should be noted that there are differences between the cauliflower and the heading broccoli. The broccoli is not quite so white and often a little coarser in texture than the true cauliflower, and it is ready for harvest at a different time of year.

Of the two, broccoli is easier to grow. It is much hardier and less demanding in its soil requirements, and will do well in most soils if they are in a good, fertile condition. It does not need freshly-manured soil – in fact it does better without it. With broccoli, as with spring cabbage, the aim is to produce a plant that is large enough and hardy enough to stand through the winter. Lush, sappy growth should be avoided.

Preparing the soil

As the plants do not need to be planted out until mid or late summer (June or July) they make a good follow-on crop to the first broad beans, peas or potatoes. If the ground was manured for the previous crop, simply prick over the top few centimetres of soil with a fork. A top dressing of superphosphate of lime, at 70g per sq m (2 oz per sq yd), is a beneficial addition. Remember, also, that broccoli, like all the brassicas, likes firm ground.

Sowing times

Seeds can be sown from mid spring to early summer (March to May) according to variety. The harvest season (except for calabrese) extends roughly from late winter to mid summer (January to early June). Those that mature in late winter and early spring (January and February) will be mainly confined to the milder, frost-free districts. In colder areas choose varieties to harvest from mid spring (March) onwards.

If you are growing more than one row, then use several varieties; that way you will have a succession of curds.

Sow the early varieties of both heading and sprouting broccoli in mid or late spring (March or April), and the later varieties in late spring (April) except for those which do not mature until early or mid summer (May or June): these need not be sown until early summer (May). Sow the seeds thinly in a seedbed, in drills 13mm (½ in) deep and 25cm (9 in) apart. Make sure that each variety is labelled before the rows are raked in. Sprinkle calomel dust along each seed drill as a precaution against club root and where cabbage-root fly is a problem, use either a bromophos or diazinon insecticide according to maker's instructions.

Thinning and transplanting

As soon as the plants are large enough to handle, thin them to 5cm (2 in) apart. This thinning (which is too often neglected) makes for good, straight plants.

The move into their final quarters can be made when the plants are about 15cm (6 in) high. Dull, showery weather is the best time to move the plants, but it is not always possible to wait for these conditions. If the ground is dry and hard, water the plants well a few hours before moving them.

To transplant, first ease the plants with a fork and lift them carefully. Keep as much soil on the roots as possible and plant them in their new quarters straight away. Allow 60cm (24 in) between plants and rows; if space is a problem you can reduce this to 50cm (20 in). Plant firmly so that the lower leaves of each plant are just clear of the soil, and then water them in. If your plants are strong and well-grown, and if you move as much soil with them as possible, the check from transplanting will be minimal.

Buying ready-grown plants
If you were unable to sow seeds, plants are usually available from garden centres and market stalls. Always find out the variety and when it is likely to mature. Do not choose plants which are weak and spindly. Ensure the plants are sturdy and about 13–15cm (5–6 in) high. Providing the rootball is not too badly damaged they should settle down quickly in their new positions.

Perennial broccoli and calabrese
An unusual member of the broccoli family is the perennial broccoli, usually listed as Nine Star Perennial. This plant produces from six to nine heads instead of the usual one. They are smaller than the normal heading types, but much larger than the heads of sprouting broccoli. The plant will continue to produce heads for several years providing you do not allow it to seed. The plants need extra room in which to develop, so allow 90cm (3 ft) between plants. They are best put out alongside a path or fence where they can be left undisturbed. After their first flowering, top-dress the plants each spring with some well-rotted manure or compost.

The green Italian sprouting broccoli, more commonly known as calabrese, deserves a special mention. Large quantities of this are now grown commercially and used in the frozen vegetable trade. It is becoming increasingly popular with housewives and is as easy to grow as the sprouting broccoli. Some varieties have a large, central green head which is followed by a limited number of sideshoots; other varieties have a smaller head and more spears. The shoots are tender and of first-rate flavour.

Sowing and cultivation are the same as for sprouting broccoli, but the plants mature in autumn and early winter, not in the spring. Their main season is mid to late autumn (September to October) but in an open autumn they will continue to produce their shoots into early or mid winter (November or December).

Above right: purple sprouting broccoli
Right: white sprouting broccoli

RECOMMENDED VARIETIES

Type	Variety	When to sow	When to transplant	When to cut
	*St Agnes	mid to late spring	mid to late summer	early to mid spring
	*Snow-white	mid to late spring	mid to late summer	mid spring
	Veitch's Self-protecting	mid spring	mid summer	mid winter
	St George	late spring	mid to late summer	late spring
	Walcheren Winter	mid spring	mid summer	late spring to early summer
	Late Queen	early summer	late summer	early to mid summer
	Mirado	early summer	late summer	mid summer
	*Not completely hardy – for mild areas only			
Sprouting broccoli	Early White	mid spring	mid to late summer	early to mid spring
	Early Purple	mid spring	mid to late summer	early to mid spring
	Late White	late spring	late summer	mid to late spring
	Late Purple	late spring	late summer	mid to late spring
Perennial broccoli	Nine Star Perennial	late spring	mid summer	mid spring
Calabrese	Express Corona (F.1 hybrid)	mid to late spring	mid summer	early to mid autumn
	Autumn Spear	late spring	late summer	late autumn to early winter

Key to seasons

early spring (February)	early summer (May)	early autumn (August)	early winter (November)
mid spring (March)	mid summer (June)	mid autumn (September)	mid winter (December)
late spring (April)	late summer (July)	late autumn (October)	late winter (January)

Harvesting broccoli

Like cauliflowers, heading broccoli tend to mature quickly if the weather conditions are suitable. Cut them as soon as they are at their best, when the edges of the curd are just beginning to open; the head is then usually 15–20cm (6–8 in) in diameter.

The sprouting broccoli are ready for picking when they look like miniature cauliflowers about 15cm (6 in) in length. It is not necessary to wait until the curds can be seen. The plants will produce further small curds over several weeks.

Pests and diseases

Although this is a relatively easy crop to grow, there are a few pests and diseases which you may encounter.

Club root Often known as 'finger and toe', this attacks the root system and causes swellings which deform the roots. This, in turn, causes the plant to wilt and look stunted. There is, as yet, no cure but the disease can be prevented. Club root is always worst on acid soils, so if your soil is acid give a dressing of 100–135g per sq m (3–4 oz per sq yd) of garden lime prior to planting and sprinkle calomel dust along the seed drills. When transplanting, make a paste from calomel dust and dip the roots in it.

Below: picking off shoots of broccoli

Cabbage-root fly This insect lays its eggs against the plant stems. From the eggs little white grubs hatch out and burrow down into the soil where they attack the roots. It is always advisable to give the ground a routine dressing of bromophos or diazinon to prevent this pest.

Cabbage whitefly This pest is particularly bad on all members of the cabbage family and can make many vegetables almost unusable. Spray at the first sign of an attack with a pesticide based on resmethrin.

Cabbage white butterfly During the summer and autumn, keep a close watch for the cabbage white butterfly. The caterpillars which hatch out from the eggs have a voracious appetite and, if they are not dealt with quickly, the plants will soon look like lace curtains. Do not wait for this stage, but as soon as a butterfly is seen spray the plants with derris or trichlorphon or malathion and repeat the spray whenever necessary.

Flea beetle This pest can be a problem after germination. Spray or dust with a BHC compound as a precaution.

BRUSSELS SPROUTS

It is not surprising that the brussels sprout should be among the most popular members of the brassica family. With its ability to grow in most soils, its hardiness and its long period of use it is one of the most valuable of winter vegetables.

You can choose from tall, half-tall and dwarf varieties of sprouts. The dwarf and half-tall types are especially useful for small gardens and exposed sites. There are now a number of F.1 hybrids that give uniform sprouts of medium size and these are specially recommended for freezing.

Plants are readily available from market stalls or garden centres; choose plants that are a healthy green and not too large.

Preparing the site

Choose an open site where the soil is 'in good heart'. Sprouts need plenty of nourishment and will not do well in poor soils. A medium to heavy loam is the best choice, but they will do quite well in lighter soils providing the site has been prepared several months in advance.

This early preparation is all-important. Dig in as much manure or compost as you can spare. Farmyard manure is still the best, but is often difficult to come by. Useful alternatives are spent mushroom compost, deep litter from poultry houses, or garden compost. It does not matter if the compost is not fully rotted as the process of decomposition will be continued in the soil. Try to complete the manuring and digging by the end of the year and leave the soil rough.

If garden lime has not been used recently, apply it during early or mid spring (February or March) at about 135g per sq m (4 oz per sq yd); but do not apply it within 3–4 months of manuring. In mid spring (March) break down the soil with a cultivator.

One of the disadvantages of growing sprouts is that ground must be reserved for them; unlike cabbages or cauliflowers they cannot be used for double cropping as the planting period is too early. Planting should be completed before late summer (the end of June) and preferably a couple of weeks earlier.

However, by careful planning, the ground can be cropped until the sprouts are quite well grown. Lettuce, radishes, spring onions and summer spinach, or turnips, beetroot and carrots for pulling young, may be sown in rows 60–75cm (2–2½ ft) apart. It is then a simple matter to plant out the sprouts between the rows of the earlier crops. These will be cleared by the time the sprouts need the space.

When and how to sow

When you sow depends on when you want to harvest. For a very early crop – in

Left: good, even-sized sprouts. Below: recommended variety Irish Elegance

mid autumn (September) – sow in an unheated greenhouse in late winter (January). When the seedlings are big enough to handle, prick them off, 5–8cm (2–3 in) apart, into trays about 15cm (6 in) deep. Alternatively, sow outdoors in early or mid autumn (August or September) and then cover the young plants with cloches later. Four rows, 10cm (4 in) apart, can be accommodated under a barn cloche.

There is, however, little point in having brussels sprouts while there is still a selection of autumn vegetables available. Many gardeners consider that sprouts taste much better after the first frost. For a mid season picking from late autumn to mid winter (October through December), sow outdoors in early to mid spring (late February or March). Where this early sowing is likely to present problems (as in cold areas or on heavy soils), place cloches in position a few weeks in advance of sowing to warm up the soil.

For a late picking from the middle of winter (late December) onwards, sow in mid to late spring (March or the first week or two in April). Plants from these sowings should be ready for moving in early or mid summer (May or June). Sow the seeds thinly in short rows 13mm ($\frac{1}{2}$ in) deep, and when the seedlings are big enough to handle, thin them to 5cm (2 in) apart. This gives straighter and stronger plants. Dust the seedlings with derris to protect them from flea beetle.

How to transplant

When the plants are about 20cm (8 in) high they are ready for transplanting. Ease them out with a fork, then separate them carefully and move them with as much soil as possible. A showery period is the best time for transplanting but this cannot always be arranged! In dry periods water the seedbed well a few hours before transplanting.

To protect the young plants from cabbage-root fly, either dip the roots of each plant in a paste made from calomel dust or sprinkle a small teaspoonful of the dust around each plant.

It is important to plant firmly, with the lower leaves just clear of the soil. A dibber or trowel is needed for this work; a trowel is better as it makes a bigger hole and avoids cramping the roots. A simple test for firmness is to pull gently at the topmost leaf of a plant. If the plant 'gives' it is not firm enough; if the end of the leaf tears, all is well.

The planting distances for sprouts are 68–75cm ($2\frac{1}{4}$–$2\frac{1}{2}$ ft), all ways, for taller varieties and 60cm (2 ft) for the dwarf varieties. These should be regarded as minimum distances, for sprouts need room in which to mature.

Tending growing plants

Unless your site is a sheltered one, you may need to stake taller plants. Where the plants are grown in a block it will be the corner plants that are most at risk, particularly those facing the prevailing wind. With the approach of autumn, draw a little soil up to the plants to give them better anchorage. Feeding should not be necessary if you prepared the ground well in the first place, but sprouts do respond to foliar feeding, and this is an extra boost that can be given at about fortnightly intervals during the peak growing period of late summer and early autumn (July and August).

Snap off any lower leaves that go yellow during the late summer and put them on the compost heap. If you leave them on the plants they may cause the lower sprouts to go mouldy or rotten.

'Blown' sprouts are those which remain open and refuse to button up into solid sprouts. Loose soil is often the cause and this is one reason why you should prepare the site early, particularly on light soils.

Above: early-maturing crops like lettuce can be grown between rows of sprouts
Below: transplant when sprouts have 4 leaves; test for firmness by pulling a leaf

Above: bend buttons sharply down to pick
Below: stake corner plants to avoid damage

Overfeeding with nitrogenous fertilizer is another cause of 'blown' sprouts.

One method of building up the sprouts is to pinch out the growing point of the plant when its optimum size has been reached – usually in late autumn (October). This practice is known as 'cocking'. Remove only a small piece, about as big as a walnut, but don't confuse this with the practice of removing the whole top of the plants.

Below: red sprouts taste like red cabbage
Below right: recommended variety Peer Gynt is a half-tall early cropper
Bottom: a fine crop ready for picking

These cabbage-like heads do make an excellent vegetable and are preferred by some people to the sprouts – but do not remove them too early. The outer leaves of the plant, and its head, are there to protect the sprouts from the winter weather. If you remove them too soon this protection will be lost. It is better to leave them in place until mid spring (March), when the worst of the winter is over, and then make use of them. The topmost sprouts will then fill out.

One of the advantages of sprouts is that they yield their crop over a period. You can remove a few sprouts from each plant as they become ready, and leave those higher up the stem to grow up to size.

To gather the sprouts, hold the plant with one hand, take off the leaves as far up the plant as you intend to remove the sprouts, and then snap the buttons off with a downward pressure of the thumb. If, as sometimes happens, the buttons are so tight and close together that removal is difficult, use a sharp knife. Whatever method you use, take the sprouts off cleanly so that no portion is left to go mouldy or rotten. In late spring (April) any sprouts or tops that have not been used will burst open and throw up seed stems. Do not allow these to flower, for it is at this stage that the plants are taking most nourishment from the soil. Chop off all the green leaves and stems and dig them in. The roots should be forked out and burnt on your next bonfire. The greenstuff will eventually rot down into humus and will, in the meantime, help to keep the soil open. Late spring (April) is the time for planting potatoes, which like a loose soil, and there is no better crop than potatoes to follow brussels sprouts.

Pests and diseases

Brussels sprouts are vulnerable to the pests and diseases that commonly attack the brassica family.

Cabbage-root fly The transplanting period is the time when precautions should be taken against this pest that lays its eggs against the stems of the plants. The maggots that hatch from the eggs burrow into the soil and attack the stems below soil level. Affected plants wilt in sunshine and will eventually collapse. Sprinkle a small teaspoonful of calomel dust around each plant or dip the roots and stems of the seedlings in a paste made from the dust prior to planting out.

Club root A fungus disease that causes swollen and deformed roots. There is (as yet) no cure, but it can be controlled if lime is used as recommended in the section on preparing the site. Calomel dust will also give some control.

RECOMMENDED VARIETIES

Early Half Tall Produces a very early crop of large, good-quality sprouts.
Bedford Filbasket Mid season variety with large, tightly-packed sprouts.
Irish Elegance Tall, mid season variety.
Cambridge No. 5 Tall, late variety.
Peer Gynt (F.1 hybrid) Early, half-tall variety with medium-sized sprouts; recommended for freezing.
Citadel (F.1 hybrid) Mid season variety, recommended for freezing.
Red Produces sprouts that look and taste like miniature red cabbages.

CABBAGE

The cabbage, despite its rather unglamourous reputation, is a useful vegetable which no garden should be without. Not only is it a valuable food source, containing calcium and vitamins A and C, but it is available all year round and is easier to grow than most brassicas.

Cabbages can be divided into five main groups: spring, summer, winter, savoy and red. There is also Chinese cabbage.

Preparing the soil
Like all brassicas, cabbage does best in a firm and preferably alkaline soil. A light to medium soil is ideal, but it will grow quite happily in all soils, providing they are well drained.

In many cases cabbages will be planted as a follow-on crop to other vegetables. If the ground was manured for the previous crop a further manuring is not necessary, but you could usefully apply a general fertilizer at 70g per sq m (2 oz per sq yd).

Sowing and transplanting
Cabbages are easily raised from seeds sown in a seedbed. Most of the summer varieties can be sown for succession and it is better to make several small sowings rather than one large one. As with broccoli (see page 64), sprinkle calomel dust along each seed drill as a precaution against club root, and where cabbage-root fly is a problem, use either a bromophos or diazinon insecticide, according to the maker's instructions.

When the seedlings are large enough to handle, thin to 5cm (2 in) apart. This gives them room to make good, sturdy plants.

The move into their final quarters should take place when the plants are about 15cm (6 in) high. Ease the plants up with a fork and separate them carefully. Leave as much soil on the roots as possible and plant them at once. A dibber can be used but a trowel makes a bigger hole and gives the roots more room. Plant so that the lower leaves are just clear of the soil, firm around the roots and water the plants well in. Then keep the plants free from weeds and see they do not lack water during dry periods.

Spring cabbage
Spring cabbage have a distinct 'nutty' flavour of their own, as well as having much else to commend them. They mature in spring when vegetables are scarce; there is usually no caterpillar

1 Cabbage seedling ready to transplant
2 Transplanting to final growing position
3 Thinning out for use as spring greens
4 Earthing-up with a swan-necked hoe

Left and above: summer cabbage Golden Acre Baseball and winter Avon Coronet

problem; being late they often miss the cabbage-root fly and they are seldom attacked by club root, which is not active during the winter months.

Sow in late summer or early autumn (July or August) and transplant during mid or late autumn (September or October). It is as well to make two sowings, about three weeks apart, and take the best plants from each. If the weather is dry at sowing time, water the seed drills well a few hours beforehand.

Spring cabbage usually follow one of the summer crops. They are ideal for following potatoes, and in this case the soil will only need lightly forking over before the plants are put out. Do not give them any manure, and use no fertilizers until the spring. The aim is to grow a strong plant to withstand the winter.

One mistake often made with spring cabbage is to give them too much room. Planted closer together they protect one another. For the smaller varieties, allow 38cm (15 in) between the rows and for the larger ones 50cm (20 in). Small cabbages can go as close as 30cm (12 in) between plants, but the larger ones will need 45cm (18 in). If enough plants are available it is a good plan to halve the distance between the plants and then take out every other plant in mid or late spring (March or April) for use as 'spring greens'.

In mid spring (March) a top dressing of a high nitrogen fertilizer will give the plants a useful boost. Hoe it into the soil and let the rain wash it in.

The main enemy of spring cabbage is not the weather but wood pigeon. In severe weather they will be desperate enough to attack plants in home gardens. Cover them with cloches – large barn cloches will cover two rows – to protect them from attack and produce an earlier crop. The thin, plastic strawberry netting also gives good protection. Make sure, though, that it hangs well clear of the plants.

Summer cabbage
The season for summer cabbage is late summer to late autumn (July to October). You can make a first sowing of an early variety in early spring (February) if you have a frame or cloches. During mid and

Winter cabbage
Sow winter cabbage in late spring or early summer (April or May) for harvesting from late autumn to early spring (October to February). Winter cabbage comprise the Dutch-type white cabbages like Winter White, the Christmas Drumheads selection and one outstanding variety known as January King. They are noted for their ability to stand several weeks without cracking open. Use them to bridge the gap between the summer cabbages and the savoys, and as a follow-on crop if planted out in late summer (July). If the variety Winter White is dug up by the roots and hung head downwards in a shed or cellar it will keep well for weeks.

Savoy cabbage
The leaves of the savoy cabbage are dark green and heavily crimped, and they will survive even a severe winter. Sow in late

RECOMMENDED VARIETIES

Type	Variety (P) pointed hearts (others are round)	Size
Spring cabbage	April (P)	small
	Durham Early (P)	medium
	First Early market (P)	large
Summer cabbage	Greyhound (P)	small
	Golden Acre	medium
	Winnigstadt (P)	large
	Hispi (P)	small
Winter cabbage	Winter White	large
	Christmas Drumhead	medium
	January King	medium
Savoy cabbage	Savoy King	medium
	Ormskirk Rearguard	medium
Red cabbage	Large Blood Red	large
	Niggerhead	medium
Chinese cabbage	Pe-tsai	
	Nagaoka (F.1 hybrid)	

Key to seasons
early spring (February)
mid spring (March)
late spring (April)
early summer (May)
mid summer (June)
late summer (July)

late spring (late March or April) make successional outdoor sowings, with a final sowing (again of an early variety) in early summer (May).

They will be ready for planting out from early to late summer (May to July). Those that you leave till later in the summer (late June or July) can make use of ground vacated by the first potatoes, peas or broad beans. You may also be able to do some intercropping by planting early summer cabbage between rows of peas or dwarf beans. In the first instance the peas will be cleared by the time the cabbages need more room, and in the second the cabbages will have been cut by the time the beans are at their peak.

Above: hardy savoy cabbage Lincoln Late
Right: hardy, slow-growing red cabbage

spring or early summer (April or May) to harvest from mid winter to late spring (December to April). There are early and late varieties. You can even plant out the late varieties in early autumn (August), making a useful follow-on crop.

Red cabbage
Although red cabbage is mostly used for pickling, it also makes quite a good table vegetable. As it needs a long period of growth, sow not later than mid spring (March). An early spring (February) sowing under cloches is better. The finest red cabbage of all comes from a sowing

Planting distance rows	plants	When to sow	When to transplant	When to harvest
38cm (15 in)	30cm (12 in)	mid to late summer	mid to late autumn	late spring to mid summer
45cm (18 in)	38cm (15 in)	mid to late summer	mid to late autumn	late spring to mid summer
53cm (21 in)	45cm (18 in)	mid to late summer	mid to late autumn	late spring to mid summer
38cm (15 in)	30cm (12 in)	early spring to early summer	early to late summer	late summer to mid autumn
45cm (18 in)	45cm (18 in)	late spring	mid to late summer	mid to late autumn
53cm (21 in)	45cm (18 in)	late spring to early summer	mid to late summer	mid to late autumn
38cm (15 in)	30cm (12 in)	mid spring to autumn	early summer to late autumn	late summer, autumn and spring
53cm (21 in)	53cm (21 in)	late spring	late summer	early to mid winter
53cm (21 in)	45cm (18 in)	late spring	late summer	early to mid winter
53cm (21 in)	53cm (21 in)	late spring	late summer	mid winter to early spring
60cm (24 in)	53cm (21 in)	late spring to early summer	late summer	mid winter to early spring
60cm (24 in)	53cm (21 in)	late spring to early summer	late summer to early autumn	late winter to late spring
60cm (24 in)	60cm (24 in)	early to mid spring or late summer to early autumn	early to mid summer	mid to late autumn
53cm (21 in)	53cm (21 in)	early to mid spring or late summer to early autumn	mid to late spring	mid to late autumn
75cm (30 in)	20cm (8 in)	late summer	do not transplant	mid to late autumn
75cm (30 in)	20cm (8 in)	late summer	do not transplant	mid to late autumn

rly autumn (August)
id autumn (September)
te autumn (October)

early winter (November)
mid winter (December)
late winter (January)

made at the same time as spring cabbage in late summer or early autumn (July or August). The plants grow more slowly than spring cabbage and, as they are perfectly hardy, can be left in the seedbed until mid or late spring (March or April).

Chinese cabbage

Although described as a cabbage, this vegetable closely resembles a large cos lettuce. Its crisp, delicately-flavoured head can be boiled like cabbage or used in salads.

The plants are easily grown from seed but should not be transplanted. A good, medium-to-heavy loam suits them best; on poor, light, hungry soils they tend to go to seed quickly.

Because of this tendency towards seeding, it is better to delay sowing until late summer (July), and this means that they are useful for following earlier vegetables. A good site is in the lee of a taller crop that will give the plants some shade for part of the day. Sow the seeds in drills 6mm (¼ in) deep and 75cm (2½ ft) apart. The easiest and most economical way is to sow a few seeds every 30–38cm (12–15 in) and then thin to the strongest.

Beyond keeping them free from weeds, the plants need no special attention, but see that they never lack water.

Pests and diseases

Some pests and diseases affect cabbages badly. Watch out for signs of trouble.

Club root (known as 'finger and toe') attacks the root system and causes swellings which deform the roots. This, in turn, causes the plant to wilt and look stunted. There is, as yet, no cure – but the disease can be prevented. Club root is always worst on acid soils, so if your soil is acid, give it a dressing of garden lime at 100–135g per sq m (3–4 oz per sq yd) prior to planting, and sprinkle calomel dust along the seed drills. When transplanting, make a paste from calomel dust and dip the roots in it.

Cabbage-root fly This insect lays its eggs against the plant stems. From the eggs little white grubs hatch out and burrow down into the soil where they attack the roots. It is always advisable to give the ground a routine dressing of bromophos or diazinon to prevent this pest.

Cabbage whitefly This pest is particularly bad on all members of the cabbage family and renders many vegetables almost unusable. Spray at the first sign of attack with a pesticide based on resmethrin.

Below: lettuce-like Chinese cabbage

Cabbage white butterfly During the summer and autumn, keep a close watch for the cabbage white butterfly. The caterpillars which hatch out from the eggs have voracious appetites and, if they are not dealt with quickly, the plants will soon look like lace curtains. Do not wait for this stage, but as soon as a butterfly is seen spray the plants with derris or trichlorphon or malathion and repeat the spray whenever necessary.

Flea beetle This pest can be a problem when the seedlings have germinated. Spray or dust with a BHC compound.

CAULIFLOWERS

The cauliflower is one of the most popular of the brassicas, though not one of the easiest to grow well. The name actually covers two types – the summer and autumn cauliflowers, and the cauliflower broccoli which is in season in late autumn and spring. This section deals with the true cauliflower – the summer and autumn varieties.

Cauliflower seeds are expensive (but not, of course, as expensive as cauliflowers themselves) and you may not wish to buy several new packets every year. But fortunately the seeds remain viable for several years and there is no reason why a packet should not be spread over two seasons. A better method is to buy new seeds each year and share them – and the expense – with another gardener.

Preparing the ground

Cauliflowers are gross feeders and like a rich, deep loam. They will not thrive on heavy, badly-drained clays, on very light loams which dry out in the summer, or on poor, hungry soils. If you plant them in these conditions they tend to retaliate by forming only small heads (a process known as 'buttoning') which open quickly and shoot up to form seed.

Choose, if possible, a site in full sun and with some shelter from cold winds. Dig this over during the autumn, working in as much compost or manure as can be spared. If you have not limed the ground recently spread a dressing over the soil surface at 135g per sq m (4oz per sq yd) and let the rain wash it in.

Sowing for all seasons

There are different varieties for different periods, so you can plan for a succession of harvests.

Cauliflowers for cutting in mid and late summer (June and July) should be sown in mid autumn (September) and overwintered under glass. Those for heading in early and mid autumn (August and September) are sown in mid or late spring (March or April), and those for maturing in late autumn and early winter (October and November) should not be sown until early summer (May).

There are several ways of raising plants of the early varieties. You can, for instance, sow the seeds outdoors in mid autumn (September) and then prick off the plants into trays of potting compost as soon as they are big enough to handle. Keep the plants in a cold frame or a cold greenhouse throughout the winter. Or you can thin the plants where they stand and cover them with cloches. In either case leave about 8cm (3 in) between the plants; this will give them room to make strong, healthy growth. Transplant them, with a good soil ball, in the spring.

If you miss the mid autumn (September) sowing you can sow in a warm greenhouse in late winter (January) or in a cold one in early spring (February). Sow two or three seeds at 8cm (3 in) intervals in one of the soilless composts, as these encourage the formation of a good rootball. Thin to the strongest plant. Although the plants need protection during the winter you should ventilate them during the daylight hours whenever possible. Begin to harden them off in mid spring (March) so that they can be put out into their final positions during late spring (the second half of April).

Maincrop sowings are made outdoors in late spring (April). Thin the plants, as soon as you can handle them, to stand 4–8cm (2–3 in) apart. Don't leave the rows overcrowded; bent, spindly plants will be the result.

One of the drawbacks to growing cauliflowers in the past has been the fact that so many of them mature together, giving a glut one week and none the next. You can offset this to some extent by making two sowings – with a fortnight between – instead of one. If you have a deep-freeze the problem of coping with a surplus becomes less important as the summer varieties can be frozen for future use at your convenience.

Buying plants

Although plants can be bought from market stalls and garden centres you would do far better to raise your own. Some of the soil is bound to be knocked off the roots of bought plants in transit and very few of them are named. If, for any reason, it becomes necessary to buy plants, choose those with a good colour and straight stems. Avoid plants that are too big; one of about 15cm (6 in) will tolerate the move better and establish itself more quickly than a larger plant.

How to transplant

The importance of transplanting healthy plants with a good rootball cannot be stressed too much. Any check to the growth of cauliflowers is liable to cause

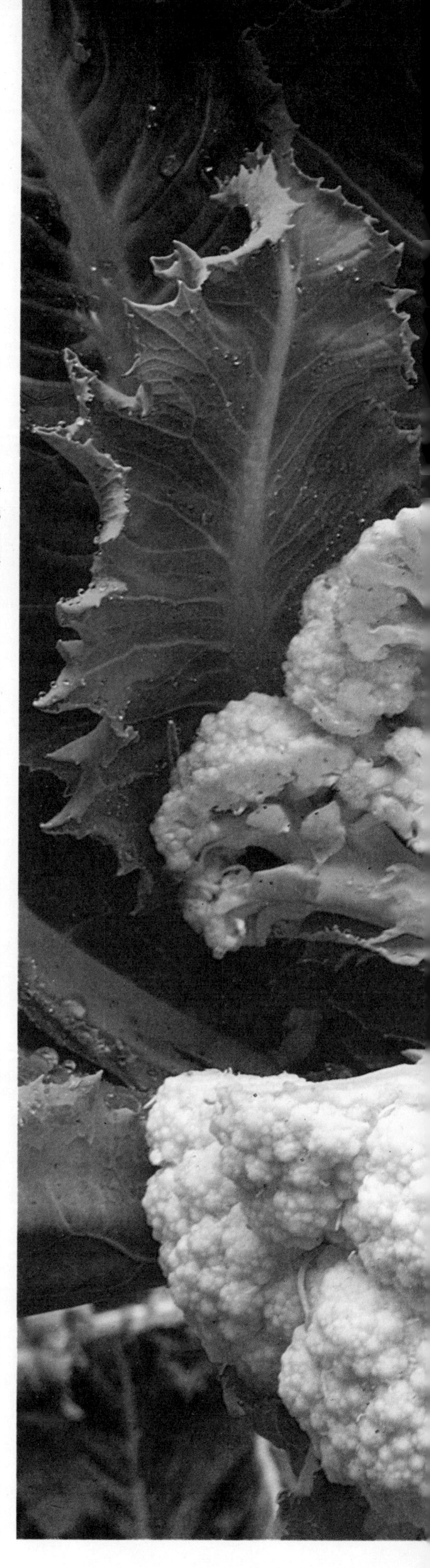

buttoning, and transplanting is one of the danger periods. The best method is to ease up the plants with a fork, then lift them out with as much soil as possible and put them straight into their final positions. Plant firmly, with the lower leaves just clear of the soil, and water them well in.

Plants of the early varieties should be spaced 45cm (18 in) apart all ways. The summer varieties will need 55cm (22 in) and the later ones 60cm (24 in).

As the later varieties are not ready for transplanting until late summer (July) you can use them as a follow-on crop to peas or early potatoes. There is no need to dig the plot over; simply prick over the top few centimetres with a fork, apply a general fertilizer at 70g per sq m (2 oz per sq yd) and rake level.

Tending and harvesting

In periods of drought give the plants as much water as possible in order to keep them growing, for drought can check growth and cause premature heading, ruining your crop.

When the plants are growing strongly they will appreciate doses of liquid manure at weekly or fortnightly intervals. Use either a proprietary liquid manure or a home-made solution, made by suspending an old sack containing several fork-loads of manure in a tub or tank and leaving it for a few days. Dilute the manure water until it has the appearance of weak tea. Young children should be kept well away from it.

Keep a close watch on the crop once the curds (florets) begin to form as they come quite quickly, especially during the summer months. Bright sunlight turns the curds yellow; to prevent this, snap the stems of a few of the outer leaves and fold them down over the developing curd to shut out the light. The same protection can be given to the late varieties if frost threatens. However, the modern strains of late cauliflowers are mostly 'self-protecting' – the inner leaves fold over the curd naturally and therefore give good protection.

Fresh cauliflowers will keep in good condition for about a week if you dig them up by the roots and hang them, head downwards, in a cool, dark place. If the soil is at all dry, water them well an hour or two before lifting.

This firm-headed cauliflower with crisp white curd has been carefully tended in rich, well-prepared soil, given plenty of water in the growing season, shielded from frost and bright sunlight and protected from pests and diseases

Pests and diseases

Cauliflowers, unfortunately, are subject to quite a variety of pests and diseases.

Birds The tender young leaves of newly-transplanted plants may be attacked by birds. Use black cotton, or flashing strips of foil to keep them off.

Rabbits On open allotments, and sometimes even in home gardens, rabbits can be terribly destructive. The only really effective remedy is to surround the whole brassica plot with 90cm (3 ft) high chicken-wire. Although this is expensive initially, you can use it over and over again. You can also try spraying or dusting with an animal repellent – quite harmless to pets.

Cabbage-root fly A more subtle, but no less dangerous, enemy that lays its eggs at the base of the plant. When the maggots hatch they burrow into the soil and attack the stem below ground. The first sign of trouble is when the leaves begin to flag. Later, the leaves turn yellow and the whole plant collapses. At this stage the maggots can often be found in the stem. You must then dig up and burn affected plants.

If the fly can be deterred from laying, or killed, there will be no eggs and no maggots. So as soon as the leaves have straightened up after transplanting sprinkle calomel dust around the plants – a small teaspoonful to each plant. As an alternative method, mix some of the powder in water to form a paste, and then dip the roots and stems in the paste as you are transplanting.

Above: Flora Blanca type cauliflowers with large, solid, very white curds

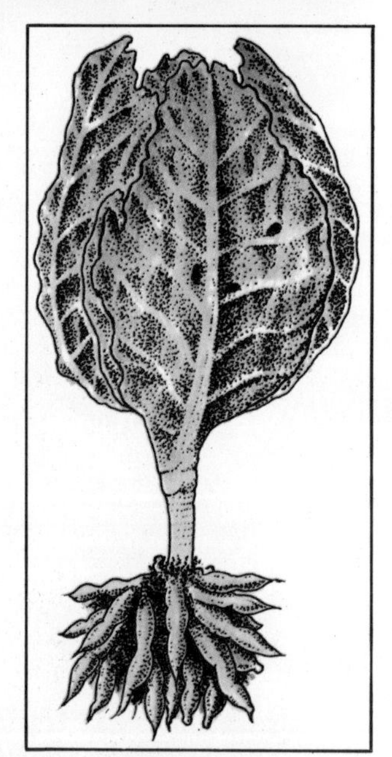

Right: club root disease turns the fine roots into thick, swollen 'fingers'

Below: protect from sun or frost by snapping leaves over the curd

If, in spite of this treatment (or due to lack of it), you find that cabbage-root fly has taken hold do not write the crop off. If the attack is not too severe you can encourage the plants to overcome it by forming new roots. They will do this if earth is drawn up under the lower leaves so that the stems are covered. Providing that you never allow them to dry out, these new roots will be enough to carry the crop through.

Caterpillars Summer varieties are especially vulnerable to the caterpillars of cabbage-white butterflies. The best remedy is to pick them off by hand, but this is time-consuming and not for the squeamish. A spray or dust with derris is effective, but you may need several applications. Derris has the advantage of being safe to use right up to the time of heading. Do not wait for trouble – at the first sign of any cabbage-white butterflies spray at once.

Club root (known in some areas as 'finger and toe'). This is the disease that you have most to fear from when growing any of the brassicas. Affected plants are stunted and sickly and the roots are swollen and deformed.

There is, as yet, no cure for club root but it can be controlled. Adequate liming of the soil helps to discourage it. Calomel dust is another good method of control; sprinkle in the drills before sowing and use it again (as described above) at transplanting time. You can 'starve out' the disease by ceasing to grow brassicas on the diseased soil but this takes a long time. Where incidence is severe it is wise to omit brassicas from the cropping plan for a few years. Remember that turnips and swedes are also members of the brassica family and are liable to be attacked.

RECOMMENDED VARIETIES

EARLY SOWINGS under glass for summer cutting:
Snowball; Mechelse Delta; Dominant.

MAINCROP SOWINGS – late spring (April) for summer cutting:
All the Year Round; Flora Blanca; Kangaroo.

MAINCROP SOWINGS for late autumn to early winter (October to December) cutting:
South Pacific; Flora Blanca No 2 (formerly Veitch's Autumn Giant); **Igea** (also known as Snow White).

SUCCESSIONAL SOWINGS
All the Year Round

KALE

The kales may well be described as the Cinderellas of the brassica family. Over the years they have acquired the reputation of being 'stop-gap' vegetables and lacking in flavour. This does not do them justice and has arisen largely through errors in picking. The leaves and shoots of kale should always be gathered while still young and small; it is the large leaves that are unpalatable.

On the credit side the kales are easy to grow and exceptionally hardy. Even a severe winter does not usually harm them. In addition, they are not exacting in their soil requirements and are more resistant to club root disease than the other brassicas.

Types of kale
In most seed catalogues this vegetable is listed as Borecole or Curly Kale. This is something of a misnomer, as not all kales are curly. They fall mainly into two groups – the curly and the plain-leaved. The curly kales are also often referred to as 'Scotch' kales. The dwarf form of the curly kale is of special value in open allotments or in exposed gardens, as it is much less subject to wind damage. Of the plain-leaved forms the best known are Cottager's kale and Thousand-headed kale; cut the centre out of these and they will produce tender young shoots. A new hybrid called Pentland Brig is a cross between the curly kale and plain-leaved kale and is gaining an excellent reputation for hardiness and heavy cropping.

Right: Dwarf Curled kale at RHS Wisley
Below: detail of Dwarf Curled variety

Two other types worth mentioning are Asparagus and Russian kale. The former is not quite so hardy as the others mentioned, while the latter is quite the opposite. This unusual plant is very hardy and has fine, deeply-indented leaves. Unfortunately neither of these varieties is widely distributed, but some specialist seedsmen still list them.

There is another variety, Hungry Gap kale, that needs rather different treatment. This is the latest and hardiest of all kales and picking can continue until mid summer (June). Unlike the others it does not transplant well and should be grown *in situ* (where it is to mature). This does not present any difficulty as the seed need not be sown until late summer or even early autumn (July or early August).

Sow the seeds in drills 2–3cm (1 in) deep and 45cm (18 in) apart, and then thin the plants to stand 30cm (12 in) apart. It is a useful vegetable for that period in late spring when fresh vegetables are scarce.

Soil requirements

Most soils will support kales as long as there is good drainage. The plants do not mind a heavy soil providing it is not waterlogged. A rich soil is not necessary and they will grow in relatively poor soils, but like most plants, they will give a better return if the ground is in good heart. As they are not planted out until late summer or early autumn (July or August) they make a good follow-on crop to earlier vegetables such as peas, early potatoes or broad beans. Where the soil was manured for the earlier crop it will be in good heart for the kales. If the site was not manured during winter digging, apply a general fertilizer at 70g per sq m (2 oz per sq yd). This will be enough to bridge the gap.

Like most of the brassicas, kales prefer a firm soil and it is neither necessary nor advisable to dig the plot over when the earlier crop has been cleared. Simply prick the ground over with a fork and then rake the soil down again. If fertilizer has been applied, this can be pricked in at the same time.

Growing from seed

Kales are quite easy to raise from seed, and the seed is relatively cheap. While plants of cabbages, cauliflowers or brussels sprouts can readily be found on market stalls or in garden centres during the planting season, it is much more difficult to find kales. Occasionally plants of curly kale are offered, but for the most part the onus is on the gardener to produce his own.

Being a winter and early spring vegetable there is no point in having them ready too early. A sowing towards the end of spring or in early summer (late April or May) will give plants for putting out in late summer (July) and these will be ready for picking from late winter (January) onwards. Sow the seeds in a little nursery bed and, when the young plants are big enough to handle, thin them to stand 4–5cm (1½–2 in) apart. This gives good strong plants for transplanting.

Left: Thousand-headed, a plain-leaved type. Below: Tall Curled 'Scotch' kale

Tending the plants

Treat the seedlings with derris dust as a precaution against flea beetle; remember that you will need to renew the treatment after rain. Growth is rapid at this season and the plants are soon out of danger. When transplanting, sprinkle a little calomel dust around each plant to help ward off club root disease and cabbage-root fly.

Firm the plants in well and water them if the weather is dry. If you move the plants when they are about 15cm (6 in) high and with as much soil as possible on the roots, they will soon re-establish themselves. Most of the kales need 55–60cm (21–23 in) of spaee, all round, but the dwarf curly kale will be quite happy with 45cm (18 in).

No special cultivation is necessary after transplanting. Simply hoe to keep down the weeds and water in dry periods. With the approach of winter it helps to give the plants better anchorage if a little soil is drawn up around the base of each plant. In early to mid spring (February or March) a sprinkling of nitrogenous fertilizer round the plants will give them a welcome boost.

Pests and diseases

Kales are susceptible to several of the diseases that commonly affect brassicas.

Flea beetle Like the seedlings of all the brassicas, kale seedlings may be attacked by the flea beetle, which eats holes in the tiny leaves. Derris dust will deal with this pest but it will need renewing after rain.

Club root Although not immune to club root, the kales do seem to have some resistance to this disease as they are not generally affected badly by it. As a precaution, apply calomel dust around the plants when transplanting.

Cabbage-root fly Kales do not seem to be as sought after by this pest as other members of the brassica family, but apply calomel dust when transplanting as a preventive measure.

RECOMMENDED VARIETIES

Tall Curled and Dwarf Curled Standard varieties of curly 'Scotch' kale.

Fribor (F.1 hybrid) New variety with finely-curled leaves.

Pentland Brig (F.1 hybrid) New hybrid of special merit.

Thousand-headed Plain-leaved and extremely hardy.

Hungry Gap A recent variety; so far the hardiest of all.

LEGUMES

BROAD BEANS

Young, fresh broad beans make a dish fit for a king. They must, however, be picked while the pods are still green and before the skins of the seeds begin to get tough.

A medium to heavy loam gives the heaviest crops, but broad beans can be grown in any well-drained soil. They are lime-lovers and if their patch hasn't been recently limed, give it a dressing at 70g per sq m (2 oz per sq yd), before sowing.

Choose Aquadulce Claudia for an early-season crop. It has white flowers (above) and fine, long pods (below)

When to sow

The two sowing periods are early to mid winter (November to December) for an early crop; early to late spring (February to April) for a maincrop harvest.

An early winter sowing is debatable, for though reasonably hardy, broad beans are not immune to frost. Fortunately cloches give the plants adequate protection. Outdoor crops may succeed in warmer areas, but cloches are probably necessary until late spring (end of March) in colder northern regions.

Don't sow cloche crops until early winter (mid November), or the plants may reach the glass roof before it is safe to de-cloche.

Broad beans are usually grown in a double row 25cm (10 in) apart and 20cm (8 in) between the seeds, which are spaced out in a drill 5cm (2 in) deep. Sow the seeds in staggered positions along the rows. If you intend growing more than one double row allow 60cm (24 in) between each pair. Single rows should also be set 60cm (24 in) apart.

First unprotected sowings can be made from early spring to early summer (late February to May), with the heaviest crops coming from the earlier sowings. If outdoor conditions are unfavourable, begin sowing in early spring (February) in a cold greenhouse. Fill a 10cm (4 in) seed tray with compost and put the seeds in 2·5cm (1 in) deep and 8cm (3 in) apart. Transplant in late spring (April).

Care of growing plants

Tall varieties can grow to about 1·2m (4 ft) high and staking is usually necessary. Insert bamboo poles on each side of the rows and firmly wind garden wire or tough string from cane to cane.

Blackfly is the greatest pest menace to the broad bean, particularly later sowings; a severe infestation can cripple a whole crop. They attack the soft-growing points of the plant; once the first flowers have set, cut out the damaged tips.

In early summer (May) spray the plants with derris or a reliable aphicide and continue spraying until the pests have been eliminated.

Mice are broad bean nibblers and can quickly cause havoc to your crop. Set traps or spray a strong repellent around the base of the plants.

Chocolate spot disease is prevalent in heavy rainfall areas. It appears as dark brown blotches on leaves, stems and pods, and a severe attack can drastically reduce your crop. Check it in the early stages by spraying with Bordeaux mixture fungicide.

RECOMMENDED VARIETIES

The two main types are the Longpod and the Windsor. The latter is less hardy but is considered by many to be the better flavoured.

A lesser-known broad bean is the Dwarf type. This breaks (makes side shoots) to form several stems. The seeds are sown 30cm (12 in) apart with 40cm (15 in) between each row. They crop heavily over several weeks and have a good flavour.

LONGPOD: **Aquadulce Claudia** (autumn sowing); **Dreadnought** (winter sowing); **Bunyard's Exhibition** (winter sowing); **Imperial White** (winter sowing); **Imperial Green** (winter sowing).

WINDSOR: **Giant Green** (spring sowing); **Giant White** (spring sowing).

DWARF: **The Sutton** (successional sowing).

The pods of the French (or kidney) bean are smaller than those of the runner bean and have a distinctive flavour of their own.
Normally the pods are eaten like runner beans, but some varieties can be grown for the seeds, that are usually dried for winter use and are then called haricots.

FRENCH BEANS AND HARICOTS

Above: bamboo canes and string provide ample support for dwarf types
Overleaf: climbing French bean in flower with (below) Romano, a good variety

FRENCH BEANS

Some varieties of French bean are flat-podded; others are round. The round varieties are sometimes called 'snap' beans – the test for quality and freshness being that the pods break cleanly when they are snapped in half.

Most varieties of French bean are dwarf, the plants forming a little bush 30–38cm (12–15 in) tall, but there are also climbing varieties that will grow to a height of 1·5–1·8m (5 or 6 ft). These give a heavier crop and are especially useful where you have a trellis or boundary fence to support them.

French beans will grow in most soils provided the drainage is good. Light to medium soils are preferable as they warm up more quickly than cold, heavy soils in which the seeds tend to rot. A soil that was manured for the previous crop will suit them, and if lime has not been applied recently, work in a dressing at 100g per sq m (3 oz per sq yd) a few weeks before you start sowing.

Sowing under glass

Unfortunately, French beans are tender subjects and cannot be planted outside while frosts are expected. But you can get an early crop by sowing the seeds in a cool greenhouse in mid spring (mid March), using 9cm ($3\frac{1}{2}$ in) pots. When the plants have made their first pair of true leaves they can be planted in the greenhouse border, or under cloches outside.

An alternative, where staging is used, is to grow the plants in 25cm (10 in) pots and keep them on the staging. Sow six or eight seeds in a 25cm (10 in) pot and then select three of the best for growing on. When the flowers begin to appear, syringe the plants night and morning with clear water to ensure good fertilization.

Sowing outdoors

For outdoor crops a sowing can be made *in situ* under cloches in late spring (April) or without protection from early summer (mid May). A late sowing in mid to late summer (the second half of June) will give pickings until the first frosts, and if this sowing is cloched in mid autumn (September) the period of cropping will be extended for a few more weeks.

Sow the seeds in drills 5cm (2 in) deep, spacing them 15cm (6 in) apart. Sow two seeds at each spacing and if both germinate pull one seedling out. Put in a few extra seeds at the end of each row for filling up any gaps that may occur. If the plants are to be grown in single rows, allow 53–60cm (21–24 in) between the rows. Another method is to grow the plants in double rows. If it is necessary to move any plants to fill up gaps, do this with a trowel, taking as much soil as possible with each plant.

Tending, staking and picking

The French bean stands drought better than the runner, but if watering becomes necessary give the plants a good soaking and then mulch them with good compost, lawn mowings (not too thickly) or moist peat.

Some kind of support is essential for the climbing varieties. If a trellis or wire fence is not available then tall brushwood, as used for tall peas, is ideal. Large-mesh netting is a good alternative.

For the dwarf varieties all that is needed is something to keep them upright. If they keel over, the lower pods will touch the ground and slug damage may result. Twiggy sticks, pushed in among the plants, is one way of supporting them. Another good method is to push in bamboo canes at intervals down each side of the row, and then run string from cane to cane about 15cm (6 in) above ground.

Begin picking as soon as the pods are large enough to use. It is better to pick on the young side than to let the pods go past their best and get tough. Pick several times a week, and take off all the pods that are ready whether they are needed or not. Any surplus can be frozen or salted.

Pests and diseases

The two pests most likely to be encountered are slugs and blackfly.

Blackfly Keep a close watch for these insects and spray with derris or malathion at the first sign of trouble.
Slugs In addition to eating any pods that touch the soil, slugs may also attack seedling plants. It is always a good plan to scatter a few slug pellets along the rows when the seedlings are pushing through.

HARICOTS

Apart from being dried for winter use, the seeds of haricot varieties can also be eaten in the green state – when they are known as flageolets.

Haricot varieties are grown in the same way as the other dwarf beans, but the plants are allowed to form seeds from the beginning. As the seeds ripen, the pods turn yellow and then brown and papery. At this stage they can be detached from the plant and the beans shelled out.

In a warm, dry autumn the ripening process may be completed on the plants, but in cooler, showery weather some help may be needed. If the pods have not dried off by late autumn (October), pull the plants up, tie them in bundles and hang them on a sunny wall to dry. Alternatively, pull the plants up and cover them with cloches. The ends of the cloches must be left open so that air can blow through.

When you have shelled the beans, spread them out on paper in a warm room to finish drying. They can then be stored, preferably in jars, though paper bags will do. Leave the jars open and give them an occasional shake; this prevents any mould forming.

RECOMMENDED VARIETIES

FRENCH BEANS – dwarf
The Prince Popular variety with long, slender pods.
Tendergreen Early variety with round, fleshy pods.
Remus Bears its pods above the foliage, making picking much easier.
Kinghorn Waxpod Round, slightly curved, yellow pods.

FRENCH BEANS – climbing
Earliest of All Heavy cropper with white seeds that can be used as haricots.
Largo Round pods and white seeds.
Romano More recent variety with fleshy, stringless pods.

HARICOTS
Comtesse de Chambord Popular, white-seeded haricot variety.
Granda Slightly larger than Comtesse de Chambord.
Purley King This new bean has a high protein content.

RUNNER BEANS

Few vegetables give a better return for the time and money spent on them than runner beans. From the time the plants begin to flower until the first frosts cut them down, they will continue to produce their pods, and only a little of those pods is lost when they are prepared for cooking. They can also be ornamental.

Runner beans will grow in most soils. On heavy soils which warm up slowly do not sow too early, and on very light soils you may find it difficult to keep the plants sufficiently well watered. These are the extremes, however, and in between them the runner bean requires no special consideration. If lime has not been given recently, apply it at about 135g per sq m (4 oz per sq yd) when the site is prepared.

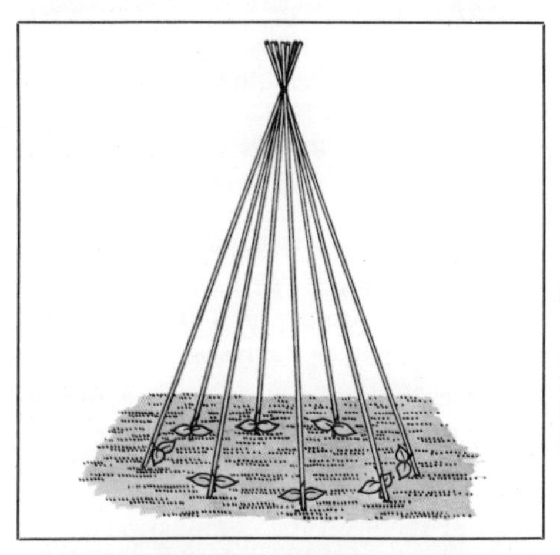

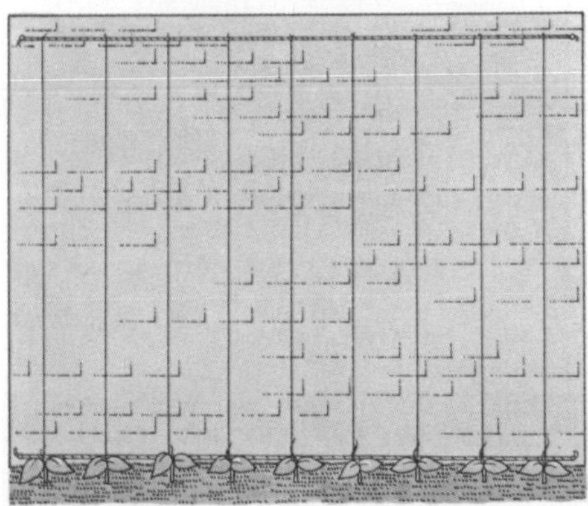

Top: staking runner beans by a wigwam of poles drawn together and fastened at the top. Above: beans can be grown up a wall by erecting a 'fence' of strings for them to cling to. Right: the most common way of staking is to use bean poles made of larch wood or heavy-grade bamboo

Preparing a trench

For best results dig out a trench 90cm (3 ft) wide and a spade's depth. Shovel out the loose soil and then break up the subsoil with a fork. As the soil is put back, mix in some compost or well-rotted manure. Leave a shallow depression at the top of the trench to help with watering later on. The trench should be prepared well in advance of sowing time – mid spring (March) is a good period.

Some gardeners line the bottom of the trench with thick layers of newspaper which are then thoroughly soaked with water. The newspapers hold some of the moisture and give it up when the plant roots need it.

If manure or compost cannot be spared for the runners, open up the trench in the autumn. Keep every scrap of kitchen waste in an old bucket, well covered. When the bucket is full, empty it into the trench and cover the waste with an inch or two of soil. Continue this process, with an occasional sprinkling of lime, until the trench is full. Although in good, fertile soil the beans will grow without any special preparation, better results can be achieved by trenching, and it is worth the extra trouble involved.

Sowing the seeds

Make an early start by sowing seeds in a cold greenhouse or frame in late spring (April) and transplanting them later. Plant one seed in a 9cm (3½ in) pot, or put the seeds 8cm (3 in) apart in a tray 10–15cm (4–6 in) deep. J.I. No 1 or one of the soilless composts makes a good medium. When the seedlings are through, give them as much light as possible with good ventilation during the day, and then harden them off before planting out.

An alternative to this is to sow the seeds directly into the soil where they are to mature and cover them with cloches. Do not sow until late on in spring (mid April) or the plants may grow too big before it is safe to decloche them. Barn cloches will cover two rows 45cm (18 in) apart. The plants must be staked as soon as the cloches are removed.

The conventional way of growing runner beans is to sow two rows of seeds 5cm (2 in) deep with 30 cm (12 in) between the seeds and 60cm (2 ft) between the two rows. The sowing can be made at the beginning of summer (first half of May in the warmer areas and about two weeks later in cooler districts). If the plants have been raised under glass, put them out in two rows early in mid summer (the first two weeks of June). The seeds, or plants, should be directly opposite each other in the rows.

Staking the plants

Bean poles are usually made of larch wood and can be bought from garden centres, but poles cut out from other brushwood will do just as well. They should be about 2–2·5m (7–8 ft) long. Wooden laths 2–3cm (1 in) square are sometimes used instead, or heavy-grade bamboo canes.

Place the butts of the poles a few centimetres into the soil. Draw together the tops of two opposing poles and cross them about 20cm (8 in) from the top. Do this all down the row. Then lay other poles horizontally above where the upright poles cross, and fasten securely at each junction.

A row of runners in full leaf and crop presents a large area to the wind, so be sure to build the supporting palisade carefully. If the plants are blown down in a summer gale it is a very difficult job to get them up again.

If cloches are not being used, it is easier to put the poles up first and then put one plant, or two seeds, against each pole. If both seeds grow, pull one out.

Harvesting Streamline runner beans. This variety produces vigorous plants and crops over a long period. The long, fine-flavoured pods are borne in clusters

Making a wigwam

Another method of growing runner beans is to grow the plants in circles or 'wigwams'. Mark out a rough circle 1·2–1·8m (4–6 ft) in diameter, and put the poles in round the circumference. Draw all the poles inwards towards the centre and fasten them at the top. Then put the plants or seeds in against the poles in the usual way. The circles take up less room than a straight row and can often be fitted into odd corners, and as they do not present a straight surface to the wind they are far less likely to blow down.

Growing along a fence

A third method of growing is to sow or plant a single row at the foot of a fence and let them climb up it. A temporary fence can be made with a few stakes, horizontal strands of garden wire at the top and bottom, and lengths of string stretched vertically between the two wires. The plants will climb the strings without difficulty.

Once the runners have twined round the poles they will soon begin to climb. When they have reached the top, pinch out the growing points to keep the row uniform and make the plants bush out. Where they are climbing up a fence they can be left to fall over and cover the other side. Keep the rows free from weeds and in dry weather give them plenty of water.

Growing without stakes

It is also possible to grow runners without stakes. In this method the seeds are sown 20cm (8 in) apart in single rows 90cm (3 ft) apart. The plants run along the ground and form a continuous row. If the runners reach out too far and threaten to become entangled in the next row, pinch out the growing points. To pick, lift up the foliage on each side of the row in turn.

The obvious advantage of this method is that it is easy because no stakes are required. In hot weather the pods, being mostly under the leaves, do not become old so quickly. The disadvantages are that in wet weather some slug damage is likely, and that where the pods touch the ground they no longer grow straight. But for the gardener who has little time to spare and is not short of space in his vegetable plot, this method has its points.

Dwarf varieties reaching a height of only about 75cm (18 in) need little or no staking. A few twiggy sticks pushed in amongst the plants keeps them upright.

Ailments and pests

There are a few problems that may affect your growing plants, so take precautions.

Bud-dropping The flowers do not open properly and fall off without being fertilized. This can be caused by cold winds, rapid changes of temperature, or dryness of the root system. Spraying with clear water night and morning may be of some benefit, but it does not take the place of a good watering around the roots. During a very hot summer, it shows clearly that beans which are watered regularly bear far more pods than plants left to fend for themselves.

Blackfly (aphides) can sometimes be a nuisance, especially if they have already infested broad beans in the vicinity. These aphides will gather round the tender tips of the shoots, inhibit flowering and make the plants unpleasant to handle. Do not let them reach this stage. Keep an eye open for them and at the first sign of trouble spray with derris or malathion.

If the attack comes late, when pods have already formed, use only derris as malathion is poisonous for a few days after application. Repeat the spraying until the plants are clear.

Frost warning

The runner bean is not a hardy plant and cannot be put out while the danger of frost is present. If a late frost threatens after the plants are through the soil, or just after they have been transplanted, cover them with newspaper, plant-pots, straw, leaves or anything else that will protect them. Plants which are only touched but not killed by frost will shoot again, but the crop will be later.

Picking the beans

When cropping begins, look over the plants every few days. Pick the pods while still young, before the beans have started to form in them, as old pods will be 'stringy'. If pods are missed and have become too old at the next picking never leave them on the plants. Pull them off and put them on the compost heap. Do not be tempted to leave them for seed, for as soon as the plants are permitted to form seed the production of young beans rapidly falls off.

If it is intended to save seed, leave one or two plants at the end of a row and do not pick any pods from them. When the pods have become dry and papery pull them off, shell out the beans, and store them in a dry, cool place.

RECOMMENDED VARIETIES

DWARF

Gina New white-flowered dwarf bean with a distinct runner bean flavour.

TALL

Streamline, Enorma, Crusader, Achievement, Kelvedon Marvel, and **Fry** (F.1 hybrid).

PEAS

Garden peas have to be home-grown to be fully appreciated. No bought peas can equal a dish of those picked in their prime, and shelled and cooked soon after.

There are tall, medium and dwarf varieties of peas. The choice will to some extent depend on what time and staking materials are available, and whether the site is sheltered or exposed.

A row of tall peas generally gives the best return but, on the other hand, rows of dwarfs can be grown closer together.

Peas prefer a deep, moisture-retentive soil in which their tap roots can thrust well down. They do not thrive on cold, sticky clay soils; nor do they like light, gravelly ones. Fresh manure, while not harmful, is not recommended because peas do not occupy a site long enough to make use of it; a strip that was manured for a previous crop is more suitable.

Sowing time

A sowing can be made in early winter (November) for picking in early summer (May). In favoured districts on a sunny, sheltered border the crop could come through winter without protection; in other areas it is wise to use cloches.

Round-seeded varieties are hardier than the wrinkled-seeded and should be used for an autumn sowing. For summer picking, seeds can be sown from early spring to early summer (February to May). Use round-seeded peas for an early spring (February) sowing, then move on to a wrinkled-seeded variety.

Tall peas are also sown in late spring and early summer (April and May) and take about 14 weeks to mature (about two weeks longer than dwarf types).

For sowing from mid to late summer (June to July) turn to the wrinkled-seeded varieties.

How to sow

Peas can be sown in a broad drill 15cm (6 in) wide and 5cm (2 in) deep, containing three rows of seeds, or in a narrow drill of only one row. A broad drill is better for tall peas. Space the seeds about 5 cm (2 in) apart. The distance between each row is the same as the height of the plants.

To save space tall peas can be sown alongside a path. Trenching will get the best results from here, but it needs to be done well in advance of sowing. Dig out a trench 60cm (2 ft) wide and a spade's depth. Shovel out the loose soil and break up the subsoil with a fork. Add good compost or well-rotted manure before returning the soil.

Fat, ripe pea pods ready for harvesting, the result of careful cultivation

Other types of peas

There are several less common types that are well worth growing.

Sugar pea (mangetout) When the peas can be felt in the pods, but before they have filled out, is the time to cook them whole for eating pod and all. Sow in late spring to early summer (April to May).

Petits pois These are smaller than the ordinary pea but many consider them to be of better flavour. Sow from mid spring to mid summer (March to June). Staking is advisable.

Asparagus pea (winged pea) This type has reddish flowers that are followed by small three-sided pods. The flavour is supposed to resemble that of asparagus, hence the name. It is not as hardy as an ordinary pea and should not be sown before late spring or early summer (April or May).

Sow the seeds 10cm (4 in) apart in drills 2–3cm (1 in) deep and 60cm (2 ft) apart. The plants grow up to 60cm (2 ft) and some twiggy support is advisable. Gather the pods when they are about 4cm (1½ in) long.

Care of growing plants

Peas must be hand-weeded, especially when they are in a broad row, and it is best to do it when the plants are 15–23cm (6–9 in) high. If left too long, the weeds cannot be pulled out without disturbing the peas. Keep the hoe going between the

RECOMMENDED VARIETIES

Dwarf (round-seeded)
Feltham First, 60cm (2 ft) early winter sowing.

Dwarf (wrinkled-seeded)
Kelvedon Wonder, 60cm (2 ft) and Early Onward, 75cm (2½ ft), mid and late spring sowings; Onward, 75cm (2½ ft) and Hurst Green Shaft 75cm (2½ ft), late spring and early summer sowings (the latter has mildew resistance); Little Marvel, 45cm (18 in), mid to late summer sowing.

Tall-growing
Alderman, 1·50m (5 ft), Lord Chancellor, 1m (3½ ft) and Miracle 1·20m (4 ft), late spring and summer sowings.

Other types of peas
Sugar pea (mangetout) – tall-growing Carouby de Maussane, 1·50m (5 ft); **dwarf** Sweetgreen, 45cm (18 in) and Grace, 75cm (2½ ft).
Petits pois – tall-growing Gullivert, 1–1·5m (3–3½ ft).
Asparagus pea (winged pea) – dwarf, 45cm (1½ ft).

rows for as long as possible.

When peas are about 15cm (6 in) high they can be sprinkled with superphosphate of lime at about 30g per metre run (1 oz per yard), along each side of the rows. Keep it an inch or two away from the plants and hoe it in.

Peas have root nodules which contain a nitrifying bacteria so they require little, if any, additional nitrogenous fertilizer.

Watering can pose a problem because peas are deep-rooting. During a drought this is an asset, providing you water them thoroughly. A mere sprinkling from a watering can, however, will do more harm than good.

Mulching with compost, lawn-mowings, old mushroom-manure or peat, will help to conserve moisture. Spread the mulch along each side of the rows, but not touching the plants; leave about 5cm (2 in) of bare soil either side so that rain can get through. The mulch should be 5cm (2 in) deep and put on when the soil is moist – *never* when it is dry.

Two rows of netting such as this give maximum support (below left); hold bine as well as pod when picking (below)

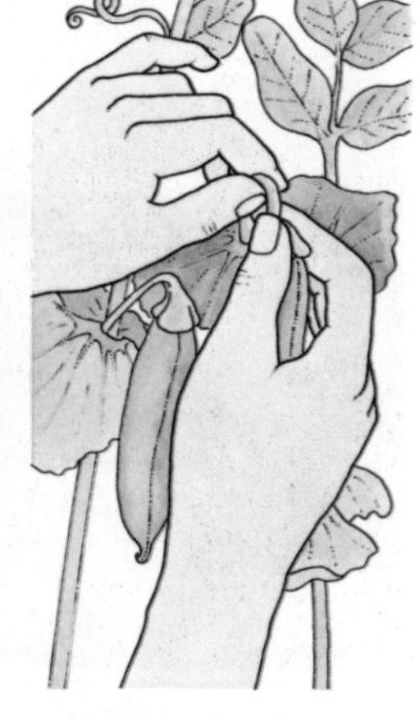

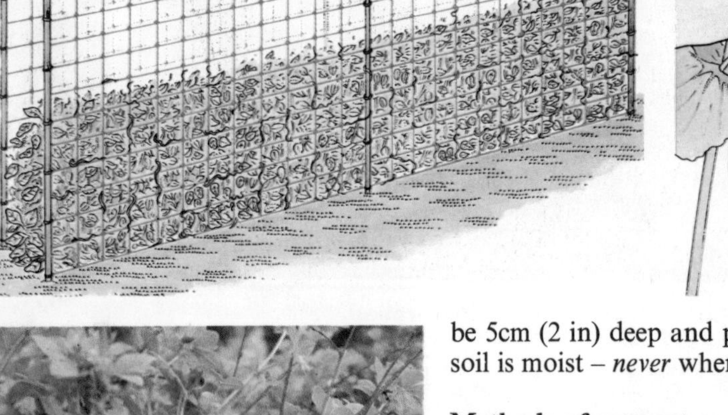

Asparagus pea pods are eaten whole. Pick the pods young, before they get stringy

Methods of support

Tall peas need staking and, although dwarfs are not supposed to need it, you will find that anything more than 45cm (18 in) tall will do better if staked. Twiggy sticks are ideal, though often difficult to come by. If you grow raspberries, you can use the prunings from the raspberry canes. Trim them and then push them into the soil on each side of the peas, leaning them inwards, so that they come together at the top.

Cord or plastic netting is used for tall-growing crops. You will find the thin 15cm (6 in) plastic-mesh type satisfactory, but it must be firmly erected and kept taut. The weight of a row of tall peas at peak harvesting time is considerable and once blown down it cannot be put back. A strong stake should be driven in at each end of the row and tall canes inserted at 2m (6 ft) intervals.

It is best to put netting up each side of a row and let the peas grow in between. Modern varieties do not climb as readily as the old kinds and are easily blown away from a single row of netting.

How to harvest

A good row should give at least three pickings, starting with the lower pods which fill out first. When picking hold the pea bine (haulm or stem) in one hand and pull off the pod with the other. This prevents damage to the bine; if it gets bent or bruised the top pods will not fill.

When the crop is finished cut off the bines at soil level and leave the roots in the ground so that the nitrogen from the root nodules can be released into the soil. This will benefit any plants that may follow.

Pests and diseases

Mice Always guard against mice, especially with autumn sowings; it is advisable to set one or two traps after sowing.

Sparrows These birds have a liking for the first tender leaves and can create havoc with a crop. Pea-guards, made from wire netting fixed over a wooden frame, helps keep the birds at bay, but when the leaves eventually grow through the netting the guards have to be removed.

Pea weevil This tiny, beetle-like creature eats holes in the leaves of young plants and inhibits their growth. As soon as the seedlings are through, dust with derris and re-apply if rain washes it off. When the plants are 10–15cm (4–6 in) high, the danger period is over.

Grubs The pea moth makes its appearance when flowering begins and the grubs may be found inside the pods. Spray the flowers with a reliable insecticide as they open, and again 10 days later.

Thrips (thunder flies) Sometimes appearing in large numbers, thrips make silvery streaks on the leaves and flowering may be affected. Control these pests by spraying with an insecticide such as BHC or liquid malathion.

Mildew A common disease among peas, the powdery form of mildew covers leaves and stems with a white dust. It can be kept in check by spraying with dinocap. Unlike downy mildew, which appears as a grey fungus on the undersides of young leaves, it is more prevalent during a dry season. Late sowings suffer most from it and the best safeguard is to ensure that the peas have an open, sunny position with a good circulation of air.

CUCURBITS

MARROWS AND COURGETTES

During the last few years the image of the marrow has come a long way from those unappetizing slabs of boiled vegetable, covered with white sauce, that were the usual offerings. Nowadays, few people want a really large marrow unless it is to win a prize at a village show. Newer varieties of marrow have been developed, giving smaller fruits which are ideal for stuffing. Courgettes (baby marrows), can be cooked whole, sliced and fried, or used in salads, and their popularity is rapidly increasing.

As well as ordinary marrows and courgettes, there are the custard marrows which are flat in shape and have scalloped edges. They are considered by many people to have a better flavour than the ordinary marrows. There is also the newer and curious vegetable spaghetti marrow. This is boiled whole, and when it is cut in half the inside can be forked out like spaghetti.

With the marrow enjoying a new following, it is fortunate that it is neither demanding in its soil requirements nor difficult to grow. Marrows will grow in any good soil, but they prefer a loam which does not dry out too quickly, and a sunny position. There are two types of plants, the trailing marrows and the bush. The trailing type sends out long runners or vines on which the fruits form, while the bush type is contained in a rough circle. The bush type is better for the small garden as it takes up less space.

If trailing marrows are chosen, some thought should be given to siting them. They are not suitable neighbours for crops such as lettuce, carrots or onions, where the rows are close together. They may be allowed to wander into the greens or potatoes, or be sited next to peas or some other early crop which will be cleared before the marrows need more room. One suitable method is to leave out a couple of tubers at the end of a potato row and plant a marrow instead.

Preparing the stations

As the trailing marrows need 1·8m (6 ft) between plants and the bush marrows 1m (3 ft), the most economical way of manuring for them is to prepare a special station for each plant. Dig out a hole 60cm (24 in) square and about 45cm (18 in) deep, and half fill it with well-rotted manure or good compost. If this is not available, fresh lawn-mowings are better than nothing and will generate a little heat as they rot. Prepare the sites several weeks in advance of sowing or planting so that the soil has time to settle down again.

Sowing under glass

For an early crop raise the plants in a cold greenhouse or frame from mid spring (March) onwards. Fill some 9cm (3½ in) pots with a good potting compost or one of the soilless composts. Plant one seed in each pot, edgeways, burying the seed about 13mm (½ in) deep. Fill several extra pots in case some seeds do not germinate. Alternatively plant two seeds in each pot and pull one out if both grow.

Keep the plants in a good light so that they do not become drawn (too tall and spindly), and then, during early summer (mid May) begin to harden them off ready for planting outdoors. If single cloches are available to cover the plants for a few more weeks they can go straight out into the prepared stations.

Below: the yellow custard marrow. Right: Long Green Trailing produces a heavy crop of large fruit and is excellent for winter storage

Top: Long White Trailing has large creamy-white fruits that make excellent jam

Above: constant cutting ensures a heavy crop with these Golden Zucchinis

Planting out

The marrow is not frost-hardy, and it cannot be planted out until all danger of frost is past. This usually means towards the end of early summer (late May in the south of England and one or two weeks later farther north).

Marrows are not the easiest plants to transplant and care should always be taken when moving them. If the plants have been raised in pots made of clay or plastic, water them well a few hours before transplanting so that the rootball will slip easily out of its pot. Peat or fibre pots have an advantage as they can be planted out intact. If using these, keep the soil moist until the pot disintegrates, for if it dries out the roots will be constricted. To give the roots additional freedom, tear off the bottom of the pot and slit it up one side before planting.

Sowing into the ground

Another method of growing is to sow directly into the ground in late early summer (mid to late May). To make sure of a plant at each prepared site, push three seeds into the soil, spacing them in a triangle about 15cm (6 in) apart. Thin bush marrows to a single plant, but with trailing marrows two plants can be left at each position and trained to go in different directions. Train the vines early as they resent being disturbed once they have taken hold of the soil. If a trailing marrow just wanders on and on without forming fruits, pinch out the growing point. This will encourage it to produce side-shoots.

Care of growing plants

Once the young plants are growing strongly see that they do not lack water. A mulch of peat or lawn-mowings will help to conserve moisture. Liquid manure or diluted soot water (see Carrots, page 113) can be given at intervals.

Trailing marrows are also climbers. Planted at the foot of a wire fence the vines will naturally climb up the wire. Some tying in of the vines is advised, and once the fruits begin to swell they will need some support to prevent large fruits from pulling the vines down again. Choose the smaller-fruiting varieties for this method, which is particularly useful in small gardens.

Fertilization of the female flowers is generally done quite adequately by insects. If, however, the flowers fail to set, strip off the petals from a male flower and push it gently but firmly into the heart of a female flower. The two are easy to distinguish as females have a tiny marrow behind the flower.

Top: vegetable spaghetti is an unusual and delicious vegetable borne on trailing plants. It is easy to grow and yields a large number of medium-sized fruit. Above: Table Dainty matures early and produces a good crop of fairly small marrows

Sometimes the fruits fall off while still small. This can be caused by lack of water, a poor soil or inadequate fertilization.

Do not spray the plants with insecticides, or give fertilizers to plants at the fruiting stage, as they encourage the production of seeds.

The only pest which may trouble them is red spider mite, but these almost invisible creatures are not a serious pest outdoors. Attacked leaves have a rusty, shrivelled appearance and should be cut off and burned. Spraying with clear water night and morning will discourage the pest as it prefers dry conditions. Occasionally, cucumber mosaic virus will attack marrows; the plants gradually turn yellow and die. Unfortunately there is no cure for this disease.

RECOMMENDED VARIETIES

MARROWS – trailing
Long White Trailing (medium to large)
Long Green Trailing (medium to large)
Table Dainty (medium)
Moore's Cream (medium)
Vegetable spaghetti (spaghetti marrow)

MARROWS – bush
White Bush (medium to large)
Green Bush (medium to large)
Smallpak (medium)
Custard White (custard variety)
Custard Yellow (custard variety)

COURGETTES – bush
True French (green)
Green Bush, F.1 hybrid (green)
Golden Zucchini, F.1 hybrid (yellow)

Picking and storing the fruits

As the fruits ripen they change colour and the skin hardens. White fruits turn yellow and green ones, if striped, show a darker tinge in the stripes. The neck (where the fruit joins the stem) also hardens and is more difficult to cut. Leave the fruits on the plants until the first frost threatens; then cut the remaining ones and take them indoors. This will normally be about mid to late autumn (late September or early October).

If the fruits come faster than they can be used, leave some of them to ripen for winter use. It must be remembered, however, that once the fruits are permitted to ripen on the plant, the production of new fruits will slow down. Choose fruits of good shape for storing. Never select any that are pointed at the butt end (the end away from the stalk) as these usually go bad.

The ripe fruits can be used throughout the winter months and will keep perfectly well if stored properly. Damp outhouses, and garden sheds which are not frost-proof, are not suitable. A dry room with a fairly even temperature of 10°–15°C (50°–60°F) is ideal. Handle the fruits carefully at all times and never store them on top of one another. Stored marrows should not touch each other. Years ago, in the days of the oak-beamed ceilings, it was the custom to put them in nets or broad bands of cloth and hang them from the ceiling. This method is still the best.

An extra bonus from the ripe marrows is the seeds, which can be extracted from the pith, dried on a sheet of paper in front of a fire, and then stored for future sowings the following year.

PUMPKINS, SQUASHES AND MELONS

Pumpkins and squashes are closely related to the marrow and are cultivated in much the same way. They need a site in full sun and a good fertile soil, but otherwise are not difficult vegetables to grow in your garden.
Cantaloupe melons can also be grown outside, but only in regions with mild winters and hot summers; otherwise use a cool greenhouse.

PUMPKINS AND SQUASHES

As squashes need to be 90–120cm (3–4 ft) and pumpkins 1·8m (6 ft) apart, you can make more economical use of your compost or manure by preparing 'stations' for the seeds. Do this some weeks in advance, taking out a hole about 60cm (24 in) square and about 45cm (18 in) deep, and half-filling it with well-rotted manure or compost. Prepare the stations in mid to late spring (the beginning of April) so that the soil, when returned, has time to settle down before planting. Leave the station in the form of a slight mound.

Sowing and raising plants

Raise the plants in a greenhouse, frame or even in a sunny window by sowing individual seeds in 9cm (3½ in) pots of J.I. No 1 or a soilless compost. Push each seed (on edge) down about 13mm (½ in) into the soil. The end of spring (second half of April) is early enough for this sowing as the plants are not frost-hardy and cannot go outdoors until there is no risk of frost.

Bear in mind, however, that neither squashes nor pumpkins move easily and that transplanting, if done, must be carried out with as little disturbance to the roots as possible. For this reason the expendable cardboard pots or soil blocks are to be preferred to ordinary pots.

Where cloches are available it is much easier to sow *in situ* in late spring to early summer (the last week in April or the first week in May) and then cover each prepared station with a single cloche, de-cloching in mid summer (the middle of June) when the risk of frost is over. Sow three or four seeds at each station, some 8cm (3 in) apart and 13mm (½ in) deep. If more than one seed germinates, thin to the strongest plant. If protection cannot be given, delay the sowing until early to mid summer (the second half of May).

In dry periods see that the plants do not lack water. A mulch of lawn mowings, compost or peat can be spread around the plants (but not right up to the stems). This helps to keep the root-run moist.

Generally, pollination is done naturally by insects. Hand pollination can be done by taking the petals off a male flower and pushing it firmly into the centre of a female flower. This is best done at midday when it is warmest. Female flowers are easily identified: they have a swelling behind the flower which is the immature squash or pumpkin.

Ripening, harvesting and storing

Some varieties of squash are classed as 'summer' squashes and others as 'winter' squashes. The summer squashes are cut in an immature state for use during the summer months. The winter squashes are left to ripen and are stored for winter use.

In the case of pumpkins, limit the number of fruits to two or three per plant. For culinary use it is better to have two or three fruits of medium size than one monster specimen. But should you want a

Right: Butternut squash, a sweet variety
Below: two trailing pumpkins, (left) orange-skinned Mammoth (and right) fine-flavoured Hundredweight

larger one, it is not a difficult matter. Let several fruits set on a plant and then choose the best one. Cut the others off and prevent the plant from setting any more by pinching off each female flower as it appears. When the fruit is swelling, feed the plant at fortnightly intervals with weak liquid manure or soot water. Before the fruit becomes too big, lift it carefully and slip a flat tile or piece of board under it. This will help to keep it clean and prevent possible slug damage.

As they ripen, the fruits of squashes and pumpkins turn a deeper colour. Leave them on the plant until the first frosts are expected, then cut them from the plant with stem still attached. Store in a light, dry, cool and frost-free place.

OUTDOOR MELONS

Outdoor melons (cantaloupes) are not difficult to raise in a cool greenhouse, frame or sunny window. Sow two seeds on edge in a 9cm (3½ in) pot, 13mm (½ in) deep. Make the sowing in late spring (middle of April); if both seeds germinate in each pot, pull out the weaker. Keep the seedlings in full light and transplant them into their permanent positions in early summer (middle of May).

For best results make up a soilbed in the frame by putting down some well-rotted manure or good compost and covering it with 15cm (6 in) of sifted soil. A frame 1·2m (4 ft) long and 75–90cm (2½–3 ft) wide will take one plant. For growing under cloches prepare stations as described for pumpkins and squashes, and allow 90cm (3 ft) between plants.

Tending and harvesting

When a plant has made five leaves, pinch out the growing point. Two sideshoots will break from each stop. For cloche cultivation these sideshoots are trained in opposite directions along the cloche run. In frames stop the sideshoots again after the fourth leaf so that they also produce two shoots (making four in all) and train one shoot into each corner of the frame.

To prevent the cloches or frames becoming a mass of leaves as further sideshoots are made, some judicious stopping and thinning of surplus shoots is usually necessary. Allow three or four fruits to each plant and when these have set, pinch back the fruit-bearing shoot at the second leaf beyond the fruit.

Fertilization is usually a natural process, but if the fruits are slow in setting, pollinate by hand – as described for pumpkins and squashes.

Melons like sunshine, and shading should be needed only during the hottest part of the day. Ventilate freely in warm weather and water regularly. Spraying the plants with clear water night and morning helps to keep the red spider mite away.

To tell when a melon is ripe for cutting, press the fruit gently at the end opposite the stem; if the fruit 'gives' to this pressure it is ripe.

Some varieties crack slightly against the stalk and give off a delicious smell.

Left: small and round Ogen melon raised on flower-pot to avoid slug damage
Below: much larger Burpee Hybrid has firm, orange flesh

RECOMMENDED VARIETIES

PUMPKINS

Mammoth (trailing) Orange-skinned with yellow flesh.

Hundredweight (trailing) Very large orange pumpkin; good flavour.

SQUASHES – SUMMER

Butternut (trailing) Sweet with bright orange flesh.

Baby Crookneck (bush) Bright yellow fruits.

SQUASHES – WINTER

Hubbard Squash Golden (trailing) Excellent variety for winter storing.

OUTDOOR MELONS (CANTALOUPES)

Sweetheart (F.1 hybrid) Pale green with firm, salmon-pink flesh; tolerant of low temperatures.

Ogen Small, round, deliciously-sweet fruit.

Dutch Net (F.1 hybrid) Orange flesh of fine quality and flavour.

Burpee Hybrid (F.1 hybrid) Large, round golden fruits with orange flesh; firm and juicy.

ONIONS

GARLIC AND LEEKS

There is a widespread belief that garlic is difficult to grow. This may come from its association with warmer climates, and the fact that the standard variety is listed as Best Italian. Whatever the cause, the belief is a mistaken one, as garlic is quite hardy and easy to cultivate.
Leeks are also very easy to grow, and few vegetables are more accommodating. The leek can be used as a follow-on crop to early vegetables; it is not much troubled by pests or diseases; it is perfectly hardy; and it matures during winter and early spring when a change of vegetable is welcome.

GARLIC

The best soil for garlic is a light to medium loam, well supplied with humus. Prepare the site, which must be in full sun, in mid autumn (September) by digging in some well-rotted manure or compost. The bulbs can be planted as early as late autumn (October), but early to mid spring (February to March) is preferable as they make little growth in the winter.

Planting the bulbs

Each bulb of garlic is made up of a number of segments or cloves. Bulbs can be planted whole to give larger bulbs, but it is more economical to plant the best cloves separately. Insert them 2–3cm (1 in) deep and 25cm (9 in) apart, in rows 30cm (12 in) apart. Buy bulbs from a leading seedsman; you can, however, use those bought for the kitchen. After the first year select some of the best quality bulbs for the next planting.

Garlic requires no special cultivation beyond keeping the weeds at bay. The

Left: garlic bulbs hanging up to dry
Below: when dry, remove loose skin and dead foliage from bulbs, and store

plants are usually free from pests and diseases. Watering is not necessary, except in very dry seasons. Pinch out flower-heads if they appear.

Lifting, drying and storing

In late summer or early autumn (July or August), according to the time of planting, the foliage begins to yellow, starting at the leaf tips. This is the signal to lift the bulbs and spread them out to dry. Put the bulbs in an empty frame with the lid raised to admit air, or in a cloche or two with the ends left open, or simply tie them in bunches and hang them on a sunny wall. When the bulbs are thoroughly dry, rub off any loose skin and dead foliage, and store them in a dry, light and frost-proof place.

LEEKS

Leeks will grow in most soils, but they do best where the soil's pH is 6–6·5. If it is lower than this, apply hydrated lime according to maker's instructions. As the plants are not put out until late summer or early autumn (July or August), they usually follow an earlier crop, and if manure was used for this crop the soil will be in good condition. If the site was not manured earlier, dig in some good compost if available. As leeks are deep rooting, the compost must be put down where it will retain moisture and the roots can take hold of it.

Sowing from seed

The plants are easily raised from seeds, which should be sown in mid to late spring (March or early April) in shallow drills 6mm ($\frac{1}{4}$ in) deep. If onions are being grown from seed, sow leeks at the same time alongside the onions. If the seeds are sown thinly, no further thinning out will be necessary. Gardeners who miss this sowing can obtain plants from markets or garden centres during the transplanting period.

Planting out

Where only a few leeks are required, an excellent way of obtaining the best results is to dig out a trench 60cm (24 in) wide and a spade's depth. Shovel out the loose soil, break up the subsoil with a fork, and then put in a layer of well-rotted manure or compost. Return about half the topsoil and mark the site of the trench with sticks. Do this a few weeks before planting so that the soil has time to settle. The trench will take two rows of plants 38cm (15 in) apart. Allow 20cm (8 in) between the leeks, and stagger the two rows.

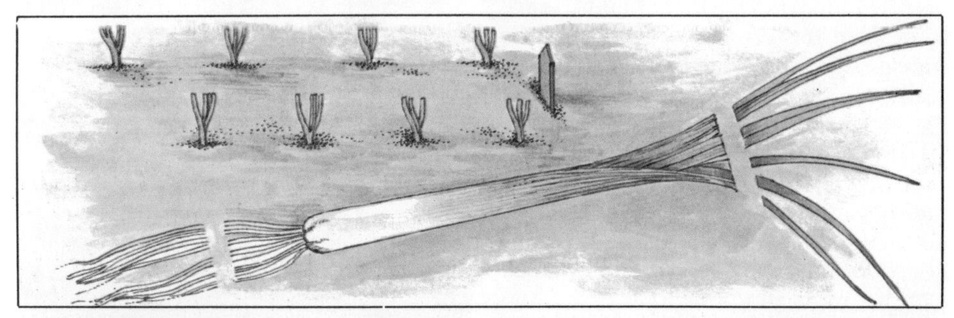

Top: composition of trench suitable for planting out a few leek seedlings
Above: before planting leek seedlings, cut back roots and trim leaves as shown

Right: mid-season leek, Musselburgh

For harvesting in midwinter, plants will need to go out in late summer (July). An early autumn (August) planting will give leeks from late winter (January) onward. As there is usually no shortage of other vegetables before this time, there is little point in planting out too early.

To transplant from the seed row, first ease the plants with a fork, then pull them up and separate them carefully. Throw out any plants that are bent or very short in the stem – these will never make good leeks – and take off any loose skin. Cut back the roots to about 4cm (1½ in) from the stem, and shorten the tops by about half. This does not harm the plants, which soon form fresh roots, but it does make transplanting much easier. The plants are ready for moving when they are about 15–20cm (6–8 in) long, usually about 10–15 weeks old.

A dibber is the best tool for planting but a trowel can be used. Make a hole deep enough to take the plant up to its lowest leaves, drop it in, trickle a little soil over the roots and pour some water into the hole. It is unnecessary to fill the hole in, as this will be done during subsequent cultivation.

When the plants are put out in the open ground, allow 20cm (8 in) between them and a minimum of 30cm (12 in) between the rows; 38cm (15 in) is better, and if you are intending to earth the plants up a little, 45cm (18 in) will be required.

1

2

To transplant leeks: **1** *draw drill with hoe;* **2** *make planting holes with a dibber;* **3** *drop plantlets into holes;* **4** *trickle soil over roots, and pour in water, but don't fill in hole*

3

4

Care of growing plants

Take care when hoeing that the stems of the leeks are not nicked with the hoe, as any wound is an entry point for pests and diseases. Being deep-rooting, the plants do not suffer too quickly from drought, but if it becomes very dry they will appreciate a good soaking of water. An occasional application of liquid manure or soot water will also be beneficial.

The edible part of the leek is the blanched stem, and this area can be increased if a little soil is drawn up the stems. Do this only when the soil is dry and friable and will run through the hoe; to plaster wet soil against the plants will do more harm than good. A dry day in late autumn or early winter (late October or November) is the time to choose. With a draw hoe, carefully pull up the soil to each plant and take care that soil does not fall into the heart of the plant. Where the plants are being grown in a trench the remainder of the dug-out soil is returned to the trench as the plants grow.

Pot leeks

The pot leek differs from the ordinary leek in having a shorter but much thicker stem. Its culture is the same as that of ordinary leeks, but its popularity is limited and mainly confined to certain northern areas of Britain.

Pests and diseases

As a rule leeks are trouble-free, but they may be attacked by onion fly or white rot.

Onion fly This pest can become a menace around the time when the seedlings are transplanted. If there is a history of onion fly in the garden, sprinkle calomel dust up each side of the row while the plants are still in the seedling stage, or dust with BHC.

White rot Calomel dust will also protect against white rot, a white fungal growth at the base of the plant. If this occurs, destroy infected plants and do not grow leeks there again for several years.

Harvesting and storing

Leeks are dug as required and present no storage problem. If severe frost threatens it pays to dig up a few leeks and keep them in the garden shed with the stems covered. An alternative method is to surround a few plants with peat or short litter (composted manure). This will absorb most of the frost and make it possible to dig up the leeks even when the surrounding ground is frozen.

Leeks will continue to grow from the time of planting to the onset of winter. The rate slows down with the arrival of colder weather, although some growth may still be made in mild periods. In mid to late spring (March to April) there is a surge of new growth that culminates in the formation of seed heads. Any plants still left in the ground at the end of spring (late April) should be lifted. These can be stored for a few weeks in a shady corner of the garden, with a little soil over the roots and the blanched stems covered to exclude light.

When digging, make sure that the spade is thrust well down, or the bottom of the leek may be chopped off. The leek makes a mass of fibrous roots, and these help to break up heavy soil.

RECOMMENDED VARIETIES

GARLIC

Best Italian Standard variety, readily available, prolific and easy to grow.

Jumbo Recent variety that can be grown from seed to maturity in about 18 months.

LEEKS

The Lyon (also known as Prizetaker) Popular early variety with long stems and mild flavour.

Marble Pillar Early variety with long white stems.

Musselburgh Mid-season variety, has long, thick stems and broad leaves.

Winter Crop One of the hardiest of the late-cropping leeks.

ONIONS
from sets and seeds

Onions used to have a reputation of being difficult to cultivate, but modern varieties offer types to suit most conditions so no gardener need be without them. Even so, the right preparation is still essential.

Onions do best in a medium to heavy loam; although lighter soils will produce good crops, the bulbs may be smaller.

Prepare the plot early so that winter frost and rain will settle the soil naturally; be sure your digging is completed by mid winter (December). Dig in as much manure and compost as possible, leave the ground rough and finish off with a dusting of lime.

In early or mid spring (February or March) when the soil is dry enough, break down the lumps with a cultivator and a rake. Tread it firmly to a fine tilth. There is a certain artistry and a lot of satisfaction in making a good onion bed.

You can grow onions in the same site year after year – *providing there is no soil-borne disease present.* To do so encourages a rich, fertile soil to build up over succeeding years.

Sowing

Onions will start to form bulbs about late summer (July), irrespective of when the seeds are sown. A late sowing will not mean late bulbing, but smaller bulbs. In general therefore, the earlier the seeds are sown, the larger the bulbs.

Grow onions in rich soil (far right) to produce beautiful golden bulbs like the Rijnsburger Yellow Globe (above)

Outdoor sowings can be made from early to late spring (February to April) whenever the ground is suitable, with a target date of mid spring (March) if possible. Sow the seeds thinly and evenly in drills 13mm (½ in) deep and 25–30cm (10–12 in) apart.

Sowing in autumn (August to October) gives the plants a longer time of growth and as autumn sowings come to maturity earlier than spring ones, the bulbs can be lifted early in the following autumn (August) while drying-off conditions are still favourable. If you do not time the sowing carefully the plants may get too far advanced by spring and go to seed.

The best sowing date for your area can be determined only by trial and error but, as a rough guide, you should reckon on the beginning of autumn (first week in August) for colder regions; one to two weeks later (mid August) for milder areas; and three to five weeks later (end of August or first week in September) for the more favourable climatic regions. Later sowings will need the protection of cloches throughout winter.

Planting onion sets

Growing onions from sets is an especially popular method in less favourable climates. An onion set is a small onion in an arrested state of development; when replanted it grows to full size. Some years ago sets were viewed with suspicion because of their tendency to go to seed, but with today's varieties this is less likely to happen. Some seedsmen are now combating the problem by storing the sets in a high temperature for several weeks. This kills the embryo flower-bud without harming the set.

Experience has shown that only a small percentage of treated sets go to seed, so they are worth the extra cost.

Plant onion sets towards late spring (March–April) in rows 30cm (12 in) apart allowing 10–15cm (4–6 in) between the bulbs (the closer planting will give bulbs large enough for kitchen use). Draw a drill just deep enough to cover the sets. It is sometimes recommended that the tips should show above the soil, but many gardeners prefer to cover them as this stops birds from pulling them out again.

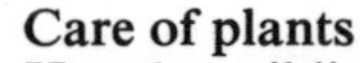

Care of plants

Hoe the soil lightly so that the roots are not disturbed. Keep autumn-sown plants weeded as long as possible or they may be so choked by spring that rescuing them could prove tedious and difficult.

Watering will help in a dry spell, but stop once the bulbs have formed and the tops (leaves) start to topple. The tops fall over when the bulbs begin to ripen as the supply of sap to the leaves is cut off. You can hasten the process by bending the tops with the back of a rake, but do be careful or the leaves may get bruised or broken. You would do better to let the tops go over naturally.

Ease up gently with fork before lifting

Plant onion sets in shallow drills

Shuffle along drill to cover with earth

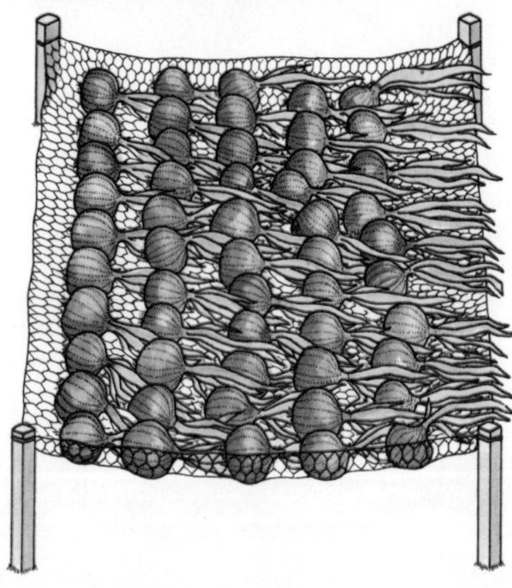

Before storing spread onions out on a bed of wire netting (above) with their roots facing south so that they receive the maximum amount of sun.
Onions are ready for lifting and drying off when their tops fall over (left)

Large onions

If you prefer large onions you will need a greenhouse that can be heated to 10°C (50°F). Make a start in late winter (January), sowing two or three seeds thinly every 4cm (1½ in) in trays of J. I. No 1 seed compost and thin to the strongest plant.

Harden them off before planting out in late spring (April). The plants must be 20–30cm (8–12 in) apart, with 30–40cm (12–15 in) between each row.

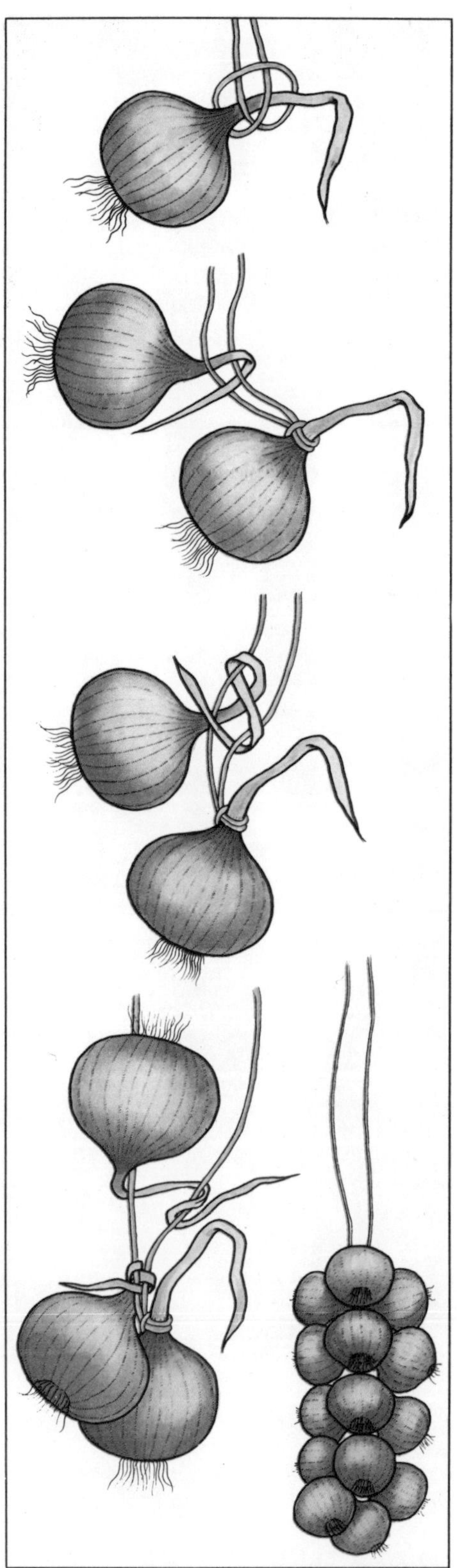

Pickling onions (top) need neither rich soil nor thinning out. For storing choose one of the long-keeping varieties such as Bedfordshire Champion (above)

Harvesting and storing

Beware at this stage of thinking that all the important work is behind you! More onion crops are ruined by poor harvesting and storing than by any other cause. They are ready to harvest when the leaves have turned yellow and the scales of the bulbs are brown. Ease them gently loose with a fork, pull them up and spread them out to dry.

Before storing make sure the bulbs are thoroughly dried off: leave them out in the open, turning them occasionally; place them in an empty frame, or on a path or wire netting suspended above the soil. An excellent drying method is to cover the bulbs with cloches, leaving the ends open to allow the wind to blow right through.

When the tops feel papery and the brown scales on the bulbs can be rubbed off, the onions are ready for storing. Put them in shallow boxes – tomato trays on legs (available from a greengrocer) are ideal as the air can circulate around them. Onions must be stored in a dry, airy place. They will stand some frost, but should be brought indoors during severe weather.

Making an onion string

A space-saving and popular idea is to string the onions together and hang them up instead of storing them away. Take a length of rope or cord and tie a large onion to one end. Using this as an anchor, secure the rest round the rope, building up from the bottom. Hang the completed onion string in a shed, garage or on a sunny wall.

White Lisbon (above) is one of the most popular spring onion varieties. For a constant supply sow 'little and often' throughout the spring and summer

Salad and pickling onions
Salad onions can be sown successionally from mid spring to mid summer (March to June). You can sow the seeds more thickly than for 'keeping' onions, and the rows need be only 15cm (6 in) apart. The plants are pulled while still green, starting when they are about pencil thickness. In dry periods water them well before pulling, and firm any plants that are left to grow on.

Thinnings from autumn and spring sowings of your keeping onions can also be used.

Pickling onions are easy to grow and they don't need rich soil. Sow the seeds thickly in a drill about 15cm (6 in) wide during late spring (April); no thinning is required. Harvest the bulbs in late summer (July).

Other types
There are several other kinds of onion which, although not so popular, are interesting to grow.
Welsh onion Forms a small, brownish, flat base; its stock can be raised from seeds sown in early or mid spring (February or March). Use the stems for salad onions. Keep a few clumps to plant again; split them up and replant in spring or autumn.
Japanese bunching onion Grows from seeds sown in late spring (April) and reaches full size in its second year. Like the Welsh specimen, use its shoots and leaves for salads and replant the clumps.
Everlasting onion Sow in spring or autumn. It is similar in habit to the Welsh and Japanese onions. Unfortunately it isn't widely distributed and might be difficult to obtain other than through catalogues of specialist growers.

Pests and diseases
It is as well to be forewarned of the likely attacks on your cherished plants.
Onion fly is the major hazard. It lays eggs at the base of the plants during early and mid summer (May and June) and the grubs burrow into the soil and attack the immature bulbs. Affected plants turn yellow, then collapse; they must be pulled up and burned. Make sure no larvae are left in the soil. The best safeguard is to apply calomel dust on each side of the rows when the plants are still at the 'crook' stage (before the seedlings have straightened up) and again about ten days later.

The pests are more active in light soils and with spring sowings. Autumn-sown bulbs and onion sets, although not immune, are less vulnerable to an attack.
White rot Fungus disease that causes the leaves of the plant to turn yellow and die. Roots rot and the base of the bulb is covered with a white mould. There is no cure and diseased plants must be burned.
Downy mildew Leaves die from the tips down and are covered with a fine, fluffy growth. It is also incurable, so burn any sick plants.

RECOMMENDED VARIETIES

For early and spring sowings
Ailsa Craig; Bedfordshire Champion; Blood Red.

For autumn sowings
Solidity; Reliance; Express Yellow.

Onion sets
Untreated: Stuttgarter Giant; Sturon.
Treated: Rijnsburger Wijbo (formerly called Giant Fen Globe).

Salad onions
White Lisbon

Pickling onions
Paris Silverskin; The Queen; Cocktail.

SHALLOTS

The shallot is a smaller member of the onion family. Gourmet cooks often substitute it for onions and it is widely used for pickling.

There is an old gardening tradition that shallots should be planted on the shortest day and harvested on the longest. This seldom occurs in practice, but it is an indication of the hardiness of this vegetable. The more usual times of planting are early or mid spring (February or March), but there is no reason why the bulbs should not be planted earlier than this if weather conditions permit.

Preparing the ground

A medium loam is the best soil for shallots but they will do well in heavier soils provided the drainage is good. Although not quite so demanding in their soil requirements as onions, they do like a good soil. If you are planting in early or mid spring (February or March), prepare the site in autumn as soon as the autumn-maturing crops have been gathered. Dig in some manure or compost and leave the soil rough. If you cannot prepare the site quite so early as this, only well-rotted manure or compost should be used.

Sowing and planting

Shallots can be grown from seed but few seedsmen list this item. Sow in mid spring (March) in drills 13mm (½ in) deep and 30cm (12 in) apart; then thin the seedlings to 15cm (6 in) apart. Bulbs produced by this method should not be saved for replanting as they will go to seed.

The other method of propagation, and that followed by nearly all gardeners, is to plant selected bulbs 20cm (8 in) apart with 30cm (12 in) between the rows. These bulbs may be purchased from most seedsmen during the planting season; alternatively, you may find that friends or neighbours have some to spare. These bulbs come from a non-flowering type of shallot, although occasional flowering shoots may be sent up (especially in a hot, dry season). If flowering shoots appear, pinch them out.

Bulbs of this type may be selected and reselected from year to year; simply pick out some medium-sized bulbs that are quite firm and of good shape and colour, and put them on one side when the crop is sorted for use.

It is sometimes recommended that shallots should be pushed into the soil until only their tips are showing, but this is not the best method of planting. Pushing them in will often leave them sitting on a hard pan of soil and the roots, in trying to penetrate this hard layer, will tend to push the bulbs upwards.

A much better way is to take out a little hole with the tip of a trowel and sit the bulb in the hollow. Pull the soil back until just the shoulders and tip of the bulb are showing.

Tending the plants

Birds can be a menace to the newly-planted bulbs by pecking the tips and pulling them out again. Blackbirds seem to be particularly guilty. Whether it is curiosity or devilment on their part is hard to say. You can, however, outwit them by stretching black cotton (positioned a few centimetres above the bulbs) between sticks. Pea guards placed over the bulbs also give excellent protection. Once the tips show green the bulbs have rooted and the danger is over.

During the summer keep the plants free from weeds but do not hoe too close to the bulbs. When the clusters of bulbs have formed and are approaching maturity, draw a little soil away from them with your fingers to aid ripening.

Lifting and drying

The time to lift the bulbs is when the foliage has yellowed, a process that begins at the leaf tips. This may tie in with the longest day, if the weather has been hot and dry, but in many seasons may be two or three weeks later.

Ease the clusters of bulbs with a fork before pulling them out. Do not split

Left: Dutch Yellow shallots, slightly larger than the red varieties, will often keep for up to 12 months

Left: (top) ease the clusters of bulbs with a fork and leave them in clumps to dry; (bottom) spicy and sweet Giant Red is a heavy cropper

them up at this stage but leave them in clumps to dry.

In a dry season drying the bulbs presents no problems. They can be left on the soil surface and turned occasionally. If the weather is wet or showery the roots are liable to take hold of the soil again. To prevent this, remove them to a hard path, or anywhere outdoors where they will not be in contact with the soil. One useful method is to put a few cloches over them, leaving the ends open so that the wind can blow through.

Storing the bulbs

When the clusters are quite dry they can be broken up. Check each bulb for any sign of disease and don't store any that are diseased. Correct storage of the bulbs is important. On no account should they be stored in bags (except net ones) or in deep boxes, because they will heat up and go bad. Spread them out thinly in a light, cool place. The shallow tomato trays with a leg at each corner, that can be bought from local greengrocers, make excellent containers for onions and shallots. In good storage conditions the bulbs will keep sound for eight or nine months.

Pests and diseases

Shallots may sometimes be attacked by the onion fly or by onion white rot disease, but such attacks are not common. For the most part they are easy to grow and trouble free.

Onion fly This pest lays its eggs at the base of the plant during early and mid summer (May and June) and the grubs burrow into the soil and attack the immature bulbs. Affected plants turn yellow and then collapse. Pull them up and burn them, making sure there are no larvae left in the soil. The best safeguard is to apply calomel dust on each side of the rows.

White rot Fungus disease that causes the leaves of the plants to turn yellow and die. Roots rot and the base of the bulb is covered with a white mould. There is no cure and diseased plants must be burned.

RECOMMENDED VARIETIES

Giant Red Mild, spicy and sweet; crops heavily and stores well.

Dutch Yellow Slightly larger than the red shallot; will often keep for nearly a year.

PERENNIALS

ASPARAGUS

**Asparagus has a large, fibrous root system and needs plenty of room. It is perennial, and takes several years before it comes into full production.
To maintain a regular supply during the cutting season you will need at least twenty-five plants – the minimum number, incidentally, that many growers will supply. This makes it difficult to fit an asparagus bed into a small vegetable plot, but the small grower is not ruled out entirely. It is possible to compromise and be satisfied with a dozen plants in a single row.**

Asparagus is easy to grow once its permanent bed has been well prepared.

Other than thorough preparation there are several factors you should consider before committing yourself to growing it. First, with this crop, you cannot expect a rapid return for your time, money and effort. Two or three years must elapse before it produces tender stalks that are ready to eat. Furthermore, if you are expecting to move house in the near future then your successor will be the one to benefit from your asparagus bed, just as it is beginning to give a good yield.

Finally, asparagus is space-consuming. For an average family you will need a minimum of 25 plants, planted 45cm (18 in) apart, in rows 90cm (3 ft) apart. However, there is no reason why you shouldn't grow one or two other quick-maturing crops between the stalks. A few Tom Thumb lettuce, for instance, or a sprinkling of radish can be sown and harvested without interfering with the growth of the asparagus plants.

If none of these considerations deter you, then your asparagus bed will be a worthwhile investment that can continue to yield for 20 years or more.

Choosing the site

The soil of an asparagus bed must be rich but, within reason, it can vary from fairly heavy to quite light. It should also be a soil that does not dry out too easily, nor must it hold excessive water and become waterlogged in winter. In fact, regardless of soil type, it is always best to grow asparagus on a slightly raised bed. The bed should receive as much sun as possible and it should be sheltered from very strong winds.

Left: shoots develop ferny stems in summer
Below: a grand crop of sticks will reward work and patience with the asparagus bed

Preparing the ground

A light-to-medium loam in which the roots can spread freely is best for asparagus, but fine crops can be grown in heavier soils providing the drainage is good. If drainage is poor dig the plot over, digging in as much well-rotted manure or compost as possible, and then raise the bed with about 30cm (12 in) of good topsoil. On light to medium soils double dig the site incorporating as much manure or compost as you can spare. Gardeners living near the sea can use seaweed, as this is excellent for asparagus.

Prepare a strip 3m (10 ft) wide so that the spreading roots will be able to find plenty of food. The site should be an open, sunny one with, if possible, some shelter from the prevailing wind.

Asparagus may be grown either on the flat, in rows 60cm (24 in) apart, or in ridges, 1·2m (4 ft) apart. Many people prefer ridging as it gives a greater length of blanched stem and makes cutting easier. Three rows on the flat or two rows in ridges is the usual arrangement, with 45cm (18 in) between plants.

Raising or buying plants

You can either raise plants from seed or buy them as one- or two-year-old plants from nurserymen or specialist growers. Don't buy three-year-old plants; their longer roots take too long to re-establish themselves.

Sow the seeds in late spring (April) in drills 5cm (2 in) deep and 38cm (15 in) apart. The seeds will germinate more quickly if they are soaked in water overnight before sowing. When the seedlings are about 15cm (6 in) high thin them to stand 30cm (12 in) apart.

Asparagus produces both male and female plants; the females are easy to identify as they bear the berries that contain the seeds. It is generally considered that the males – having to expend no energy on reproducing – give the heaviest crop. However, as the ratio of males to females is about equal it is very difficult, unless you grow a large number of plants, to select all males. It is more important to make sure that the best plants of either sex are saved for growing on. Strong, healthy plants will be easier to pick out in the second season.

As to variety, Connover's Colossal is an excellent choice, producing an early crop of thick, succulent stalks

Transplanting the crowns

Whether your plants are raised from seed or bought, the planting procedure is the same. Plant out in late spring (April). Take out trenches 30cm (12 in) wide and 30cm (12 in) deep, then return enough soil into the trench to make a ridge about 25cm (9 in) in height. The roots of asparagus are long and spidery and the best method of planting is to sit the plants on the ridge with the roots trailing down each side. It is most important to remember that the roots must never be allowed to dry out. Do not lift them, or unpack them (if bought in) until you are ready to plant them, and fill in the trench as each plant is put in. Try to have the ground prepared beforehand so that they can be unpacked and planted as soon as they arrive. The crowns, when planted, should be about 8–10cm (3–4 in) below the soil surface.

Tending growing plants

No sticks should be cut during the year after planting; leave the plants to make their fern (leaves) unchecked. If you are growing the plants in two rows then you can grow a catch crop of lettuces, radishes, young roots or French beans in that first season. In the autumn, when the fern has yellowed, cut it down to leave about 2–3cm (1 in) of stem and clear away and burn the cut foliage to help minimize any pest or disease problems. Remove all weeds by pricking the soil over, *lightly*, with a fork, then mulch the bed with manure or compost. In mid spring (March) rake the bed clean and then apply a good, general fertilizer at about 70–100g per sq m (2–3 oz per sq yd).

In the second year after planting, if two-year-old crowns were used, you can cut a few spears (stems) but limit the number to three or four from each plant. In the third season (when the plants will be four or five years old) you can cut them over a period of about a month. After this, the bed will be in full production.

To grow the plants by the ridge method, dig out a shallow trench from between the two rows after the autumn clean-up, and heap it up over the crowns to form a ridge. In mid spring (March) after applying the dressing of spring fertilizer, fork the ridges over lightly and then mound them up again with a hoe. When you have finished cutting, level the ridges out again.

The maintenance of an established bed then falls into the same routine of cutting off the foliage and mulching in autumn, followed by a fertilizer dressing in the spring. A 'bonus' that asparagus appreciates once it is established is a yearly dressing in late spring and early summer (late April or May) of agricultural salt at around 70g per sq m (2 oz per sq yd).

If the weather is dry in late summer and early autumn (July and August) then you must keep the bed well watered as it is

Below: dig trench 30cm (12 in) deep and wide, then form ridge 25cm (9 in) high. Rest asparagus crown on top, spread out roots and cover to original soil level

Above: to cut asparagus sticks, use a sharp, narrow-bladed knife. Follow the stem down through soil and cut neatly about 8–10cm (3–4 in) below soil level

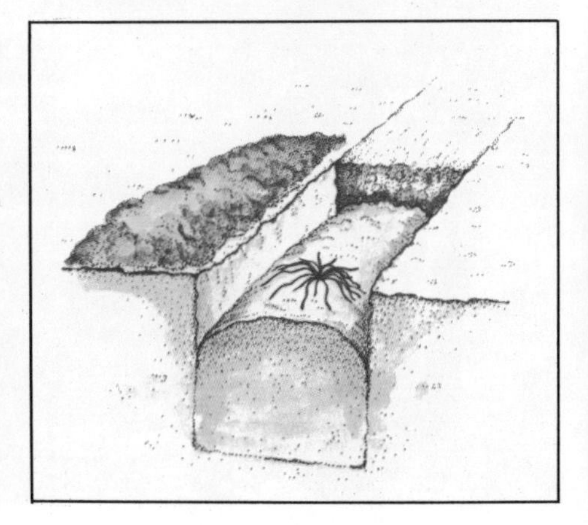

RECOMMENDED VARIETIES

Connover's Colossal Probably the best-known variety; early and reliable with thick, succulent spears.
Martha Washington Tender, delicious and a prolific cropper; has some resistance to asparagus rust.
Brocks Imperial (F.1 hybrid) Early and vigorous, producing large crops of uniformly thick spears.
Suttons Perfection A reliable, standard variety available as two-year-old roots.

during this period that the plants have to produce their ferny foliage which provides the crowns with food for the following season.

It does the crowns no good if the fern stalks are blown about in high winds, so some form of staking is usually necessary. One good way of doing this is to push in bamboo canes at intervals, and then run string around and between them to support the ferns.

Harvesting the spears

The cutting period for an established bed runs from late spring to mid summer (April to June), varying a little according to district and season. A good general rule is to cut for eight weeks after you start cutting. Resist any temptation to prolong the cutting season for another week or two as this will have an adverse effect on the following year's crop. The time to begin cutting is when the first spears are 8–10cm (3–4 in) above soil level. Emerging spears may sometimes be damaged by a late spring frost, but you can guard against this by spreading a little short litter, such as bracken or straw, evenly over the bed.

Cutting asparagus

You can buy a special asparagus saw for cutting, but this is not necessary unless your crop is very large. A narrow-bladed kitchen knife is the next best choice. The cutting must be done with great care or other shoots, still below ground, may be damaged. Sever the sticks about 8–10cm (3–4 in) below soil level. It is at this stage that the ridge system comes into its own, for it is much easier to follow a selected shoot down if it is on a ridge and you can gently draw the soil away.

Cut all the spears as they appear and then grade them according to thickness for cooking. Any surplus can be frozen for later use. Spears less than 6mm (¼ in) in thickness are known as sprue. These are useful in soups.

Pests and diseases

Asparagus is prone to one or two pests and diseases. Good hygiene, in particular the cutting and burning of old, yellowed ferns, is one of the best preventive methods.

Asparagus beetle The main pest of asparagus is the asparagus beetle. The grey larvae of this little creature is particularly destructive in its attacks on the stem and fern during late summer and early autumn (July and August). Examine the ferns from time to time and, if you find the pests, treat with derris dust. A second application, 10–14 days later, will kill any grubs that have emerged from the eggs since the first dusting.

Asparagus fly This insect lays her eggs in late spring and early summer (April and May) on the young shoots. The yellowish-white maggots tunnel into the shoots, causing them to wilt. Cut out all affected shoots and burn them. Fortunately this pest is not so common as the beetle.

Asparagus rust A fungus disease called asparagus rust appears on the stems and foliage of the plants from late summer (July) onwards. This takes the form of small reddish pustules that turn darker as the season advances. Dusting the foliage with flowers of sulphur will help to keep the fungus at bay.

Below: one new shoot of Asparagus officinalis *appearing during summer among the older stems*

RHUBARB

Rhubarb is too often relegated to some out-of-the-way corner of the vegetable garden and then forgotten. Yet, given a good start and a little care, it will crop heavily and regularly over a long period.

Four rhubarb plants should be enough for the average family and six for a large one. There are two methods of establishing a rhubarb bed: one is to buy the planting crowns and the other is to raise your own roots from seed. If time is not important, growing from seed is cheaper and not difficult, but planting crowns gives a quicker return.

Preparing the soil

Rhubarb prefers a sunny, open site. It will grow in most soils but does better in a soil that is rich and light. As it occupies the ground for a long time (a good bed should crop for at least ten years) it makes sense to give it a good start. Begin by taking out a trench 90cm (3 ft) wide and a spade's depth, and then break up the subsoil. Before returning the topsoil, fork in some well-rotted manure or compost – about a bucket load to each plant. This should be done several weeks in advance of planting so that the soil has time to settle.

Planting or sowing

You can buy crowns from market stalls or nurserymen during the planting season. Choose roots that have at least one good bud or crown. The best planting time is early winter (November) followed by early to mid spring (February or March).

Sow seed outdoors in mid to late spring (late March or April) in drills 2–3cm (1 in) deep and 38cm (15 in) apart. Thin the plants to stand 15cm (6 in) apart and then let them grow on. It may be possible, by the end of the summer, to see which are the best roots to retain when thinning, but a better selection can be made if the plants are left for another season. You can then pull stalks from the rejected plants before they are discarded; don't pull any from the chosen roots.

In early winter (November) lift the roots carefully and replant them firmly 90cm (3 ft) apart, so that the topmost bud is just about 5cm (2 in) below the level of the surrounding soil.

Pulling the stalks

No stalks should be pulled in the first year after planting. In early autumn (August) the stalks yellow and die down naturally, and the goodness in them is returned to the crowns. By pulling too soon you delay

Champagne Early has a fine flavour

Above left: give a good mulch in autumn Above: cover crowns with removable box or bin to force. Above right: yellow leaves of forced rhubarb contrast with those of a normal crop (left)

the build-up of a good crown with strong buds. In the second season after planting you can pull some (but not too many) of the stalks.

Cut off any seed-heads that push their way up through the leaves (and put them on the compost heap) as the production of seed weakens the plants. Stop pulling rhubarb after mid summer (end of June). If you then want stalks for jam, take one or two from each plant. Always leave some stalks to feed the crowns for the following year.

When pulling rhubarb, slide a hand down the stem as far as possible and then detach the stalk with a quick, outward twist. One peculiarity of this plant, that should not be forgotten, is that while the stalks are edible the leaves should never be eaten as they contain oxalic acid and are poisonous.

Tending the plants

In autumn rake off the withered leaves and mulch the area with some good compost or manure. The goodness from this will be absorbed into the soil with beneficial results. Repeat this dressing annually to help keep the bed in the best possible condition.

When crowns produce only a succession of thin stalks it is a sign that the roots need lifting and dividing. Fork them out, chop them up with a sharp spade and select only the strongest, outlying crowns for replanting. Only divide one or two roots at a time to make sure there is no break in the supply of stalks.

Forcing rhubarb

Rhubarb 'forcing' means persuading it to produce stalks before its normal season. There are two ways of doing this. For the first method you will need a greenhouse with some heating; a temperature of 10°C (50°F) is high enough. Dig up strong-growing crowns in late autumn and early winter (October and November) and leave them on the open ground so that the roots are exposed to the weather. In mid or late winter (December or January) take them into the greenhouse and plant them closely together in the soil border, or under the staging or in a deep box. If using boxes, put the crowns on a few centimetres of good soil and then cover them completely with more of the same soil.

There are two important points to remember with this type of forcing. The soil around the crowns must be kept moist, and they must be forced in the dark. Black polythene makes a useful screening material. If you are using boxes it is a simple matter to invert one box over another.

The disadvantage of this method is that, after forcing, the crowns are exhausted and are of no further use. Therefore you must either buy crowns specially for forcing, or take up valuable space in order to grow extra crowns for the purpose. But as rhubarb freezes well there is no longer the same need to take this trouble in order to have rhubarb early in the year.

The second, and easier, way is to force the crowns *in situ* in the garden by covering selected roots with bottomless boxes, buckets or tubs. An old dustbin, with the bottom knocked out and the lid used as a cover, is ideal for this purpose. The point in having a removable cover is that it enables the crowns to be inspected without disturbing the box or bin. You can gain a little extra warmth by heaping strawy manure or decaying leaves around the bin. Alternatively, fill the bin loosely with hay or straw.

This practice, although giving later stalks than the greenhouse method, has the advantage that the crowns are not seriously harmed. Providing the same roots are not used for forcing each year, they soon recover. The simplest method of all (still giving stalks earlier than from unprotected roots) is to cover the roots in mid winter (December) with 30cm (12 in) of straw. You can leave the straw in place, after the rhubarb has emerged, where it will rot down to form humus.

Pests and diseases

The only calamity likely to affect rhubarb is crown rot. This bacterial disease causes rotting of the terminal bud, and may extend right back to the rootstock. Dig up and burn affected plants.

RECOMMENDED VARIETIES

Victoria Long, cherry-red stalks of excellent quality and flavour.

Champagne Early Fine-flavoured variety with long, bright scarlet stalks.

Glaskin's Perpetual Grows well from seed and produces a good yield over a long period.

Holstein Bloodred Vigorous grower and prolific cropper with juicy, dark red stalks.

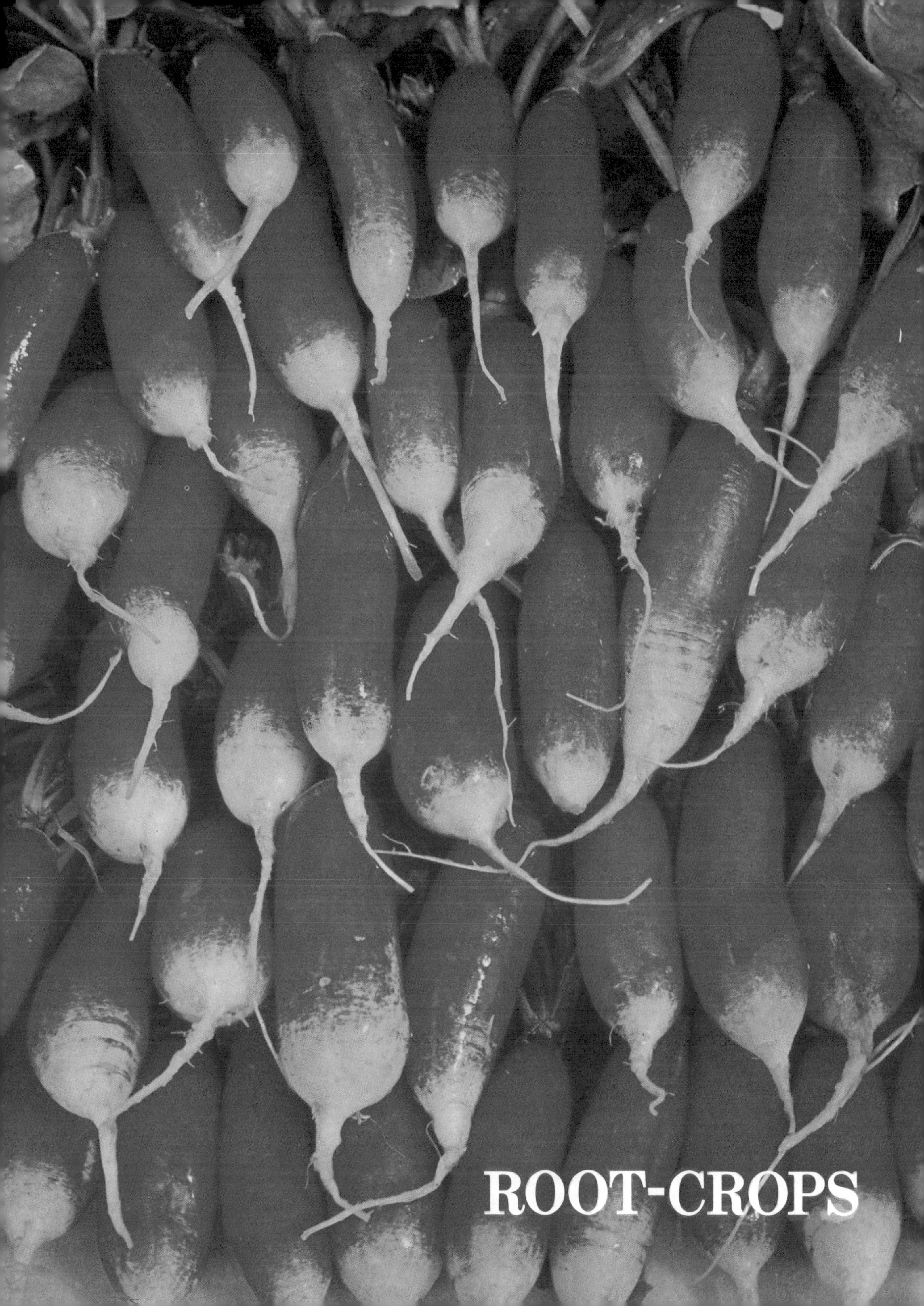

ROOT-CROPS

BEETROOT AND LEAF BEET

The first tender, succulent young roots of beetroot are one of the joys of the vegetable gardener's year. Furthermore it is a root which most people can grow without difficulty.

There are three types of beetroot – the globe beet (which is the most popular), the intermediate or cylindrical beet and the long beet. Although the long beet is still grown commercially and for exhibition, it has been superseded to a great extent by the other two kinds. For early sowings always use the globe beet. The intermediate beet is bigger but it grows more slowly, so it is more suitable for maincrop use.

Sowing the seed clusters

Beetroot is unusual in that each 'seed' is really a capsule containing several seeds. Extra care should be taken, therefore, to sow thinly. You can sow early crops in a continuous row, but where the maincrop and late sowings are concerned, it is better to sow one or two seed clusters at 10cm (4 in) intervals and then thin to the strongest plant. The drills should be 2–3cm (1 in) deep and 30cm (12 in) apart.

Sow seed capsules thinly at intervals

Early sowings

For an early crop, sow in early spring (February) in a cold frame or under cloches. A barn cloche will take three rows, 23cm (9 in) apart. Outdoor sowings can begin after the middle of spring (after mid March). Although the beetroot is a biennial plant, forming a root in its first year and seed in the second, it can telescope this process if sown early, and throw up seed stalks in the first year. Gardeners describe this as 'bolting'. For these early sowings, therefore, choose a variety with some resistance to bolting.

Maincrop sowings

Do not sow maincrop beetroot too early – towards the end of early summer (mid May to early June) is a good time. If you are sowing in late summer (July), go back to using the small, globe beet as these are the quickest to mature, providing the summer is not too hot and the autumn mild. They will give tender young roots for use in late autumn and early winter (October and November).

Long beetroot need a deep, fertile soil, free from stones. They should be thinned to 23cm (9 in) apart with 38–45cm (15–18 in) between the rows.

Tending beetroot

In periods of drought give the beetroot a good soaking of water to keep them growing. Dry weather tends to affect the eating quality of the roots; it is also one cause of the plants 'bolting'.

Be very careful when hoeing beetroot; once the leaves have begun to hide the roots do not hoe too close to the rows. A tiny nick at this stage will turn into an ugly crack later on; so if need be, hand weed around the plants.

Harvesting and storing

Beetroot are ready for pulling as soon as they are big enough to use, and some thinning of the earliest sowings can be done in this way. However, it always pays

to do a little preliminary thinning as soon as the plants are big enough to handle. Beetroot is relatively hardy but can be injured by severe frost, and it is wise to lift the roots by about the end of autumn (end of October). The foliage shows the approach of maturity by beginning to lose its bright, fresh colour.

Ease the roots up with a fork and rub off any soil adhering to them. Take great care, when digging up long beet, so that the roots are not damaged. Twist off the tops about 5cm (2 in) from the crown. Long beetroot have a much greater tendency to 'bleed' when cut than the other kinds; to prevent this always twist off their tops.

Sort the roots through, putting on one side any that are cracked or damaged for immediate use, and store the remainder in boxes of peat, sand or soil – a thin layer of roots followed by a layer of the medium, until the box is full. The medium should be just damp enough to stop the roots from shrivelling. An alternative method is to make a little clamp (as you do for carrots) in the garden.

Other types of beetroot

In addition to the ordinary beetroot there are several leaf beets that make excellent vegetables. Here the process is reversed, for it is the leaves which are used and not the roots. All the leaf beets throw up flowering stems in their second year. Let these run up (but not to seeding point), then chop them up and put them on the compost heap.

Above: twist off tops to prevent 'bleeding'
Right: pull spinach beet leaves as needed
Above left: beetroot in a straw-lined storage clamp
Left: a popular globe beet, Avonearly, and right, Detroit variety

Spinach beet Probably the best known of the spinach beets and a substitute for spinach. It also appears in the catalogues as Perpetual Spinach. The roots, when at their peak, produce lots of thick, fleshy leaves which you can boil like spinach, but without boiling them down nearly so much. To harvest, take a few leaves from each plant; fresh leaves will grow in their place.

Sow spinach beet in mid or late spring (March or April) in rows 2–3cm (1 in) deep and 38–45cm (15–18 in) apart. Thin the plants to 23cm (9 in). They require no other attention, except for hoeing and watering in dry weather. A good row of spinach beet will give pickings for a year; but if you make a sowing in early autumn (August), this will give plenty of young leaves for picking in the spring. The advantage of an early autumn (August) sowing, where space is at a premium, is that you can use it as a follow-on crop to some of the earlier vegetables.

Seakale beet or Swiss chard The plant produces large fleshy leaves with a broad white mid-rib. This is a dual-purpose vegetable, for in addition to using the leaves as spinach, the broad mid-ribs can be cut out, chopped in pieces and used as a substitute for seakale *Crambe maritima*, which is grown for its tender shoots that must be forced.

Sowing times and distances, and cultivation are the same as for spinach beet, and the early autumn sowing is particularly useful where space is a problem. The seed is usually listed as seakale beet or Swiss chard, but there is now an F.1 hybrid called Vintage Green, which is said to be more vigorous and prolific. Spinach beet and seakale beet (Swiss chard) are both forms of *Beta vulgaris cicla*, but the latter provides leaves as well as mid-rib shoots for eating.

Ruby chard An ornamental form of Swiss chard with long, bright red stalks and crumpled leaves and can be cooked in the same way as seakale beet. Sowing and cultivation are as for seakale beet.

RECOMMENDED VARIETIES

GLOBE BEETROOT
Boltardy (resistant to bolting)
Avonearly (resistant to bolting)
Early Bunch (resistant to bolting)
Crimson Globe
Burpee's Golden (for leaves and roots)
Snowhite
Detroit Little Ball (late sowings)

INTERMEDIATE BEETROOT
Cylindra
Formanova

LONG BEETROOT
Cheltenham Green Top
Long Blood Red

SEAKALE BEET/SWISS CHARD
Vintage Green (F.1 hybrid)

Pests and diseases
Blackfly and boron deficiency can be a problem when growing beetroot.

Blackfly Keep a close watch for this insect and spray with derris at the first sign of trouble.

Boron deficiency Causes the heart leaves to turn black, and black spots appear inside the roots. If you have encountered this trouble before, take preventive action by watering the plants with a foliar feed containing trace elements.

Below: Boltardy, a magnificent example of a globe beetroot
Bottom: two forms of Swiss chard, seakale beet (left) and ruby chard (right)

CARROTS

Carrots are a highly nutritious vegetable, a rich source of vitamin A. By making successional sowings and storing carefully you can have a supply for most of the year. Furthermore, they are a crop that yields a high return from a small area.

In length carrots may be short, intermediate or long. In shape they may be round, cylindrical with a blunt end (known as stump-rooted or short-horn), or tapering. From a harvesting point of view they fall roughly into four groups: early round; early stump-rooted (picked young in bunches); intermediate and long. The intermediate and long carrots are grown for storing and using during the winter months; they may either be stump-rooted or tapering.

If space in the garden is at a premium it may be necessary to drop intermediate and long (maincrop) varieties from the cropping programme and concentrate on 'bunching' carrots—young carrots from the early stump-rooted varieties.

Soil requirements

The ideal carrot soil is a light but deep loam which does not dry out too quickly. Such soils arc found naturally in various parts of the country, although they are not widespread. Fortunately, carrots will do reasonably well in most soils, with the exception of sticky clays and very light soils. In heavy loams they may split in wet weather, and in shallow soils only the stump-rooted varieties are suitable. In stony soil they may become misshapen or the roots may fork.

Fresh manure is not suitable for carrots as it may also cause forking roots, but you can use well-rotted manure or compost if it is dug or forked in a week or two before sowing. The tap root (main root) of a carrot should be able to go straight down into a soil where the food values are evenly distributed; a site previously well-manured and cultivated for a crop like potatoes is ideal. Before sowing rake in a balanced fertilizer, such as Growmore, at 70g per sq m (2 oz per sq yd).

Sowing under glass

If a heated frame is available, sow round or stump-rooted carrots in late winter (January). It is better to delay sowing in a cold frame or under cloches until early spring (mid-February). Make up a bed, about 23cm (9 in) deep, of prepared soil in the frame and sow the seeds thinly in rows 15cm (6 in) apart. The soil should be a good, riddled loam with some coarse garden sand and peat added. (The John Innes formula of 7 parts loam, 3 parts peat and 2 parts sand is a good guide.)

If using one of the modern glass-to-ground frames, fork over the bed, removing any large stones, and add some well-moistened peat and the balanced fertilizer. For sowing under cloches, prepare the soil strip in the same way. A large barn cloche 58cm (23 in) wide will take four rows of carrots sown 15cm (6 in) apart or five rows sown at 10cm (4 in) apart. Prepare the soil in good time so that you can put down the cloches three or four weeks before sowing. This will warm up the soil and give the crop a better start.

Below: easing up carrots with fork before lifting. Below left: prime examples of stump-rooted Chantenay Red Cored

Outdoor sowings

Sow (thinly) outdoors from mid spring (mid March) until late summer (mid July). Make the intermediate maincrop sowings in early summer (May or early June). It used to be recommended to sow considerably earlier than these times, but it has been found that later sowings are more likely to escape the carrot fly.

Long carrots should be sown by early summer (mid May); so limit late spring (April) sowings to small sowings of the early stump-rooted varieties which can be harvested quickly before the long varieties go in. Stump-rooted varieties can be used again in late summer (July) to give tender young roots for pulling in autumn. For outdoor sowings, allow 20–23cm (8–9 in) between rows for early short-horn varieties and 25–30cm (10–12 in) for maincrops.

Block method Another way of growing carrots is to sow a block of six rows only 8–10cm (3–4 in) apart. If sowing more than one block put a 60cm (2 ft) wide path between blocks. Plants kept in rows are easier to weed. The seeds in the blocks can be sown broadcast but this means more hand-weeding. Eventually the foliage takes over and stops further weeds from growing. An old table knife, heated and then bent over at the end, makes a useful tool for hoeing such narrow rows. The block method is space-saving and gives a heavier crop over a given area, but the individual roots may be a little smaller.

Thinning the seedlings

Theoretically you should sow carrots so thinly that no thinning out is necessary. But as this is hardly practical, just aim to sow as thinly as possible.

While some thinning can be left until the pulled roots are big enough to use, always make a preliminary thinning to 2–5cm (1–2 in). Thin maincrops to stand 8–10cm (3–4 in) apart, and the late summer (July) sowings to 5–8cm (2–3 in). Do this as soon as the plants are big enough to handle. With the late summer (July) sowings it is essential to thin the plants as early as possible or they will not have time to make usable roots.

In dry weather water the rows well before thinning. Afterwards, always firm the soil back with your feet and water again. Never leave thinnings lying around as they may attract the carrot fly. Drop them into a bucket as they are pulled out and put them on the compost heap. Do

Top: round carrots are particularly good on shallow soils. Left: cylindrical Early Nantes is excellent for the first spring sowings in frames or under cloches

not make early pullings from the maincrop rows as this also helps the carrot fly by leaving uncovered soil in which eggs can be laid; leave the roots in until harvest time comes round.

Lifting and storing

Lift and store maincrop carrots for the winter months. Although in theory carrots are hardy enough to spend the winter outdoors, in practice it is better to dig them up. Slug damage may occur during mild periods and heavy rains can cause cracking if they are left in the ground too long.

Lift the roots in late autumn or early winter (the end of October). By that time the foliage will have lost its rich green and turned a dull colour. Carefully ease up the roots with a fork before pulling them out, and rub off any soil. Cut the tops off about 13mm ($\frac{1}{2}$ in) from the crown. Put aside for first use any carrots which are split or damaged.

The sound roots can be stored in one of two ways. For storage in a garage or shed, take a wooden box and put a layer of sand, peat or reasonably dry soil in the bottom. Follow this with a layer of carrots packed head to tail. Alternate layers of covering and carrots until the box is full. The covering medium prevents the roots from shrivelling.

To store carrots outdoors, keep them in a little clamp. Pack the carrots in a conical heap with the roots pointing inward. Cover them with a layer of hay, straw, dried bracken or any dry litter which will not rot, and cover this, in turn, with about 10–15cm (4–6 in) of soil, leaving a wisp of the covering material sticking out of the top as an air vent to prevent the carrots going off. A heavier soil covering is not necessary. Although slight frost will not harm the carrots if it penetrates into the clamp, it is wise to leave them undisturbed until the frost has gone. In mid spring (March) push off the soil covering or the roots will rapidly make new growth. Rub off any new shoots that may have formed, and transfer the carrots to a box for use.

Pests and ailments

The foliage of healthy, growing carrots should be a rich, lustrous green. If it loses this richness, suspect either greenfly or carrot fly.

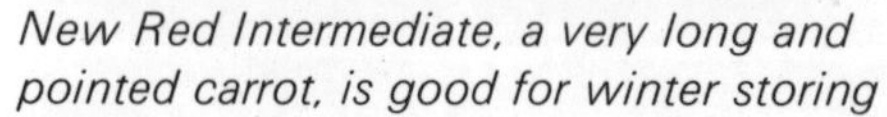

New Red Intermediate, a very long and pointed carrot, is good for winter storing

Greenfly The delicate, ferny foliage is liable to be attacked by these pests (aphides), but they can be prevented if the crop is sprayed with derris.

Carrot fly Appears any time from late spring to mid summer (April to June) and lays eggs in the soil close to the roots. As the maggots hatch and attack the roots, the foliage first takes on a reddish tinge and then turns yellow. The little cracks and tunnels made in the roots are often enlarged by slugs and wireworms until the vegetables are of little value. Prevent carrot fly by dusting the seed-drills with an insecticide such as BHC before the seeds are sown, or by spraying the young plants with a trichlorphon-based insecticide. Do not eat the vegetables within three weeks of spraying. Weathered soot (soot from house chimneys which has been stored under cover for about six months) is also a help in keeping the fly away and has a slight nitrogenous value. Although later sowings often escape the flies, they are not immune.

Bright sunlight Sometimes causes greening of the roots at the shoulders (just below the leaf stems). Although this is not a serious ailment, it does detract from their appearance. Prevent this problem by drawing a little soil up over the tops of the roots if they are exposed. Where carrots are grown close together the leaves will give adequate protection.

Below: for indoor storage, pack carrots head to tail between layers of dry sand
Bottom: carrots can be stored outdoors in a clamp made of straw and soil

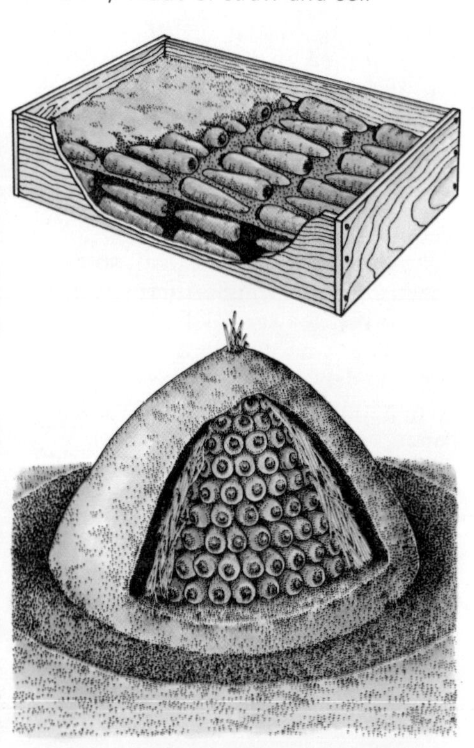

RECOMMENDED VARIETIES

EARLY ROUND
Parisian Rondo

EARLY STUMP-ROOTED (SHORT-HORN)
Amsterdam Forcing
Early Horn
Early Nantes

MAINCROP SHORT
James' Intermediate
Chantenay Red Cored
Autumn King

MAINCROP LONG
St Valery
New Red Intermediate

PARSNIPS

Parsnips are a hardy root crop and easy to grow – an ideal vegetable for the beginner. The only important point to remember is that they require a long growing season.

Parsnips do best in deep, loamy soil (shallow, stony ground is suitable only for the stump-rooted varieties). Grow them on ground that was well-manured for a previous crop; fresh manure can cause the roots to fork. If your soil is not already limed, rake in a dressing of garden lime at 70g sq m (2 oz per sq yd).

When to sow

Start sowing in early to mid spring (February to March), when the soil is easily worked to a fine tilth. You can sow as late as mid to late spring (mid April) and still get good-sized roots.

Make shallow drills (furrows) with a hoe or side of a rake, 2·5cm (1 in) deep and 40cm (15 in) apart, and sow a few seeds at 15cm (6 in) intervals.

Parsnip seeds are very light, so choose a calm day for sowing. (Alternatively you can use pelleted seeds.) They are slow to germinate, and the best way to keep weeds under control is to sow a few fast-germinating radish seeds between each parsnip station (cluster of seeds). When the radishes are large enough for eating, pull them up and hoe the soil.

Parsnip seeds soon lose their viability (ability to germinate), and any left over from a packet should be thrown away.

Tending and harvesting

Once the seeds are sown all you have to do is keep the plants free from weeds until their foliage meets. Autumn frost cuts down the foliage but does not harm the roots: in fact, unlike some crops, parsnips taste even better when they have been frosted.

Leave the roots in the ground in winter and dig them up as required. If severe weather threatens, lift a few roots and keep them in a box of sand or dry soil in a shed or garage, so that you have a supply if the ground becomes frozen.

The end of the harvesting season is mid spring (March), when new growth is seen. Dig up all remaining roots at this time before they become woody.

Parsnips are generally free from pests, but there is an incurable disease known as parsnip canker, which is encouraged by cold, damp soil. The symptoms are cracks on the shoulder of the root, followed by brown patches and, in severe cases, rotting of the crown. A wet autumn after a dry spell encourages canker to develop in the root.

Later-sown crops are not so liable to suffer an attack, and once the trouble has been encountered, the next year's seeds should not be sown before late spring (April): use a canker-resistant variety.

Smooth, long-rooted Tender and True parsnips (right), show a marked resistance to canker. Equally smooth is the stump-rooted variety (below)

RECOMMENDED VARIETIES

Improved Hollow Crown Long, well-shaped roots.
Tender and True Long, smooth roots.
Offenham Stump-rooted, with broad shoulders.
The Student Intermediate roots of good quality.
Avonresister Small, conical roots. This variety has some resistance to parsnip canker.

RADISHES

The humble radish ought to be the easiest of all vegetables to grow. Germination is usually good and the growing time is short. In practice, however, many gardeners confess to disappointments. The failure usually lies in two simple and easily-corrected faults–sowing too deeply and too thickly.
There are two sorts of radish–the popular summer kind and the less-well-known winter radish.

Radishes prefer a light-to-medium, fertile loam; they do not like cold, wet soils. The best radishes are those that are grown quickly. The summer radishes are better known, and if it takes them more than six weeks to reach the pulling stage they will usually be 'woody' (tough and stringy) rather than 'hot'.

A soil that was manured for the previous crop is the best choice. If there is some good, well-rotted compost available it can be pricked into the top few centimetres of soil. It is a good plan to mix this with equal parts of a good brand of moistened peat, to keep the soil damp.

SUMMER RADISHES

The summer varieties may be round, oval or long. For early forcing and growing under cloches the round varieties are to be preferred. Where successional sowings are to be made it is not economical to buy the seed in small packets. Buy in larger packets or by the 28g (1 oz). Nowadays, several seedsmen offer packets of mixed radish seeds. These are a good buy for the main sowings as they prolong the period of pulling.

How to sow

Make small, successional sowings to avoid having too many come ready at once, for the roots should be pulled when they are at their best. Radishes are the ideal intercrop and should never need to have ground reserved especially for them. They can be grown between rows of peas or beans, on the sides of celery trenches, or in the spaces reserved for brassicas; anywhere, in fact, where there is a patch of ground that will not be needed for the next six to eight weeks.

Three recommended varieties for summer: quick-growing Scarlet Globe (above left) has crisp, delicately-flavoured flesh; sweet-tasting Icicle (right) – seen with globe-shaped Sparkler – is also quick growing and crisp; and king-sized Red Prince (above) is a juicy, tasty newcomer

Radishes are also useful as 'markers'. If a few seeds are trickled along the drill when slow-growing crops such as parsnips, onions or parsley are sown, the radishes will come through first, thus enabling you to identify the rows and hoe between them before the other seedlings are through.

Sowings can begin in early spring (February) in frames or under cloches, or in mid spring (March) outdoors. Where lettuces have been sown under cloches, a single line of radishes may be sown between the rows of lettuce. These will be cleared before the lettuce need all the room available.

Successional sowings outdoors can be made at 10–14 day intervals. From late summer until mid autumn (late June until early September) make the sowings, if possible, in the lee of taller subjects such as peas or beans so that the radishes will have some shade for part of the day.

Except for single rows under cloches, do not sow the seeds in a V-shaped drill; instead sow thinly in a broad band about 15cm (6 in) wide. Make the sowing on the soil surface and then rake thoroughly with a rake or cultivator. This will put

most of the seeds just beneath the soil surface, which is deep enough.

Thinning and tending

If any thinning is necessary, do it as soon as the plants are big enough to handle. Ideally one plant to every 6 sq cm (1 sq in) is enough. It is not customary to weed radishes as the crop is on the ground for such a short time. Generally speaking, each radish patch can be pulled over three or four times. Any plants that are left after this will have failed to develop properly or will be too tough, so hoe them up with the weeds and put them on the compost heap.

Two recommended varieties for winter: Black Spanish, available in both round (above left) and long (above) forms, and China Rose (top). Like all winter radishes, they are much larger than summer varieties and can be used as vegetable or salad

Radishes should never be allowed to dry out, especially on light soils; in dry periods give them plenty of water to keep them moving.

Pests and diseases

Flea beetle and birds are the main enemies of the radish grower.

Flea beetle This pest eats holes in the leaves and can decimate a crop if not checked. Prevention is better than cure, so as soon as seedlings are through the soil, dust them with derris. Renew the application if rain washes it off. When the plants are past the seedling stage, the danger is over.

Birds Sparrows particularly may attack the seedlings, but a few strands of black cotton criss-crossed over the rows will be enough to drive them away.

WINTER RADISHES

The winter radishes are not nearly so well known as the summer ones, but they are not difficult to grow and seed is easy enough to obtain as most seedsmen stock the main varieties. There are both round and long types. They are much larger than summer radishes, with roots weighing up to 500g (1 lb) each. They can be used as a vegetable but are generally sliced thinly for use in winter salads.

The seeds should not be sown until late summer (July). This makes them useful as a follow-on crop to some of the earlier sowings. Sow the seeds thinly in drills 13mm (½ in) deep and 25cm (10 in) apart, and when the plants are large enough to handle, thin them to stand 20cm (8 in) apart. Keep the plants clean by hoeing and weeding and see that they do not lack water during dry periods.

The roots will be ready for use from late autumn (October) onwards. They will store well in boxes of dry sand or soil in a little clamp, but in light-to-medium loams they can be left in the ground to be dug as required. In severe weather cover the roots with a little straw or litter, to prevent them deteriorating.

RECOMMENDED VARIETIES

SUMMER RADISHES

Cherry Belle Globe-shaped and scarlet; good for forcing under cloches.
French Breakfast Red with white tips; a long radish and one of the best known.
Icicle Long, all-white radish.
Scarlet Globe Early and crisp.
Red Prince Recent introduction, two or three times the usual size.
Yellow Gold Egg-shaped, yellow radish with white flesh.

WINTER RADISHES

China Rose Oval root, about 15cm (6 in) in length; rose-coloured with white flesh.
Black Spanish Black skin and white flesh; available in both round and long forms.
Mino Early Japanese introduction with white flesh and a mild flavour.

SALSIFY, SCORZONERA AND HAMBURG PARSLEY

Salsify, scorzonera and Hamburg parsley are three lesser-known root vegetables but they are not difficult to grow and worth trying for a change. Their general cultivation is the same in each case.

Prepare the site for salsify, scorzonera and Hamburg parsley by digging and manuring it in the autumn. If this is not possible, try to choose a strip that was manured for the preceding crop. Fresh manure should not be used as it may cause the roots to split and fork. Stony soils can have the same effect. A light to medium, fertile loam, with a good depth of fine soil, is ideal.

However, by using the 'crowbar method' it is possible to produce fine-quality roots in less suitable soils. To do this you make holes with a crowbar 30–45cm (12–18 in) deep and 7–10cm (3–4 in) wide at the top, and fill them with a good compost such as the J.I. No 3 or a home-made mixture on similar lines. Tamp the soil down lightly and then sow a few seeds in the centre of each hole. When the seedlings are through, thin to the strongest plant. The holes should be 25cm (9 in) apart. Good, strong roots can be obtained by this method, even in heavy soils.

Cultivation of all three root vegetables consists mainly of hoeing and weeding. Should the weather become very dry, a good watering followed by a mulch of peat or compost will help the plants to keep going. None of these vegetables is much troubled by pests or diseases.

Salsify, scorzonera and Hamburg parsley can all be lifted as required, but it does pay to dig up and store a few roots if a period of severe frost seems likely. It is during such periods, when other vegetables may be difficult to gather, that these roots are most appreciated. The alternative, if storage space is at a premium, is to spread some peat or short litter between the rows. This will 'turn away' most of the frost and make it possible to dig some of the roots even though the surrounding soil is frozen hard.

SALSIFY

This root is also known as the 'vegetable oyster' as the flavours are thought to be similar. The plant is a biennial with narrow, grey-green leaves and a cream-coloured root.

Previous page, above: salsify crop, well established after two months' growth; and below: salsify Mammoth – the roots are delicious boiled or fried

Above: Scorzonera Russian Giant deserves to be better known. The roots (below) have a delicate flavour and after lifting they can be stored in sand or soil

Sow in mid or late spring (March or April) in drills 2–3cm (1 in) deep and 30–38cm (12–15 in) apart. Thin the plants, when large enough to handle, to 10cm (4 in) apart and later take out every other plant.

Harvesting is from late autumn (October) onwards. The roots can be stored in a box, with alternate layers of roots and sand or soil, but in most soils there is no necessity to lift them and they will be fresher if lifted as required.

In lifting the roots take care not to damage them or they will 'bleed'. Should any be damaged use them as soon as possible and do not attempt to store them. The flesh of salsify soon discolours when exposed to the open air. To prevent this, rub lemon juice on the cut surfaces.

If all the roots have not been used by the spring those that are left in the ground will produce tender new growths. These green shoots are known as 'chards', and they can be cut and cooked when they are about 15cm (6 in) in length. The shoots can be used green, or they may be blanched and used like the chicons of chicory.

SCORZONERA

These roots are often linked with salsify and in some regions are known as 'black salsify', but the plant is a perennial and not a biennial. It has narrow, pointed strap-like leaves and long, tapering dark-skinned roots with white flesh that are thinner than salsify. In the past the root was used as a medicine as well as for culinary purposes, and it is still said to be good for the digestion.

Do not peel the roots; when they have been steamed or boiled you can remove the skin quite easily.

Sow in mid or late spring (March or April) in drills 2–3cm (1 in) deep and 38cm (15 in) apart, and thin the seedlings to stand 20cm (8 in) apart.

Like salsify the roots are used during the autumn and winter and can be stored in boxes of sand or soil. However, they are just as hardy as salsify and it is better to dig them as required. Lift them carefully as the long, thin roots are easily broken. If the roots do not reach a good size in their first season – 5cm (2 in) thick at the top can be considered a good size – leave them down for a second season.

HAMBURG PARSLEY

This root is shorter than those of salsify and scorzonera. It sometimes appears in the seed catalogues as 'turnip-rooted parsley'. In shape and size however the roots are like parsnips but with a much smoother skin. The flavour is distinct and pleasant, somewhere between parsley and celery. You can use the parsley-like foliage for garnishing. In the summer pick a few of the tenderest and youngest leaves to add a new flavour to salads.

Sow the seeds in mid or late spring (March or April) in drills 13mm (½ in) deep and 38cm (15 in) apart. They will grow quite successfully in partial shade. Hamburg parsley is occasionally attacked by parsnip canker, but this is the exception rather than the rule.

The roots are perfectly hardy and can be dug as required during late autumn and winter (October to January). If peeled they tend to discolour and lose some of their flavour. Because the roots are smoother than parsnips, a good wash and light scrubbing is enough to prepare them for cooking. They can also be used in soups or grated for winter salads.

Above right: use foliage of Hamburg parsley for garnish and in salads
Right: distinctively-flavoured roots of the easy-to-grow Hamburg parsley look like parsnips

RECOMMENDED VARIETIES

SALSIFY
Mammoth The best-known variety.
SCORZONERA
Russian Giant The only variety on general offer.
HAMBURG PARSLEY
Usually appears under the parsley entries of seed catalogues and is listed by name only.

TURNIPS AND SWEDES

Turnips are not difficult to grow, have a long season of use and will thrive in any good garden soil which does not dry out too quickly. Swedes are larger and sweeter than turnips; they are also hardier and store well.

Turnips and swedes all belong to the cabbage (brassica) family and their treatment is very similar.

Turnips are grouped according to whether they are ready for harvesting in spring and summer, or in autumn and winter. The autumn and winter varieties can be stored, but spring and summer varieties (which take about 10 weeks to mature) do not store well.

Right: Green-top white turnip
Below left: Purple Top swede, one of the most popular varieties

Spring and summer turnips

If you have a cold frame you can make a sowing of turnips in early spring (February). You will need a soil depth of at least 15cm (6 in). A sowing can also be made under cloches – one row for tent cloches and three rows, 25cm (9 in) apart, under barn cloches.

Start outdoor sowings from mid to late spring (mid March) in rows 13mm ($\frac{1}{2}$ in) deep and 30cm (12 in) apart. Sow the seeds thinly along the drill, or else in clusters 15cm (6 in) apart. In either case, thin the plants to some 15cm (6 in) apart. Make successional sowings throughout early summer (May) to mature in late summer and early autumn (July and August). These sowings may suffer if the weather is hot and dry as turnips dislike such conditions. It is, therefore, a good plan to site these sowings in the lee of a taller crop; this will give turnips some shade for at least part of the day. Water well in a dry spell. The summer turnips, especially, need to be 'kept moving'; if they take too long to mature they tend to become stringy or woody.

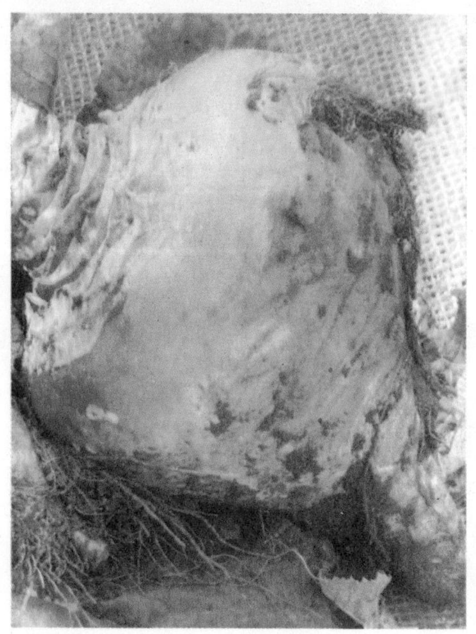

Autumn and winter turnips

Sow autumn and winter varieties in mid summer (June) in drills 13mm ($\frac{1}{2}$ in) deep and 38cm (15 in) apart. These can be grown as a follow-on crop in the ground vacated by the first peas or potatoes. Thin the plants to 20cm (8 in) apart. These varieties take a little longer to mature and will be ready from mid autumn (September) onwards. About the end of autumn (late October) lift any roots that are left and store them in boxes of sand or soil, or in a little clamp in the garden. Leave about 2–3cm (1 in) of stalk on top of the turnip and shorten the roots a little – but do not trim them right back.

Turnip greens

Late varieties of turnip can also be sown in early or mid autumn (August or September) to provide turnip tops for use in the early spring. These turnip greens are rich in iron. For the production of tops, sow the seeds thinly in a continuous row and do not thin them. Allow 30cm (12 in) between the rows.

Pests and diseases

Flea beetle and a condition resulting from boron deficiency are the main enemies.

Flea beetle This attacks the seedlings as soon as they have formed their first leaves. It is often referred to, rather vaguely, as 'the fly'. A severe attack can cause a row of seedlings to disappear overnight. Do not wait for trouble; as soon as seedlings appear, dust the rows with derris and repeat the application if rain washes the dust off. The danger is over once the plants are through the seedling stage.

Boron deficiency Occasionally turnips may suffer from boron deficiency, a condition which shows itself in a brown rot when the roots are cut open. The remedy is to apply borax; only a tiny quantity is needed – about 2g per sq m (1 oz per 20 sq yd). To obtain an even distribution, mix it with sand.

SWEDES

Swedes are milder and hardier than turnips. Sow the seeds thinly in early or mid summer (May or June), in drills 13mm ($\frac{1}{2}$ in) deep and 40cm (15 in) apart. Thin out to 20cm (8 in) apart.

They are hardy enough to remain outdoors all winter and can be lifted as required. Any remaining in the ground by spring will also produce edible tops.

RECOMMENDED VARIETIES

TURNIPS
Early (spring and summer)
Model White
Early Six Weeks
Snowball
Tokyo Cross (F.1 hybrid)
Late (autumn and winter)
Golden Ball
Manchester Market
Green-top White

SWEDES
Purple Top
Chignecto (resistant to club root)

SALAD AND FORCING CROPS

AUBERGINES AND SWEET PEPPERS

When in fruit aubergines and sweet peppers are ornamental as well as useful. They are often looked upon as 'luxury' vegetables, too difficult for the average gardener to grow. This is unfortunate, for while they do need glass protection (at least for part of their lives) they are no harder to cultivate than tomatoes, and in milder districts it is possible to grow them outdoors.

The aubergine is also known as the egg-plant because the fruits of one variety are white and look like goose eggs. In some catalogues it is listed under this name. The fruits of the more common varieties are purple and may be oblong or oval in shape. They can be sliced and fried, or stuffed like marrows. The capsicum genus includes sweet peppers, the fruits of which can be eaten when unripe and green, or when they have ripened to red or yellow.

Growing from seed

Unlike tomatoes, that are freely available at planting time, the plants of aubergines and sweet peppers are not often to be found, and you will almost certainly have to raise your own. If you are the owner of a greenhouse with some heat, then this is not a difficult process, as the seeds will germinate in a temperature of around 18°C (64°F).

A start can be made in early or mid spring (February or March), according to the facilities available and depending on how the plants are to be grown on afterwards. For instance there is no point in starting too early unless you are growing the plants on in a greenhouse. For planting in frames or under cloches mid spring (March) is early enough to sow, and where an outdoor crop is planned, delay the sowing until late spring (mid April).

Sow the seeds in seed trays filled with J.I. seed compost or in a good, soilless medium, spacing them about 2–3cm (1 in) apart. When the seedlings have formed the first true leaves, prick them out into 9cm (3½ in) pots and grow them on, making sure they have plenty of light. Should you have to delay the final planting, do not let the plants become pot-bound and stand still; move them on into 12cm (5 in) pots.

If you do not have a greenhouse you can still raise a few plants on a warm,

Above right: the large fruits of the vigorous Moneymaker, ready for picking
Right: fine, well-developed examples of Long Purple – delicious when stuffed
Far right: Slice-Rite, a heavy cropper

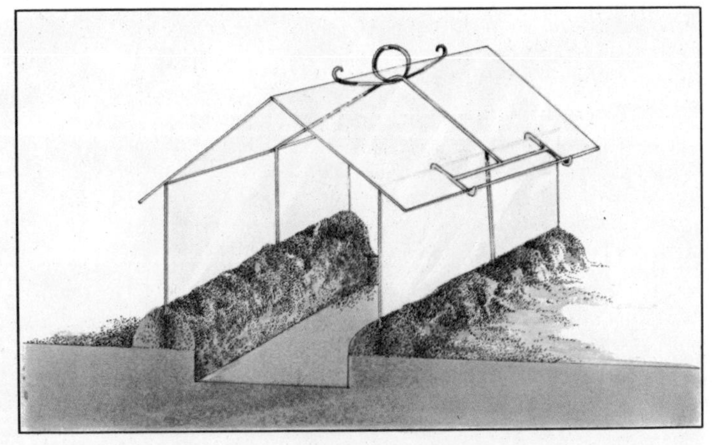

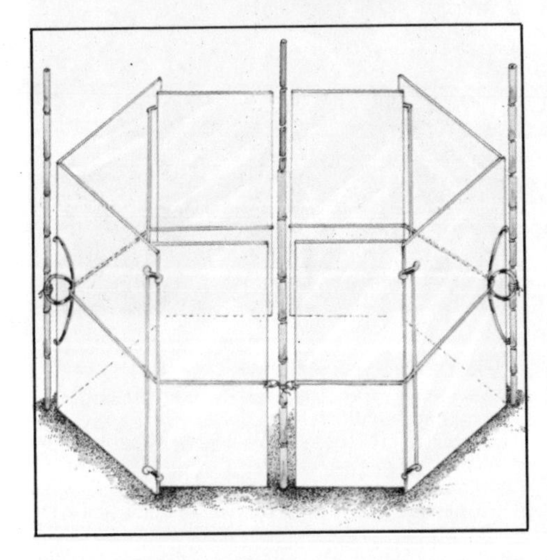

Above left: frame raised on blocks to take tall plants; above right: barn cloche over a trench gives extra space; left: another simple solution – a cloche on bricks with gaps earthed up; below left: cloches can also be stood on end

sunny windowsill. Sow the seeds in a seed tray and then prick them out into separate pots. Keep the pots close to the light and remember to turn them daily so that the plants grow evenly.

Growing on in the greenhouse

In the greenhouse, aubergines and sweet peppers may be planted directly into the soilbed, or you can grow them in pots on the staging. A good plant may reach about 75cm (30 in) in height. A few weeks before planting into the soilbed, fork in some well-rotted compost or manure. When planted out, aubergines should be 60cm (24 in) apart and sweet peppers 45cm (18 in).

For growing in pots use J.I. No 3 or one of the soilless mediums. Should good, well-rotted compost be available, mix some of this in at a rate of about one part in four. For aubergines the final move should be into 23 or 25 cm (9 or 10 in) pots; sweet peppers will fruit in 18 or 20cm (7 or 8 in) pots.

Frames and cloches

If you are using a frame it is more than likely that you will have been growing an early crop of lettuces or young root vegetables in it. If so, no other preparation will be required. Otherwise make up a mixture as described above.

Similarly, with cloche cultivation, if the ground has already been prepared for a previous crop then no other treatment is necessary. Otherwise fork some compost into the top 15cm (6 in) of soil.

For an outdoor crop choose the sunniest and most sheltered position possible. The foot of a south-facing wall, where the heat is reflected back onto the plants, is always a good choice. Remember that the soil at the base of a wall dries out quickly and water accordingly.

Other suitable places are the corner of a sunny patio where the plants can be grown in pots or tubs, or a conservatory or garden room.

Raising the headroom

One problem that may be encountered is what to do if the plants outgrow the accommodation provided. The old-fashioned type of frame with a sliding light is usually too shallow for aubergines and sweet peppers. You can, of course, use it to protect the plants in the early stages and remove the light when the leaves touch the glass, or you can raise the frame on bricks or concrete blocks.

The newer, all-glass frames are more suitable for these taller crops. Some are span-roofed, which gives welcome additional height in the centre. Special adaptors to raise the height can be bought for large barn cloches such as the Chase type; you can raise them on bricks or blocks. Fewer bricks will be needed if you place them at the corners of the cloches; soil can be drawn up to fill the gaps between the bricks.

Another method of gaining headroom is to set the plants out in a shallow trench. Make the trench some 15cm (6 in) narrower than the width of the frame or cloches. Do not make the trench too deep – about 8cm (3 in) is enough – or the plants will have to make do with the poorer soil below. Place the excavated soil along the edges of the trench to gain another few centimetres of height.

As a final resort, if the plants are still outgrowing their headroom, take off the cloches and stand them on end around the plants. But do remember to anchor them to the ground or a summer gale may badly damage your crop.

Tending growing plants

When the aubergine plants are about 15cm (6 in) high, pinch out the growing point. This makes the plants bush out and produce fruit-bearing laterals.

The same treatment can be given to the sweet peppers but is not always necessary as the plants generally break naturally. A single cane should be used to keep the plants upright.

Keep the plants clean and see that they never dry out. Once the first fruits have set, feed at fortnightly intervals with liquid manure. Remember that the soil must be moist when liquid feed is given; liquid manure should not be applied to dry soil. In dry spells, therefore, it will be necessary to water first. If you are also growing tomatoes you can use your tomato fertilizer for the aubergines and sweet peppers as well.

The Gardener's Seasons			
early spring	(February)	early autumn	(August)
mid spring	(March)	mid autumn	(September)
late spring	(April)	late autumn	(October)
early summer	(May)	early winter	(November)
mid summer	(June)	mid winter	(December)
late summer	(July)	late winter	(January)

Sweet peppers planted out – red indicates maturity. Two early fruiters are Canape (top right) and New Ace (right) both good for growing outdoors

Pests and diseases

Both of these vegetables are usually free from pests or diseases, the red spider mite being a possible exception.

Red spider mite These little creatures, that live by sucking the sap from the undersides of the leaves, like dry conditions and dislike water. Mottled leaves, that may later turn brown and fall off, denote their presence. Control can be achieved with liquid derris or malathion insecticide. Spraying with clear, tepid water, night and morning, will also help.

Ripening and harvesting

As the fruits of sweet peppers can be used when still green you can begin picking as soon as the fruits are large enough, or else leave them to turn red and develop a stronger flavour; the colder nights of mid to late autumn (late September) will eventually bring growth to a halt.

Pick off the first few flowers that appear, as this will encourage a heavier crop later on in the season.

With aubergines the fruits must be allowed to ripen. This stage is reached once the fruits are glossy and fully coloured. To obtain fruits of a good size, limit each plant to four or five fruits. When these have set, pinch out later fruits as they appear.

RECOMMENDED VARIETIES

AUBERGINES

Short Tom (F.1 hybrid) Bears a heavy crop of fruit about 13cm (5 in) long.
Slice-Rite No 23 (F.1 hybrid) Large, dark-coloured oblong fruits.
Moneymaker (F.1 hybrid) Early and vigorous with large, dark fruits.
Long Purple Large, oval fruits.

SWEET PEPPERS

New Ace (F.1 hybrid) Early and prolific; for outdoors or under glass.
Canape (F.1 hybrid) Recommended for cloches and outdoors
Californian Wonder Good, mild flavour

CELERY AND CELERIAC

Celery is not one of the easiest vegetables to grow, but it is very rewarding. Home-grown sticks – grown well – are far superior to anything that you can buy.

Celery needs a sunny open position, a rich soil and plenty of water. Very light soils and heavy clays are not suitable unless you try to improve them.

Types of celery

There are several different types of celery that you can grow. Trench celery gives the best sticks but needs plenty of room and attention. Self-blanching celery is easier to grow and, with the introduction of improved varieties, is now nearly as good in quality and flavour. Celeriac is the easiest of all to grow, though probably the least known. It produces a turnip-like, celery-flavoured root that can be grated into salads or boiled as a vegetable.

When and how to sow

The plants of all types can be raised from seed. Start them early as they need a long period of growth. Sow trench celery and celeriac in mid spring (early March) and self-blanching celery in mid to late spring (late March). A greenhouse with some heat is a distinct advantage, especially for trench celery, but plants can be raised from seed sown in a seed pan placed in the sunny window of a warm room. If this method is used it is advisable to start in the early spring (second half of February). Sow the seeds in J.I. seed compost or one of the soilless composts. Growth in the initial stages is slow.

When the seedlings are large enough to handle, prick them off into boxes, spacing them 5cm (2 in) apart all ways, and put them close to the light. If you are putting the trays in a cold frame, provide plenty of ventilation. Gradually harden off the plants in readiness for planting out in early or mid summer (late May or June).

Buying plants

If you do not have the time or the facilities for raising your own plants, buy them at planting time from nurserymen or market stalls. Most of the plants offered will be trench celery. Some self-blanching celery plants can be found but you will rarely see celeriac plants on sale.

When buying plants, choose those that are a healthy green and not too large.

Trench celery

Trench celery comes in white-, pink- or red-stemmed varieties. The white is not quite so hardy as the pink or red and is generally picked first.

Prepare the trench in early or mid spring (February or March) so that the soil has time to settle. Dig out a trench 38cm (15 in) wide for a single row, or 45cm (18 in) wide for a double row, and shovel out the loose soil. Break up the bottom of the trench with a fork and then put in a layer of well-rotted manure or good compost. Do not return all the topsoil at this stage; leave about 8–10cm (3–4 in) of the trench open. (The surplus soil can be spread along the sides of the trench and used to grow a catch-crop – such as lettuce, radish or spring onion.) To give room for earthing-up, leave about 60cm (24 in) on either side of the trench.

Weathered soot (soot that has been stored in the open for at least six months) is excellent for celery. If this is available incorporate it with the soil as the trench is filled up again.

The plants are ready for planting in the trench when they are about 15cm (6 in) high. Use a trowel for planting and space plants and rows 25cm (10 in) apart. If you are growing a double row, the plants in the two rows should be opposite each other as this makes earthing-up easier.

To dig up the sticks, remove the bank of soil at one end and follow the stems down to the root; then thrust the spade well down under it and lever the stick out.

It is a good plan to mark the site of the celery trench with sticks, and to choose a follow-on crop for the next season that will make good use of the enriched soil. A row of cauliflowers is a good choice.

Self-blanching celery

Self-blanching celery does not need earthing-up, and plants of these varieties should be planted on the flat, with 20cm (8 in) between plants and rows. Make short rows so that a block of plants is formed. As the plants grow they will exclude the light from each other, except for the plants on the outside. A simple method of blanching these is to peg boards upright around the block and fill in any gaps between the boards and the plants with straw, bracken, sawdust, or some similar 'short litter'.

A box frame that may have been used for an earlier crop makes an excellent container for self-blanching celery.

Tending growing plants

Cultivation during the growing period (until earthing-up) is the same for all types of celery. Keep the plants free from weeds and see that they never lack water.

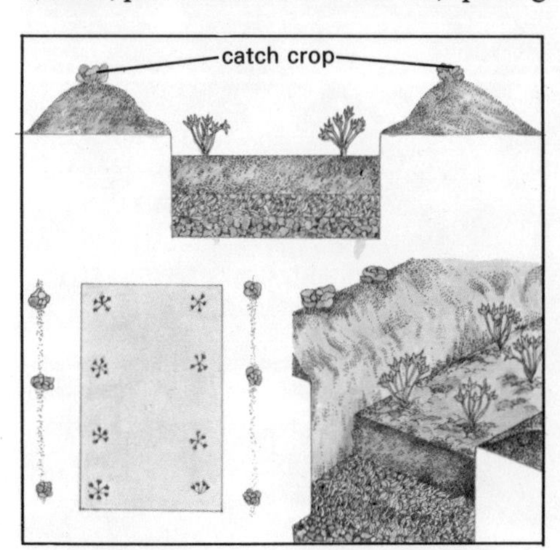

Trench celery in the early stages of growth allows for a catch crop as well

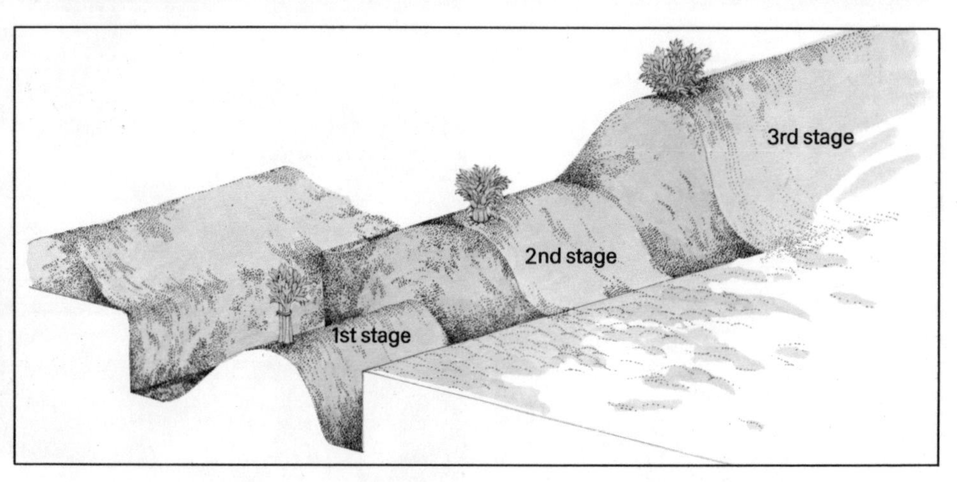

Above: the three stages of earthing-up; leave about two weeks between each one

Right: use overlapping cardboard 'collars' as an alternative method to earthing-up

During late summer and early autumn (July and August) a fortnightly application of liquid manure will help to push the plants along. Soot water, made by stirring a handful or two of soot into each can of water, is also good and has the advantage that slugs dislike it.

Earthing-up

Earthing-up should begin towards mid autumn (the end of August). Choose a dry day for this when the soil is friable. First, remove any suckers from the base of the plants and any small, outer leaves that would be buried. Draw the stems together at the top and hold them firmly with one hand. Then dig out soil from the sides of the trench and bank it up against the stems. As it is difficult to use a spade with one hand, a trowel or hand fork may be used instead. Cover the stems to about a third of their length.

Repeat the process about a fortnight later, this time taking the soil two-thirds of the way up the sticks, and after another two weeks finish off by banking the soil up to the top of the plants so that only the tips are showing. Finish off the bank by patting it smooth with the back of a spade so that surplus water will run off. Three or four weeks after the final earthing the sticks will be ready for use.

At each stage of earthing take care that soil does not fall into the hearts of the plants, or they may rot. One way of preventing this is to tie the stems loosely at the top. Another is to wrap strong paper or cardboard around them before earthing. Corrugated cardboard, with the smooth side against the stems, makes an excellent medium. Ordinary newspaper is not suitable as it will rot before the sticks are ready to use. Using a barrier of this nature also helps to foil the slugs.

In mid to late winter (end of December), if frost threatens, cover the tops

Above: trench celery Giant White shows final depth of soil after earthing-up

Below: Golden Self-blanching should be grown close together to exclude light

of the plants along the ridge with some protective straw or litter.

Trench celery without earthing
An alternative method of growing trench celery (useful on heavy soils where the drainage is poor) is to grow the plants on the flat and dispense with earthing-up, using cardboard collars instead. Overlap the edges of each collar and fill the space between the top of the collar and the tips of the leaves with peat so that light is totally excluded.

Growing celeriac
Celeriac is grown on the flat and does not need blanching. Raise plants from seed as for trench celery in mid spring (March) – with heat, if possible.

When planting, allow 30cm (12 in) between plants and 45cm (18 in) between rows. Planting should be done in early summer (late May). As the roots swell, draw the soil away from them so that the swollen root stands out. Should suckers appear, follow them down to their source of origin and cut them off. In late autumn (October) draw soil up over the roots to protect them from frost.

The roots can be left in the ground all winter, to be used as required; but in heavy soils it is better to lift and store them. Cut off the outer leaves but leave the little tuft in the centre. The roots store well in boxes of sand or dry soil.

Pests and diseases
Celery is subject to several pests and diseases, notably slugs, celery fly maggots and celery leaf spot fungus disease.

Slugs These are the main enemy of the celery family, and every effort should be made to keep them at bay. During the growing season sprinkle slug pellets among the plants or water them with a liquid slug repellant. Renew the slug pellets just before earthing-up.

Celery fly maggots The small white maggots of the celery fly burrow into the leaf tissues leaving blistery trails. At the first sign of trouble, spray with malathion. Remove and burn badly-affected leaves. A very light dusting with weathered soot at fortnightly intervals will often serve to keep the fly away. This should be done in the early morning when the dew is still on the plants.

Celery leaf spot This fungus disease takes the form of small, brown patches with black specks. It spreads rapidly and can be fatal to the plants. Pick off and burn all affected leaves. Spraying with Bordeaux mixture or zineb in the early stages of growth is a good safeguard. If, however the seed has been bought from a reliable source it will have been treated against this disease and there should be no trouble. For this reason surplus celery seed should never be used in the kitchen.

RECOMMENDED VARIETIES

CELERY – trench
Giant White Excellent variety of white celery producing good-quality plants.
White Ice Very flavoursome variety; crisp and almost stringless.
Clayworth Prize Pink Pale pink in colour and has a very sweet flavour.
Giant Pink Produces very long, heavy, pale pink sticks of excellent flavour.
Giant Red Makes robust growth and solid stems; very dark red in colour.

CELERY – self-blanching
Golden Self-blanching Very early variety; economical to grow and excellent for cooking; has solid, golden-yellow hearts with a nutty flavour.
Lathom Self-blanching Highly resistant to bolting; produces stringless sticks of outstanding flavour.
American Green A green celery that is grown in the same way as self-blanching; pale green, crisp, fine-flavoured stems.

CELERIAC
Globus Fine-flavoured roots that are excellent for cooking.
Marble Ball Large, globular roots that produce few sideshoots; fine flavour.

Celeriac variety Globus is easy to grow and gives a fine celery-like flavour

CHICORY AND SEAKALE

Chicory and seakale, although not related, have certain 'cultivation points' in common. Both produce tender, edible young shoots that must be blanched in darkness to prevent them developing a bitter flavour and both can be forced to provide winter crops.

CHICORY

Chicory is a perennial plant but is usually treated as a biennial. The root that it forms in its first season is forced into growth during the winter and early spring. The leaves of the blanched new growths are tightly folded and look rather like small, creamy-white cos lettuce. These new growths are called chicons. They can either be eaten raw in winter salads or used as a cooked vegetable.

A light-to-medium loam is the best soil for chicory, but the plants will succeed in heavier soils. Fresh manure is neither necessary nor advisable as it probably still contains toxic elements that may damage the roots. A soil that was well manured for the previous crop is ideal. Supplement this, before sowing the seeds, with a feed of general fertilizer at some 70g per sq m (2 oz per sq yd).

Sowing and thinning

Sow the seeds in early to mid summer (late May) in drills 13mm (½ in) deep and 38cm (15 in) apart. If sown too early the plants have a tendency to produce flowers in the first season at the expense of forming roots. When the seedlings are large enough to handle, thin them to 25cm (9 in) apart. Cultivation during the summer months is simply a matter of keeping the plants clean by regular hoeing and weeding.

Storing the roots

In late autumn or early winter (October or November), as the foliage is dying down, lift the roots carefully and store them in a cool, frost-proof place until needed for forcing. One method that saves space indoors is to pack the roots close together in a trench, leaving the foliage intact. Cover the roots with extra soil to keep out the frost.

How to force

To prepare the roots for forcing, cut off the foliage about 2–3cm (1 in) from the crown, taking care not to damage the growing tip, trim off any sideshoots and then shorten the roots to a uniform length of about 20cm (8 in), by cutting the tips.

There are several ways of forcing the roots, but whichever one you choose, it is essential that the chicons should be formed in complete darkness. One method is to use deep boxes and pack the roots upright in moist peat. Then cover them with a 17cm (7 in) deep layer of dry sand, light, sifted soil or more peat. Alternatively you can pack them in 25cm (10 in) pots, invert a second pot over the first one, and cover the drainage hole with a piece of slate to keep out the light. Then place the boxes or pots in a heated greenhouse or take them indoors; a temperature of about 10°C (50°F) is enough to induce growth.

Another method of producing chicons is to force the plants *in situ*, although this method will give you a later crop. The simplest way of doing this is to cut off the foliage and then earth up the roots to a depth of about 17cm (7 in). Alternatively put boards down on either side of the row and peg them upright. Fill in the space between the boards with leaves, peat or sifted soil. In severe weather give extra protection by covering the rows of chicory plants with straw or short litter.

Cutting the chicons

When the points of the chicons protrude through their covering (usually after about one month) they are ready for cutting. Remove the covering with care so

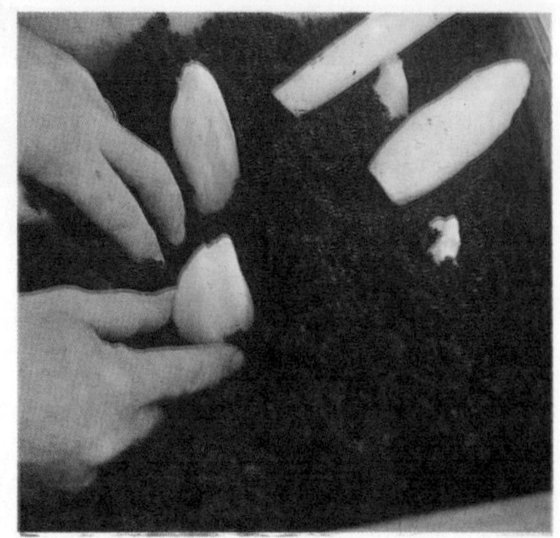

as not to damage the tender young growth, and then cut the chicon off just above the crown.

SEAKALE

Seakale is also a perennial plant and, as the roots crop for a number of years, needs a semi-permanent site. It likes a rich soil and a sunny spot. Prepare the site in autumn or winter by digging in as much manure or good compost as possible, and finish off, 2–3 months later, with a dressing of lime at 70g per sq m (2 oz per sq yd). Seaweed, if you can get it, is an excellent manure for seakale. You can raise the plants either from seeds or root cuttings.

Below left: Witloof chicory – the leaves can be used like spinach in the summer
Bottom, far left: forcing chicory in peat and cutting the forced chicons
Below: Seakale Lily White has very white, sweet shoots
Bottom: preparing seakale root cuttings, and picking a forced crop

Growing from seed

Seed is the cheapest method of raising plants but it will take you a year longer to produce a plant that is vigorous enough for forcing.

Sow in mid or late spring (March or April) in drills 13mm ($\frac{1}{2}$ in) deep and 30cm (12 in) apart. Thin the plants to stand 15cm (6 in) apart and then leave them until the following mid spring (March). Choose the best plants for transplanting; plant them in their permanent positions in rows 60cm (24 in) apart, with 60cm (24 in) between the plants.

See that the plants do not lack water during the summer months, and in mid summer (June) give a dressing of agricultural salt at about 35g per sq m (1 oz per sq yd). If flowering shoots should appear, cut them out.

Method of forcing

In autumn, when the foliage has died down, the roots are ready for forcing. If you want an early crop then lift them and force them indoors. Pack them close together in boxes or pots in the same way as for chicory, but do not cover the crowns. Simply invert another box or pot over them to keep out the light. A temperature of about 10°C (50°F) is enough to bring them on. Cut and eat the blanched shoots when they are about 20cm (8 in) in length. After forcing in this manner the roots should be discarded.

The easiest method is to force the plants *in situ* by covering them with special seakale pots, large plant pots, boxes or discarded buckets in much the same way as rhubarb. To generate a little more heat, pile leaves or strawy manure around the covering pots or boxes. This method of forcing does not harm the roots. When the last blanched growths have been cut in the spring, cover the crowns with leaves or a little compost and then prick over the soil with a fork.

Propagation from cuttings

If you already have seakale in the garden, then you can take cuttings from the side roots that form on the main roots. These side roots are called thongs. Choose the thongs that are straight and about the thickness of a pencil and cut them into 15cm (6 in) lengths. Cut the top of the root straight across and the bottom slantwise; this solves the difficulty of knowing whether you've planted them right way up.

If the thongs are taken from roots lifted for forcing, tie them in a bundle (making sure to label them) and keep them in sand or soil until planting time in mid spring (March). Plant them with the crowns about 5cm (2 in) below the soil surface.

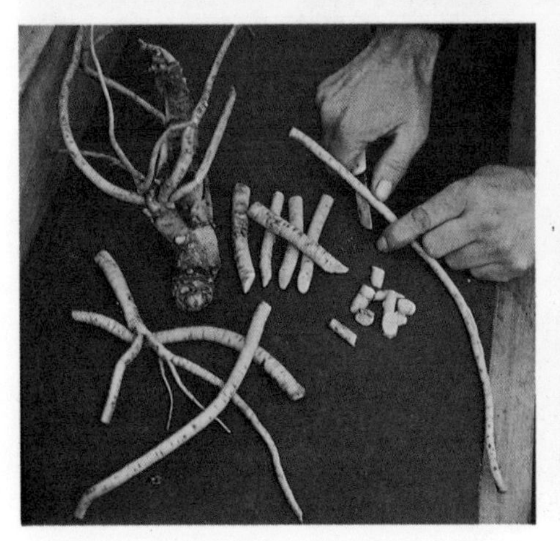

RECOMMENDED VARIETIES

CHICORY

Witloof (or Brussels) Very popular variety with large, tight, crisp heads.
Red Verona Produces pink-tipped chicons.
Sugar Loaf An excellent variety that is becoming more widely-known.

SEAKALE

Lily White The only variety in general use; produces tender, sweet shoots.

CUCUMBERS AND GHERKINS

There are three ways of growing cucumbers in the vegetable garden – in frames, under large barn cloches, and out in the open. Cucumbers like a rich soil, and for best results some soil preparation is necessary. Although the type of soil is less important than the quality, a good, medium loam is the best choice.

Where a cool greenhouse is available there is no difficulty in raising your own plants. Fill several 9cm ($3\frac{1}{2}$ in) pots with a good compost – J.I. No 1 or a soilless compost – and put one or two seeds on edge 13mm ($\frac{1}{2}$ in) deep in the soil. If two seeds sprout, remove the weaker one.

Late spring (April) will be soon enough for this sowing, as the weather will not be sufficiently warm enough to put the plants in the frame until early summer (mid May). If the pots fill with roots before conditions are suitable for transplanting, pot them on.

Gardeners without a greenhouse can still raise their own plants by keeping the pots on the sunny windowsill of a warm room. Once the seedlings are through the soil, turn the pots daily so that the plants grow upright and evenly.

How to transplant

Although cucumbers can be transplanted successfully, they do not like root disturbance and transplanting must always be done with care. For this reason, use peat or fibre pots as they can be planted out intact and will break up in the soil. Keep the soil moist until the pot has disintegrated, for if the pot dries out the roots of the plant cannot break through.

Growing in frames

Frames which have been used to grow early vegetables usually become vacant in early to mid summer (late May or early June) and will then be ready to take cucumbers. If manure was put into the frame at the beginning of the season, no more will be needed; if not, remove the soil, put in some well-rotted manure, good compost, or old rotted turfs and replace the soil. A layer of manure or compost 15cm (6 in) deep, topped by 10–15cm (4–6 in) of soil, is about right.

Burpee, the outdoor, ridge cucumber

A frame with a single light (sliding top) will take one plant; a double light will take two. Plant the cucumber in the centre of each light, and when it has made six leaves, pinch out the growing point. Allow two shoots to form and, when these have six leaves, stop them (pinch them out) in the same way. Each shoot should break into two, giving four in all. Train these four shoots into the corners of the frame and stop them when they arrive.

Sideshoots or laterals grow next, and the fruits will form on these. Quite often the plants will produce more laterals than are needed, so some judicious thinning of the weaker shoots may be required to prevent overcrowding.

When the flowers appear, the male ones should be pinched out, as they encourage production of seeds in the fruits produced by the females. Female flowers are easy to identify as there is a minute cucumber behind each one. Some modern varieties of cucumber produce only female flowers. When fruits have set, stop each lateral one leaf beyond the fruit.

Watering and spraying in frames

Never put cucumber plants in a hollow where water can gather around the stem, as this may cause collar rot (rotting at the base of the stem). It is better to plant them on a slight mound where water will drain away from the stem. A good method of watering is to sink two 13cm (5 in) pots about half their depth into the soil, one on either side of the plant stem and about 30cm (12 in) away from it, and then water into the pots. Keep a small can in one corner of the frame so that the water will be the same temperature as the frame.

Cucumbers like a moist, humid atmosphere so encourage this by syringeing the plants twice a day with tepid water.

Growing in cloches

Cucumbers can also be grown successfully under large barn cloches. There are two ways of preparing the site. One is to dig out a trench along the cloche run, 60cm (24 in) wide and a spade's depth. Loosen the subsoil with a fork, then put in a good layer of manure or well-rotted compost, before returning the soil.

The second method, more economical of manure, is to prepare stations 90cm (3 ft) apart. Dig out holes 45–60cm (18–24 in) square, and about 30cm (12 in) deep, and half fill these with manure or compost. Tread this down firmly before returning the soil. In heavy soils it is better to replace the excavated soil with a good potting compost. Mark each station with a stick. This method can also be used for glass-to-ground frames.

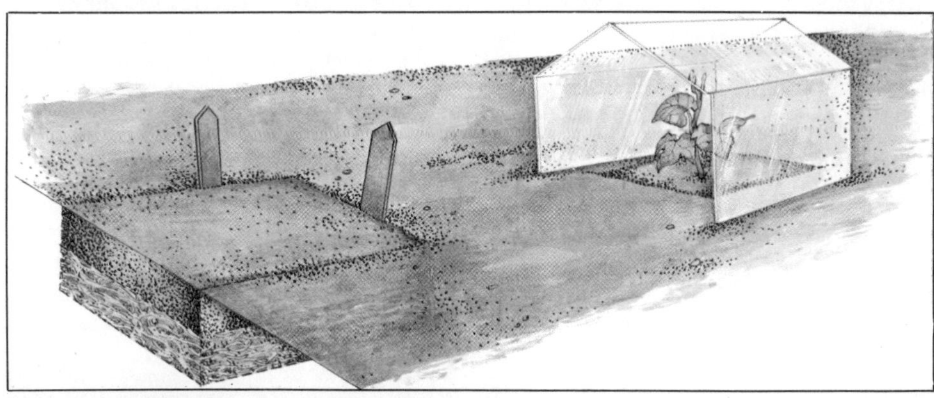

Top: cucumber seed on edge, planted 13mm (½ in) deep in potting compost, and a frame cucumber planted on a slight mound, with two 13cm (5 in) pots sunk to half their depth into the soil on either side to assist watering; above: under barn cloches, set in stations 30cm (12 in) deep, half-filled with manure and topped up with soil

Cultivation under cloches is the same as for frames except that the plants are stopped only once. The two shoots which form are then trained in either direction along the cloche row.

Cucumbers dislike strong sunlight, and some protection should be given to frame and cloche crops. This can be done by flecking the glass with a coloured solution, preferably white, or draping something over the glass that will break the sun's glare without cutting out too much light (old lace curtains are ideal).

Purchasing plants

If you have to buy cucumber plants, choose them with care. Select dark green, short-jointed plants, and avoid any that are light in colour, lanky or have thin stems. These will have been forced along too quickly. Your best plan is to find a good local nurseryman, or an amateur grower who has a few plants to spare.

Growing ridge cucumbers

Outdoor cucumbers are also known as ridge cucumbers, from the time when market gardeners grew large quantities of them on specially-prepared ridges. For the gardener who needs only a few plants, it is much easier to prepare stations 75cm (2½ ft) apart, in the same way as you cater for cloche plants.

If the plants have not been raised in

Apple-Shaped, a prolific cucumber strain

advance, you can sow seeds directly into the soil towards the end of early summer (late May). Push in three seeds, on edge, about 13mm (½ in) down and 8cm (3 in) apart, and then thin to the strongest plant.

If the nights are cold when the seedlings come through, protect them with a single cloche or a jam jar. Screens of lath and polythene, about 60cm (24 in) high are easy to make and give good shelter from cold winds. Stop the plants when they have made six leaves, to encourage the production of laterals, and keep them well supplied with water. Do not remove male flowers from ridge cucumbers, as this variety needs to be pollinated to produce fruit.

In an average summer, ridge cucumbers can be a worthwhile crop. In recent years improved varieties have appeared; these have thicker fruits that are a little shorter and have a rougher skin than frame varieties.

Japanese climbing cucumbers

Another group of outdoor cucumbers is the Japanese climbing type. By tying them in carefully, you can train them to climb up a fence or trellis.

Pests and diseases

Red spider mite and cucumber mosaic virus are the main enemies of the cucumber.

Red spider mite This pest sucks the sap from the leaves, giving them a mottled, and later a rusty, appearance. Cut off and burn badly affected leaves. Fortunately, the mite dislikes water and regular syringeing will help keep it away. Red spider mites rarely attack outdoor plants.

Cucumber mosaic virus A serious disease of cucumbers is the cucumber mosaic virus. Affected plants turn yellow, wilt and then die. Unfortunately, there is no cure. The virus is spread by aphides, and keeping the greenfly population down by spraying regularly with an insecticide such as derris or malathion is the best safeguard against the disease. Pull up and burn any infected plants as soon as they are seen.

Growing gherkins

The cultivation of gherkins, the little pickling cucumbers, is the same as for ridge cucumbers. Gherkins crop prolifically so one or two plants will produce enough for the average household. Cut the fruits when they are 5–8cm (2–3 in) long, and examine the plants every few days, as the fruits form quickly.

RECOMMENDED VARIETIES

CUCUMBERS FOR FRAMES AND CLOCHES

Butchers Disease Resisting Prolific variety, remarkably disease resistant.
Conqueror Heavy cropper, excellent for frames or cool greenhouses.
Greenline Recent variety, proved successful in frames.
Telegraph Improved Thrives in a cool greenhouse or frame; reliable cropper.

CUCUMBERS FOR OUTDOORS

Baton Vert (F.1 hybrid) Produces long, slender fruits of excellent flavour.
Burpee Hybrid (F.1 hybrid) Does well outdoors or in frames.
Burpless Tasty Green (F.1 hybrid) Produces excellent fruit, easy to digest.
Nadir (F.1 hybrid) Long-fruited, very prolific, outdoor variety.
Perfection Longest ridge cucumber, very prolific, and will crop well into autumn if fruits are cut before they get too old.
Apple-Shaped Unusual variety that produces egg-shaped fruits, very prolific and will grow well outdoors or under cloches.
Kyoto Japanese climbing cucumbers; fruits have good flavour and few seeds.
Kaga Japanese climbing cucumbers; produces very early, heavy crop of crisp fruits.

GHERKINS

Hokus Recent variety which crops well and is very prolific.
Venlo Pickling One of the most popular gherkins for pickling.

La reine, female-flowering cucumber

ENDIVE AND CORN SALAD

useful winter salad crops

These vegetables, once neglected but now increasingly in demand, can be a valuable addition to the salad bowl at a time when lettuce is scarce; corn salad, for example, is said to be best eaten with game.

Endive and corn salad can be grown in their own right but it is more common to find them used as a substitute for lettuce, especially during the autumn and winter months when good lettuces are at a premium. The leaves of corn salad are used in the green state but endive, which is allied to the chicory family, is bitter and needs blanching before it is eaten. Neither crop is difficult to grow and it is surprising that salad lovers, in particular, do not make more use of them.

ENDIVE

In appearance, endive is like a rather loose-leaved lettuce. There are two types of endive – the curled-leaved, that is generally preferred for summer use, and the plain-leaved or Batavian. The Batavian is a little hardier than the curled and is more suitable for winter use.

Endive prefers a light to medium soil but will grow in heavier soils that have plenty of humus and are well drained. A soil that was well manured for the previous crop is always a good choice. Nitrogenous fertilizers should not be used as they tend to promote lush growth that may lead to heart rot during the autumn and winter months.

Successional sowing

The plants take about three months to reach full size and may be sown from late spring to early autumn (April to early August). Where they are intended as a substitute for lettuce, the best time for sowing is during the late summer (late June to end of July).

The seeds should be sown thinly in drills about 13mm (½ in) deep and 30–38cm (12–15 in) apart. When the seedlings are big enough to handle, thin them to stand 30cm (12 in) apart. If you want a second row, it is a good plan to thin the plants to 15cm (6 in) and then, a week or two later, take out every other plant to form a second row. This row of transplants will form a natural succession to the earlier row. Move the plants carefully, taking a good ball of soil with each plant, so that the check to growth is reduced to a minimum. Transplanted endive, moved carelessly, are apt to run up to seed.

Protecting your crop

Keep the plants clean by hoeing and weeding, and see that they never lack water. With the advent of colder weather in late autumn some form of protection is advisable. Endive will stand some frost, but not severe frost unless given the protection of frames or cloches. Straw or short litter worked in amongst the plants is a help, but cloches of some kind are undoubtedly the best method of defence.

Blanching

A simple method of blanching is to draw the outer leaves of the endive up over its heart and gently tie them together about 10cm (4 in) from the top. This gives a blanched heart, although it wastes the outer leaves. An alternative method, and a much better one, is to cover the whole plant with a box or large flowerpot. If you use pots, remember to cover the drainage holes. The leaves of the selected plants must be completely dry before blanching begins, or the hearts will rot – another good reason for using cloches.

The time it takes to obtain a good blanch varies with the season. In early autumn it may be only one or two weeks; later on, probably three weeks or four. Inspect the plants from time to time and, as soon as they are fully blanched, cut them for use. Cover only a few plants each week; it is a mistake to blanch too many at once as they will not remain in good condition for many days after being blanched. In their green state they should stand for several weeks.

CORN SALAD

There is a wild form of this plant that grazing sheep are fond of and this has given it an alternative name of 'lamb's lettuce'. The cultivated type has larger and more succulent leaves.

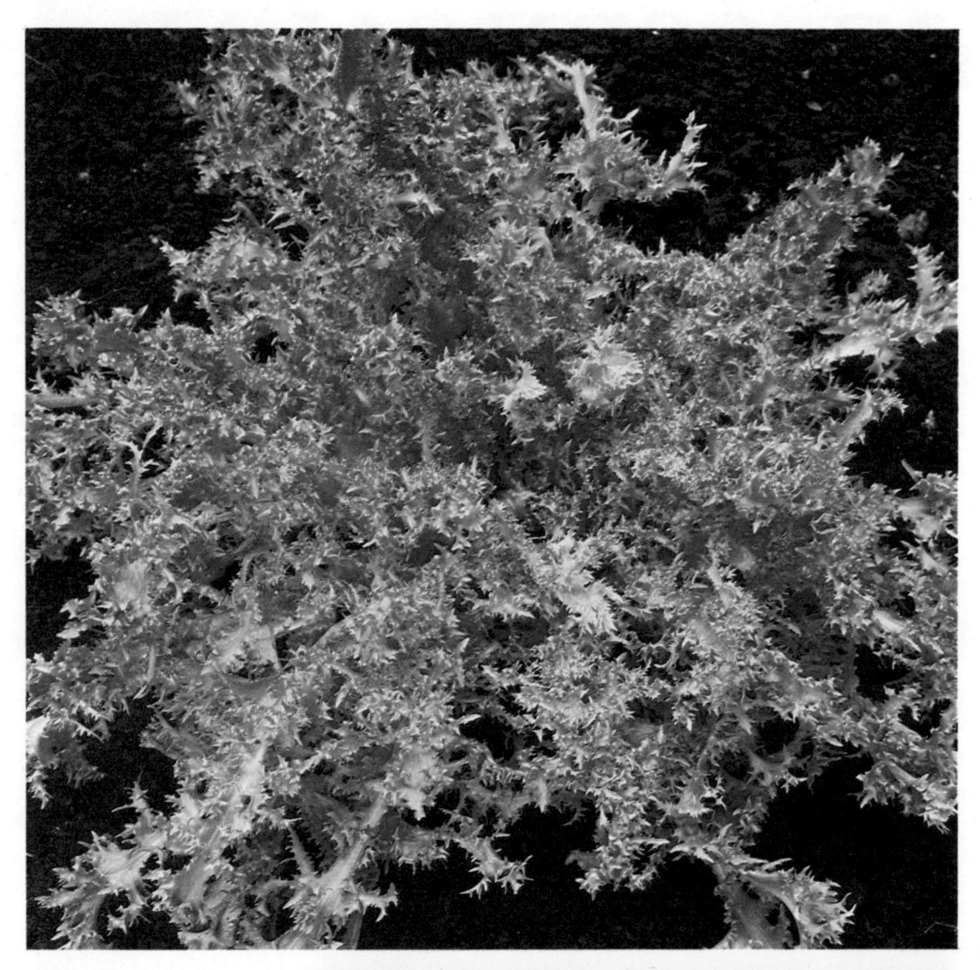

Previous page: Batavian Green plain-leaved endive, an excellent lettuce-substitute for autumn and winter months
Above: Green Curled endive needs to be blanched before eating
Right: corn salad, or 'lamb's lettuce', needs no manuring but likes a sunny, sheltered position

This plant is hardier than endive and will grow in most soils that are in good condition. A sunny, sheltered position is best. Fresh manure is neither necessary nor advisable – a soil manured for the previous crop will suit it well enough.

Sowing and cropping

For an early crop, a sowing can be made in mid spring (March). The main sowings should not be made until early autumn (August) and can continue at fortnightly intervals until the end of mid autumn (September). This makes it a useful follow-on crop to earlier vegetables. These sowings will give pickings in autumn and winter, the time when they will be most valued.

Sow the seeds thinly in drills 13mm (½ in) deep and 15cm (6 in) apart. No special care is needed apart from attention to watering; the plants should not be allowed to dry out.

There are two methods of gathering the leaves. One is to pull up the entire plant and cut off the root; the other is to pick over the plants like spinach and cut off tufts of leaves as you want them. The second method is slower but has the advantage of giving a regular supply of tender young leaves. If you follow this method, do not take more than half the leaves from any plant at one picking.

Protecting your crop

Although corn salad is hardy, a better and cleaner crop will result if you cover the plants with cloches during late autumn and early winter (October and November). A barn cloche will cover four rows. If you can't get cloches, protect the plants during severe weather with a *light* covering of straw. Remove this when milder weather returns.

Both endive and corn salad are liable to be attacked by slugs. A few slug pellets, scattered at intervals between the rows, will deal with this problem. Slugs apart, the plants are generally free from pests and diseases that afflict salad crops.

RECOMMENDED VARIETIES

ENDIVE

Green Curled For first use.

Batavian Green Plain-leaved and a little hardier than the curled.

Winter Lettuce-leaved Has large leaves and stands well.

CORN SALAD

Verte de Cambrai Round, succulent leaves.

Large-leaved Italian Hardy, with large leaves.

Large-leaved English Similar to above.

LETTUCE

As lettuce is a main ingredient of many salads, its importance can scarcely be over-emphasized. Fortunately it is so easy to grow that the real skill comes in having a steady supply for the table over as many months as possible and not just a glut in mid summer.

Lettuce are not particularly fussy about their soil requirements – except that the earth must be well drained. They will grow quite happily between rows of slower-maturing plants. Whilst the surrounding soil must never be allowed to dry out, it is equally dangerous for it to become waterlogged. Cold, damp soils are not conducive to rapid growth and should be improved by the addition of sand and peat to lighten them. Light, dry soils can have their water-holding capacity increased by adding peat or other organic materials, such as manure.

Main types

With lettuce, perhaps more than with most vegetables, it is important to sow the right varieties at the right time. An understanding of the three main types is essential in order to have a steady supply over as long a period as possible. The **cabbage head** group can be subdivided into two classes: flat or smooth, that grow over a long period; and crisp or crinkled, that are mainly for summer cropping.

Cos This is a tall, pointed variety of which there are two kinds – large and intermediate. The cos is generally a summer crop that can be overwintered. While they are not nearly so popular as the cabbage lettuce, cos deserve to be more widely grown, and the intermediate ones are certainly gaining in popularity.

Loose-leaved This type does not make a heart, but produces a succession of tender leaves which can be picked as required. It has the advantage of standing well in hot weather.

Successional sowing

The aim of every salad-lover growing his own lettuce is to have a steady succession for as many months of the year as possible. This is easy to achieve on paper but much more difficult to accomplish in practise. Successional sowings, however carefully planned, have a habit of taking different times to mature according to different weather conditions – and these, unfortunately, are outside your control.

There are two ways of planning for succession. One is to make successional sowings of the *same* variety; the other is to sow two *different* varieties at the same time. Sometimes a combination of both methods will give the best results. If, for example, a flat lettuce is sown at the same time as a crisp variety, a succession

Row upon row of the beautiful pale-leaved Suzan, a smooth cabbage variety. Sow them under glass in autumn for transplanting early in the winter. The first of the crop will be ready for the table by late spring

is almost assured because, on average, the crisp varieties take longer to mature.

Transplanting is another aid to succession: transplanted plants, however carefully moved, are bound to be checked (slowed up) and so will take longer to mature than those left undisturbed.

In order to avoid having too many lettuces ready at once, the golden rule is to make small sowings at frequent intervals from mid to late spring (March to April), and transplant from these until mid summer (June). These sowings will be under glass. In summer months it is better to sow *in situ* (directly into the soil) and thin out, throwing away unwanted seedlings. This is because plants that are transplanted during this period are more liable to go to seed.

Three crisp, sweet lettuce that are sown outdoors for summer and autumn salads. Webb's Wonderful (above) and Lobjoit's Green Cos (below right) last well in hot, dry weather. Little Gem (right) is also known as Sugar Cos

Growing under glass
The use of glass will help to extend the season at both ends. Few people will want to heat a greenhouse specially for growing lettuce, but where heat is needed for other plants, a few can be grown in deep boxes or in 13cm or 15cm (5 or 6 in) pots on the staging. Lack of daylight in winter is the main obstacle, and only the specially-bred varieties should be grown.

Heated frames Where heat is provided through a soil-warming cable buried a few centimetres below the surface, a frame is much more economical than a heated greenhouse, and can be used for growing lettuce – at a minimum temperature of 10–13°C (50–55°F) – during the winter. (A transformer will be needed to reduce the voltage, for safety reasons, and it cannot be too strongly emphasized that the equipment must be installed by a qualified electrician.)

Cold greenhouses These, and especially the glass-to-ground type (which traps all the available winter light and heat), are a boon to lettuce-growers as seeds sown in late summer can be planted out inside the greenhouse from late autumn to early winter (October to November).

Alternatively you can sow *outdoors* and bring the seedlings under glass at planting time. The lettuce will be ready for cutting from mid spring to early summer (March to May). Any plants that may be in the way if you have tomatoes ready for transplanting can be pulled up and used first.

Cold frames These are useful for providing an early crop, especially the metal types with glass all round. Seedlings that have been started under glass during the winter as already described, can be planted in the soil bed and the frames then put over them.

The older type of frame with sliding lights (glass lids) generally requires a soil bed to be made up inside it, so that the soil level is raised and the plants are reasonably close to the glass.

Growing under cloches
The simplest method of growing lettuce under glass is to use cloches. The tent-shaped (inverted 'V') cloches will cover a single row (or two of a small variety) while barn cloches (shaped like miniature greenhouses), cover three rows. Glass is preferable, but there are various plastic and polythene cloches available that are satisfactory provided they can be securely anchored and are not in too exposed a position.

Sow the seeds directly into the soil – which will have warmed up a little if you place the cloches in position a week or two before sowing. Sow as thinly as possible, in drills about 12mm ($\frac{1}{2}$ in) deep. Thin out or transplant the young plants as soon as they are about 10cm (3–4 in) high. Subsequent cultivation consists simply of keeping the surrounding soil clear by weeding and hoeing, but you must take care not to damage the roots which lie just below the surface. It is also a good idea to give a liquid feed every

ten days while they are actively growing.

Lettuce do best in an open, sunny position, but some shade is an advantage for those maturing during the hottest months, so put them in the lea of a row of runner beans or other tall plants.

General pests

The main pests to guard against are slugs, birds and aphides. Slug bait will help to keep them down and spraying with a good insecticide will control the greenfly. It is wise to spray occasionally before the hearts have formed, even if no greenfly can be seen, as it is impossible to get at them once the lettuce begin to 'heart up'.

Watch out for birds as they can soon ruin a promising crop, sparrows being especially notorious for this. The old method of using black cotton (not thread) is still effective. Simply push in sticks at intervals and then run the cotton from stick to stick, just clear of the plants. A touch of the cotton on a bird's wings is enough to send it winging away. Or you can try proprietary bird repellents.

Unrivalled (left) and Tom Thumb (above left) can be sown 'little and often' for cutting from spring to autumn

Main diseases

The two main diseases are mosaic disease and grey mould (*botrytis cinerea*). Mosaic shows up as stunted growth and a yellow mottling of the leaves. It is a virus spread by aphides and once plants are attacked there is no cure, which is another good reason for early spraying against aphides.

Grey mould is much more widespread and serious. Affected plants wilt and then collapse. If a collapsed plant is pulled up you will find that the stem has turned brown and rotted at soil level. Although there is no cure at this stage, some measure of control is possible by spraying the fungicide Benlate at the first sign of trouble.

Grey mould is generally a disease of plants grown under glass or cloches and is rarely encountered outdoors. This gives us a valuable clue to its prevention – adequate ventilation. Where plants under

RECOMMENDED VARIETIES

Type	Variety	When to sow	When to transplant	When to cut	How to grow
smooth cabbage	Kwiek	early autumn	late autumn	mid winter to early spring	heated greenhouse or frame
	Premier Suzan	mid autumn	early winter	late spring to mid summer	cold frames, cold greenhouses or cloches
	Imperial	early autumn	thin out instead	early summer to mid summer	outdoors
	Tom Thumb	early spring and early autumn	thin out instead	early summer, and late autumn to early winter	outdoors; good under cloches
	Unrivalled All The Year Round	mid spring to early summer	late spring to mid summer	mid summer to early autumn	outdoors
crisp cabbage	Webb's Wonderful Avoncrisp	mid spring to early summer	late spring to mid summer	late summer to mid autumn	outdoors
large cos	Lobjoits Green Paris White	mid spring to late summer	late spring to mid summer	late summer to mid autumn	outdoors
intermediate cos	Little Gem (also listed as Sugar Cos)	mid spring to late summer	late spring to mid summer	mid summer to mid autumn	outdoors; good under cloches
	Winter Density	mid autumn	early winter, or thin out instead	late spring to mid summer	under cloches
loose-leaved	Salad Bowl	mid spring to early summer	thin out instead	mid summer to mid autumn	pick leaves as required

Key to seasons

early spring (February)	early summer (May)	early autumn (August)	early winter (November)
mid spring (March)	mid summer (June)	mid autumn (September)	mid winter (December)
late spring (April)	late summer (July)	late autumn (October)	late winter (January)

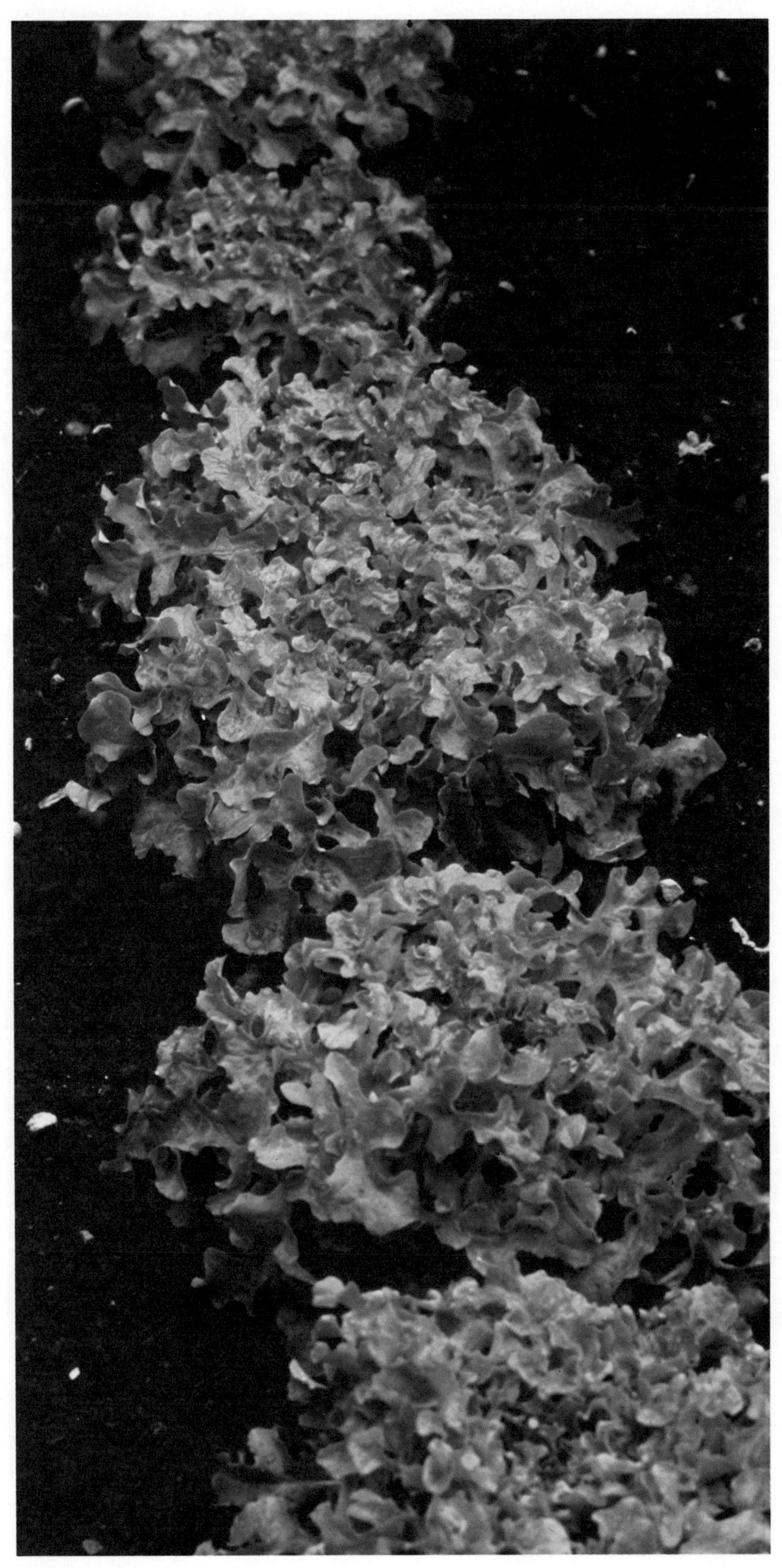

glass are given plenty of ventilation, grey mould should not be a problem. Open up frames in all but the severest weather; leave a slight gap between cloches, and where there is a ventilating pane, close it only in hard weather. Lettuce are much tougher than is generally supposed.

Another safeguard against grey mould is good hygiene. Yellow leaves, or any lying flat on the soil, should be removed, and any affected plants disposed of at once. Keep the plants free from weeds, with a good circulation of air round them.

Care of plants

When it is necessary to water lettuce in frames or greenhouses, do so early in the morning so that the soil has time to dry out before nightfall. Water the soil *between* the plants and keep it off the leaves as much as possible. There should be no need to water those under cloches during the winter, as enough water will seep in from the soil at the sides.

Outdoor varieties Most of these need about 30cm sq (12 in sq) in which to mature, but under glass this can be reduced to 23cm sq (9 in sq) so that the optimum use is made of the glass. The variety Tom Thumb is small, quick-maturing and needs only 15cm sq (6 in sq). It makes a useful crop for both early and late sowings.

Imperial is one of several varieties which can winter outdoors in a sheltered spot for maturing in early spring. These varieties will survive an average winter, though they may not come through a severe one. The increasing use of cloches, however, means that these 'winter' varieties are of less importance now, and they are being replaced by more tender ones.

Cutting time

Cabbage lettuce should be firm when pressed gently at the top of the heart; test a cos by pressing at the tip – never squeezing from the sides. With your early spring crop, it is a good plan to plant at 13–15cm (5–6 in) intervals and then to cut every other lettuce when the row begins to look crowded. These surplus plants, although not properly hearted, will be welcome, and mean an earlier start to the season.

One final point: nothing equals home-grown lettuce for freshness and flavour, but do cut them when they are at their best. Avoid the heat of the day, when they are limp and flaccid, and cut them in the early morning or late evening.

The loose curly leaves of Salad Bowl are picked individually as required

MUSTARD, CRESS, BEAN SPROUTS

Mustard and cress are traditionally grown together. White mustard is the kind grown for salads; cress can be either plain or curled. There is also American or land cress – a perennial that tastes like watercress. Newer crops such as alfalfa and adzuki beans and mung beans can provide a similar crisp ingredient for salads or be used as a cooked vegetable.

Mustard, cress and bean sprouts are all good crops for stimulating the interest of children in growing things, as they like something that grows quickly and can then be eaten.

MUSTARD AND CRESS

Packets of mustard and cress will be found among the vegetable seeds in shops and stores, but this is an expensive way of buying them. Buy 30g (1 oz) packets from a seedsman or, if you intend to make successional sowings throughout spring and summer, buy a still larger packet. Always use fresh seeds; old seed oddments may give poor germination results.

If mustard and cress are needed together, sow the mustard three or four days later, as it grows more quickly.

Growing and harvesting

As these crops are eaten in the seed-leaf stage a rich soil is not necessary. The J.I. No 1 compost is good enough. If you grew tomatoes or cucumbers in the previous season, the spent compost from these crops will make a first-rate medium for mustard and cress.

To grow, fill a seed tray with the growing medium and press it down with a block of wood until the surface is firm and level and about 13mm ($\frac{1}{2}$ in) below the top of the tray. Sow the seeds evenly and thickly. Do not cover them with soil – simply press them into the medium with the flat piece of wood. Water them in well with a fine spray, or immerse the tray in water until the soil surface turns dark as the water comes through. If the seeds are given a good watering to begin with, no more should be needed until after germination. Cover the trays with brown paper until the young shoots appear.

The main difficulty in growing mustard and cress is that the seedlings tend to bring up their seed cases and particles of soil with them. These cling to the stems and leaves and make the end-product gritty. One way of preventing this is to cover the growing medium with a layer of silver sand and press the seeds into it. Another method is to cut a piece of hessian, the size of the inside of the tray, and lay this over the seeds. Keep the hessian damp until the seeds are through. The hessian will hold the seed cases and soil in place while allowing the shoots to push through. When the seedlings are about 2–3cm (1 in) in height, carefully remove the hessian and leave them to grow on.

Mustard and cress can also be grown on moist absorbent paper (such as blotting paper or kitchen paper).

Cut the seedlings when they are about 5–8cm (2–3 in) in height with a pair of sharp scissors that will cut cleanly, then empty the tray on to the compost heap and refill with new soil.

AMERICAN LAND CRESS

This cress can be grown in ordinary garden soil and prefers a north-facing or semi-shaded position where the soil will remain moist. It needs plenty of water and should never be allowed to dry out.

The plants are quite hardy and take about 8–10 weeks to mature from seed. If they should prove difficult to establish from a spring sowing, try again at the beginning of autumn (early August). Thin the plants to about 10cm (4 in) apart and keep them free from weeds at all times. Pinching out the growing points will help keep up a steady supply of leaves.

If you sow the seeds in a block, rather than in rows, the plants can be covered in autumn with a cold frame or cloches, and the season of picking will be prolonged.

Far left: mustard (larger leaves at rear) and cress traditionally go together
Below left: American land cress likes a moist, shady spot in which to grow
Above: bean sprouts – or mung bean – are ready for eating after 4–6 days' growth

BEAN SPROUTS

Recent years have seen the introduction of several crops producing shoots that can be used either in salads or as a vegetable. First to arrive, and still the most popular, was the mung bean. The seeds of this bean can be sprouted indoors on strips of flannel or sheets of kitchen paper kept moist.

Two more recent additions are alfalfa, with a flavour similar to garden peas, and the adzuki bean. It is usually recommended that these be grown by the 'jar' method. Place a measure of seed in an ordinary jam-jar (or similar jar) and then cover it with a piece of muslin kept in place by an elastic band. Fill the jar with water, shake well and drain off again. Repeat this procedure night and morning until the sprouts are ready for use – in about 4–6 days.

One advantage of these seeds is that they can be sprouted at any time of the year. Full instructions are given on the packets or in an accompanying leaflet.

SPINACH AND SPINACH SUBSTITUTES

Spinach is an excellent 'food value' vegetable, rich in vitamins A, B1, B2, and C. It also contains useful quantities of calcium, protein and iron. For spinach lovers there are also several other leaf vegetables – perpetual spinach, New Zealand spinach and Good King Henry – that have a similar flavour.

SUMMER SPINACH

The round-seeded or summer spinach can be sown from mid spring through mid summer (March to the end of June) and is 'in pick' 8–10 weeks after sowing. It needs a fertile soil with good, moisture-retaining properties. On light or hungry soils the plants will soon go to seed.

If the ground is being prepared especially for this crop, dig in some manure or good compost during the winter months. Some well-dampened peat may also be incorporated and will help to keep the soil moist. In many cases, however, spinach can be used as an intercrop; for example, it can be grown between rows of peas or dwarf beans.

Sowings maturing during the summer will benefit from a little shade for part of the day. Good sites for these sowings are between rows of tall peas or in the lee of a row of runner beans.

Sow the seeds thinly in drills 2–3cm (1 in) deep and 30cm (12 in) apart. As soon as the seedlings are big enough to handle, thin them to stand 15cm (6 in) apart. When the plants have grown until they touch each other, take out every other plant and use them in the kitchen.

Regular hoeing will keep the weeds down by creating a loose, dry, layer of earth that acts as a mulch. Water during dry spells; do not allow the plants to dry out or they will go to seed.

Picking can begin as soon as the leaves are large enough. Cut the leaves off close to the stem, taking a few from each plant.

Even well-grown plants of summer spinach will not crop for long, and to keep up a regular supply it is necessary to make successional sowings every two or three weeks.

WINTER SPINACH

The prickly, or winter, spinach – 'prickly' applies to the seeds, not the plants – is sown in early to mid autumn (August to September) for use during the winter months. It makes a good follow-on crop to some of the earlier sowings. Before sowing, rake in a general fertilizer at 70g per sq m (2 oz per sq yd). An open site with some shelter from cold winds is preferable. Sow the seeds in drills 2–3cm (1 in) deep and 30cm (12 in) apart. Thin the seedlings to stand 23cm (9 in) apart. If the soil is dry at the time of sowing, water the drills well beforehand. Once established there should be no watering problem as the normal rainfall of an average autumn and winter will be enough for their needs.

Although the plants are hardy they give a better and cleaner crop if some protection can be given, ideally with cloches, during the winter months. Straw or short litter tucked around the plants is one way of doing this.

Picking is the same as for summer spinach, the largest leaves being taken first; but pick rather more sparingly as leaf production in the winter months is slower. In early spring a dressing of nitro-chalk at 35g per sq m (1 oz per sq yd) will help the plants along, by increasing production of leafy growth which in turn will help to give you earlier spinach pickings.

SPINACH SUBSTITUTES

In addition to 'true' spinach there are several spinach-type vegetables that have a similar flavour. All are very little troubled by pests and diseases.

Perpetual spinach This is another name for spinach beet (which was included in the section on leaf beets, page 112). The leaves of spinach beet are thicker and fleshier than those of the true spinach and are preferred by many people for this reason.

Sow in drills 2–3cm (1 in) deep and 38–45cm (15–18 in) apart, and thin the plants to stand 23cm (9 in) apart. Sow in late spring (April) for summer use and in early autumn (August) for winter use. If the winter row can be cloched, a heavier and cleaner crop will result. Pick the leaves as they become large enough and never let any leaves grow on until they become tough, or the production of new leaves will be hindered.

New Zealand spinach This half-hardy annual thrives best in a light to medium soil and in a sunny position. Unlike summer spinach it will tolerate hot, dry conditions without running to seed. It has a low, spreading habit and needs plenty of room. Allow 90cm (3 ft) between the plants.

For an early crop, sow in mid spring (March) under glass and prick the seedlings off into 9cm ($3\frac{1}{2}$ in) pots, ready for planting out towards mid summer

Above left: Viking, a comparatively new summer spinach variety
Below left: low-growing New Zealand spinach thrives in hot, dry conditions
Below: versatile Good King Henry, another spinach substitute, that can also replace broccoli on the menu

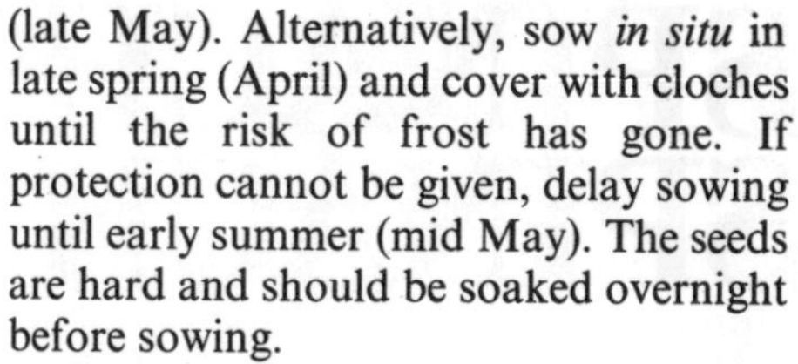

(late May). Alternatively, sow *in situ* in late spring (April) and cover with cloches until the risk of frost has gone. If protection cannot be given, delay sowing until early summer (mid May). The seeds are hard and should be soaked overnight before sowing.

Keep the plants watered in dry spells, and pinch back the shoots to encourage the production of more leaf-bearing sideshoots. The dark green, triangular leaves are smaller than those of summer spinach but picking is done in the same way (by taking individual leaves). Plants bear freely until cut down by frost.

Good King Henry This is a hardy, perennial plant, not widely known outside its native English county of Lincolnshire. It is a useful, dual-purpose plant; in the spring shoots are produced from the leaf axils and these can be cut and cooked like spring broccoli. Later the large triangular leaves can be used as a substitute for spinach.

The plants can be propagated by division or from seeds sown in late spring or early summer (April or May) in drills 30cm (12 in) apart. Soak the seeds overnight before sowing. When the seedlings are large enough, thin them to stand 30cm (12 in) apart.

Because the plant is a perennial and needs to build up its reserves for the following season, shoots should not be taken later than mid summer (June), but leaves can be removed until early autumn (August).

RECOMMENDED VARIETIES

SUMMER SPINACH

Sigmaleaf Large-leaved, round-seeded variety; can also be sown in autumn for overwintering.

King of Denmark Large, round, dark green leaves.

Longstanding Round Quick-growing with dark leaves; the standard summer variety.

Viking Excellent recently-introduced variety with dark green leaves.

WINTER SPINACH

Greenmarket Large, dark green leaves.

Longstanding Prickly Very hardy; the standard winter variety.

SPINACH SUBSTITUTES

Perpetual spinach or spinach beet (No named varieties). Has succulent spinach-type leaves.

New Zealand spinach (No named varieties). Plants have low, creeping habit and soft, thick fleshy leaves.

Good King Henry (No named varieties); useful substitute for spinach or broccoli.

SWEET CORN

Many gardeners mistakenly believe that sweet corn is a luxury crop too difficult for the average gardener, or that it can only be grown in very mild climates. In reality sweet corn is no harder to grow than outdoor tomatoes.

There are two important points to keep in mind when growing sweet corn, or corn-on-the-cob as it is also known. First, the plants will not withstand frost and cannot be planted out until the risk of frost is past. Secondly, the plants do not like being transplanted and should always be moved with care.

A sunny site is essential, with shelter from cold winds if possible. Cold, wet soils are unsuitable because they take too long to warm up, but any other good garden soil will do. Do not use fresh manure as it may induce leaf growth at the expense of the cobs. Soil that was well manured for a previous crop is ideal and will only need the addition of a general fertilizer at the rate of 70 g per sq m (2 oz per sq yd).

Sowing methods

There are three ways of growing this delicious vegetable. If you possess a cold greenhouse or cold frame you can start in late spring (mid April) by sowing two seeds in an 8 cm (3 in) pot. Pull the weaker one out if both germinate. If you use trays they must be 15cm (6 in) deep, but because of the problems with transplanting it is better to use pots.

Peat or fibre pots are good; because you can then plant out, pot and all, into the soil with the minimum disturbance of the roots. Be sure to keep the pots moist after planting so that they will rot down and allow the young roots to grow through into the soil. Slit each pot up one side and remove the bottom. If you use plastic or clay pots, water the plants well before moving them and tap the sides of the pots gently so that the soil ball slips out easily. Transplant in early summer (mid May) if the plants are going out under cloches; otherwise, wait a week or two longer.

Another, and possibly better, method is to sow the seeds directly into the soil under barn cloches in late spring or early summer (late April or early May). Draw out two drills 40cm (15 in) apart and 5cm (2 in) deep, and sow three seeds every 30cm (12 in) along the row. Leave two plants at each station. De-cloche the plants around mid summer (mid June).

The third way is to sow the seeds directly into the open ground towards mid summer (end of May), using the same sowing distances as for cloches. If you have no glass at all you can gain valuable time by starting a dozen or so plants in pots on a sunny windowsill.

Aids to fertilization

Sweet corn is an attractive and interesting plant, as it carries both male and female parts on the same stem. The male tassels at the top of the plant are the pollen bearers. When the pollen is shed it falls onto the female silks—the tufts of fine hairs at the end of each immature cob.

To assist good fertilization, set out the plants in blocks rather than in long rows. An excellent technique is to have two short rows of plants covered by cloches; then sow or plant another two rows between the cloches. The outdoor rows will mature later, but they will get quite a lot of shelter from the outlying cloches. Pollen is usually distributed by the wind, but in calm periods it helps if the plants are tapped gently about mid-day.

Tending the growing plants

Do not hoe too deeply or too closely to the growing plants, as they are not deep rooting and there is a danger of breaking the surface roots. Water the plants in dry periods, and mulch with compost, peat or spent mushroom manure to help conserve moisture. Sweet corn is a crop that

Right: fully-ripe, golden corn ready for cooking and eating. Below: corn growing under cloches with tops removed to air them in dry, sunny weather. Below right: cob still covered by sheath. Far right: very young cob with sheath removed

RECOMMENDED VARIETIES

Early Extra Sweet Said to improve in flavour after harvesting.
Golden Bantam A good yielder of medium-sized cobs.
John Innes Hybrid Vigorous hybrid, producing large cobs.
Kelvedon Glory Early maturing, very uniform, and excellent for freezing.
Earliking Produces long cobs of excellent quality.

benefits from foliar feeding (being fed through the leaves), so spray at two-week intervals until the cobs have formed: each plant usually produces two cobs—sometimes more.

Unless the plants are in a very sheltered position you will have to stake them. Extra support can be given by drawing a little soil round the base of each plant. Staking each plant is time-consuming: a better method is to drive in a stake or strong cane at the ends of each row, with perhaps a light cane in between, and then run garden wire from cane to cane and all round the block. It is then simple to tie each plant to the wire.

Sweet corn plants are generally pest and disease free, though in an indifferent summer there may be trouble with poor fertilization and some of the grains may fail to swell. Tapping the plants at midday, as suggested, will help to prevent this.

Harvesting the cobs

Part of the art of growing sweet corn lies in knowing when it is ready for picking. Apart from the natural plumpness of a ripe cob, a reliable sign is that as the cob matures the silks turn brown and dry. Also, there is often a slight cracking of the sheath against the silk.

The grains of corn are enclosed in a leafy sheath which can be gently parted so that you can look at them. In a ripe cob they will be a rich yellow. The final test of ripeness is to pierce one of the grains with a thumb nail. If the liquid that comes out is pale and watery, then the cob is not ready. Close the sheath and leave it to ripen a little longer. When the liquid is rich and creamy the cob is at its best and must be picked at once before it becomes mealy and unpalatable.

Pick the cob by cutting it off with a knife or breaking it off with a sharp, downward twist. When all the cobs have been gathered chop up the plants and put them to rot on the compost heap.

Once picked, the cobs should be cooked and eaten as soon as possible, as they deteriorate rapidly .

TOMATOES
sowing and planting indoors and out

It is the aim of almost every gardener to grow his own tomatoes. Thanks to the great deal of progress that has been made in recent years in breeding new varieties, it is now possible for the amateur to achieve a really good crop – with or without a greenhouse.

When growing tomatoes under glass, beware of starting off your tomato seeds too early. Plants which suffer a check from too low a temperature take a long time to recover. It is the *night* temperature of the greenhouse that is most important. A constant 18–21°C (65–70°F) is necessary to start the seeds off, with a follow-on minimum night temperature of about 12°C (54°F).

From late mid spring (the second half of March) or, with insufficient heating facilities, a few weeks later, you can sow seeds in a box of John Innes Potting Compost No 1 (J.I. No 1) or one of the soilless composts. Space the seeds 4cm (1½ in) apart, and cover them with a light sprinkling of compost. Water gently with a fine rose on the watering can, and keep the compost moist but not over-wet.

When the seedlings have made their first pair of true leaves (after the little seed leaves) pot them up into 9 cm (3½ in) pots containing J.I. No 2 or a similar mixture.

Ripe, heavy trusses of delicious tomatoes reward you for your weeks of loving care

Transplanting the young plants
The plants will be ready for transplanting into their final quarters when they are about 20–25cm (8–10 in) high, probably from early summer (early to mid May) onwards. If they are to be grown on staging they will need to be put into 25cm (10 in) pots.

The best results are generally obtained from plants in a 'glass-to-ground' greenhouse. Here the tomatoes can be planted directly into the soil bed, which should be enriched with good compost or well-rotted manure. It is important to dig in the compost or manure in good time, so that the soil can settle before the tomatoes have to be planted.

If you have no heating at all, it is better to buy the plants from a good nurseryman. Look for plants that are short-jointed, well-grown and a rich dark colour.

Transplant the young shoots carefully into the prepared bed, so that the soil ball is just below the soil level, and water them well, using a fine rose on the watering can. They should be spaced some 40–45cm (15–18 in) apart.

Giving support
Instead of an individual cane for each plant, a good alternative method of supporting them is to run a wire from end to end of the greenhouse above the plants and just below the roof. Strong, galvanized wire hooks are pushed into the soil close to each plant and a length of stout garden string is fastened to the hook at one end and the wire at the other. It is then a simple matter, as the plant grows, to give the string an occasional twist round the stem.

Support tomato plants by tying to canes (below), or by twisting string from wire hooks to a horizontal line (below right)

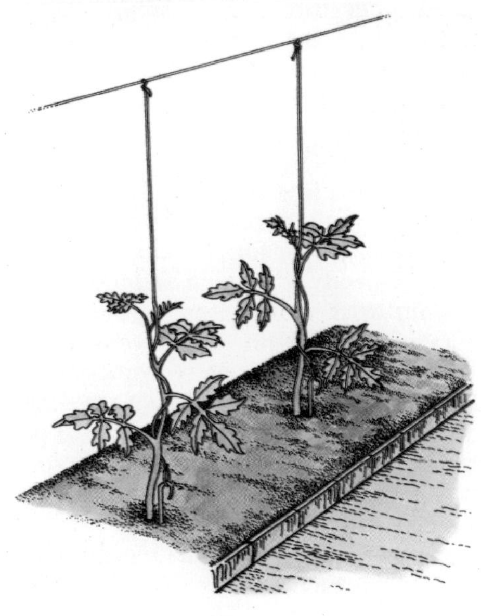

Growing by ring-culture
The drawback to planting directly into the greenhouse soil bed is that the soil soon becomes 'sick' (unhealthy in gardening terms), with the resultant risk of disease affecting your tomatoes. To avoid this, the soil bed should be dug out to a spade's depth every couple of years and then filled up with new soil.

Lining for ring-culture bed and cross-section of plants in bottomless pots, one plant in earlier stage of growth

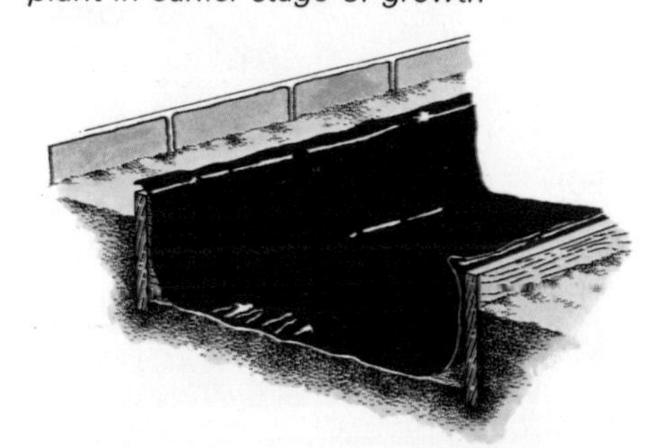

However, a less arduous way round the problem is to grow your tomatoes by the ring-culture method. Remove the soil to a depth of 15cm (6 in) and replace with pea-gravel, weathered ashes, or peat: gravel is the longest lasting. If a strong polythene sheet is laid across the bottom and up the sides of the trench before the aggregate is put in, moisture will be retained and less watering will be required.

Bottomless pots (usually sold as ring-culture pots), which can be bought from any good seedsman, are placed on the aggregate and filled with J.I. No 3, or a similar mixture; the tomato plants are then planted out into them. The object in ring-culture is to encourage the plants to form two sets of roots—one in the pot for feeding and the other in the aggregate below the pot for supplying water.

Once the plants are growing strongly and have sent out roots into the aggregate, watering in the pots should cease, except when feeds are given. If the aggregate is kept moist the plants will take up all their water from below. By using this method, contact with soil-borne diseases is eliminated.

Using 'Gro-bags'
A third method is to grow your tomatoes in the new 'Gro-bags'. These are bags of specially-prepared growing medium which are simply laid on the greenhouse soil or staging. The tomatoes are planted directly into the bags through pre-marked openings, and the only chore then is to keep the medium in the bags watered.

The cordon method
Practically all greenhouse tomatoes are grown by this artificial method that restricts all the growth to one main stem. All tomatoes, if left to themselves, will produce sideshoots that will grow on to make additional stems on which fruit can be borne. These sideshoots come from the leaf axils where the leaves join the stem. By adopting the cordon method the plant is kept from sprawling, and produces earlier and better fruits. Pinch out the sideshoots between finger and thumb as soon as they appear.

GROWING OUTDOORS
Here you have three methods of growing and three different types of plant: the *cordon* type (already described), the *dwarf* and the *bush* tomato. The dwarf tomato is a distinct type which breaks (forms sideshoots) naturally to form several stems. In the bush tomato the stems are more numerous and more pliable and the low-growing plants form a small bush. Neither dwarf nor bush tomato is suitable for greenhouse culture.

In the cold frame

If you have the old type of cold frame, with a sliding light (glass lid), it can be used to start off a few plants. Allow about 30cm (12 in) between the plants when putting them in. Provide a good enriched soil, as for the greenhouse soil bed, and cover with the light until the plants are touching the glass. Plant them in early summer (mid May) and if the nights are cold, or frost is expected, be prepared to cover the glass with old sacks, matting, or anything else that will prevent heat loss—but remember to remove the covering in the morning.

You must also be sure to ventilate the frame on sunny days; even early summer sun can 'toast' the plants badly when it is shining through glass. Remember, however, to close it again in the evening.

When the tops start touching the glass, remove the light and support the plants. You have given them a good start and every week saved is of vital importance when growing outdoor tomatoes.

For the newer types of garden frame, which have more headroom, the dwarf or bush varieties are better, and it may be possible to keep them covered throughout their growth, although adequate ventilation must still be provided if weather conditions demand it.

Under cloches

The bush and dwarf tomatoes are also ideal for growing under barn-shaped cloches. Decide on the strip of soil to be covered and prepare it well in advance. It should be 'in good heart' (that is, a good fertile soil) but not too enriched or the plants will produce plenty of foliage at the expense of fruits. Old bonfire ash makes an excellent dressing for outdoor tomatoes and should be worked into the soil as the strip is prepared. If no ash is available, sulphate of potash at about 35g per sq m (1 oz per sq yd) will help to promote strong flower and fruit production. Incidentally, if the strip has been really well prepared, additional feeding during the growing period should not be necessary. Put the plants out in early summer (the second half of May), allowing about 30–45cm (12–18 in) between plants, according to the vigour of the variety, and cover with the cloches.

If the plants outgrow the available headroom, remove the cloches carefully and stand them *on end* round the plants. Secure a cane to the handle of each cloche and into the soil so that it cannot be blown over. Later, when the weight of fruit pulls the plants down, the cloches can be put over them again to assist ripening. At the same time, cover the ground under the fruit trusses with straw or polythene to prevent any contact with the soil.

Barn cloches standing on end, anchored by canes tied to the handles, protect young tomato plants growing outdoors

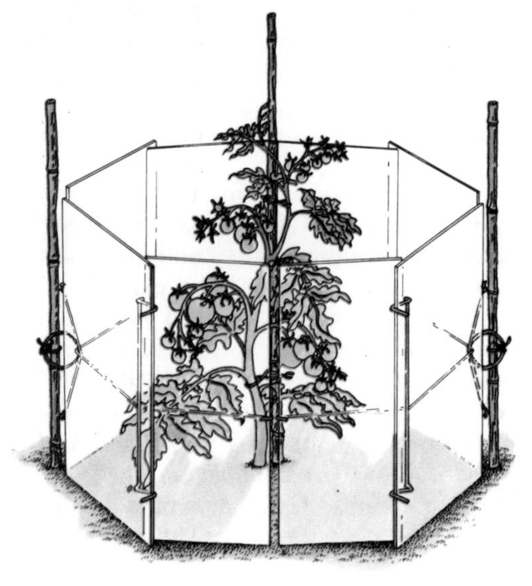

RECOMMENDED VARIETIES

FOR THE GREENHOUSE

Moneymaker Probably the best-known variety for the greenhouse. Can also be grown outdoors.
Ailsa Craig Another old favourite of first rate quality.
Alicante A more recent introduction of fine flavour.
Big Boy Very large fruits, fleshy and meaty; needs extra support. Not suitable for outdoors.
Golden Sunrise A fine yellow variety. The yellow tomatoes deserve to be more widely grown. A little sugar sprinkled over them helps to bring out the flavour.

FOR OUTDOORS

Outdoor Girl Cordon type. Sometimes produces a few misshapen fruits but is a heavy cropper. Outdoors only.
Pixie Dwarf type. Specially suitable for frames with headroom of 60–90cm (2–3 ft). Attractive fruits of good quality.
French Cross Dwarf. A heavy cropper of first-class fruits. For frames or cloches.
The Amateur Bush type. Perhaps the best-known bush variety. Fine for cloches.
Yellow Perfection Cordon type. Good quality and flavour.
Sleaford Abundance Bush type. Quality fruits and a good cropper but rather later than Amateur.

Growing without glass

While many thousands of tomato plants are sold each year for planting outdoors, they are nearly all cordon varieties. Very few nurserymen offer dwarf or bush varieties as young plants. This means that if you want to grow them, you must raise them from seed. If you have neither greenhouse nor frame, you can still get results by sowing the seeds in a pot or seed tray placed in the window of a warm kitchen and then following the method already outlined. When the seedlings are ready, set out the number you require into 9cm ($3\frac{1}{2}$ in) pots and keep them in the window, turning the pots each day so that growth is even. Gradually harden them off by moving them to an unheated room and then to a sheltered sunny position outdoors during the day (but bring them in each evening), before planting them out into their final positions.

For plants which have to grow and fruit without any glass protection at all, choose the sunniest and most sheltered spot available. A border facing south, backed by a house wall or close-woven fence, is ideal. Another good site, often overlooked, is the corner of a sunny patio which will accommodate a few plants in large pots or tubs. If the plants have to be grown right out in the open, some shelter can be given by putting in short stakes on the north side and fastening old sacking or sheets of plastic to them. Make sure, however, that this barrier is quite firm and that there is no danger of it blowing down onto the plants.

While all three types can be grown outdoors, the cordon varieties are usually preferred. Because the growing season for outdoor tomatoes is relatively short, it is usually accepted that a plant cannot be expected to set more than five trusses of fruit with any hope of ripening them. So when the stem has reached two leaves beyond the fifth truss, pinch out the growing point with your finger and thumb. You can also use the ring-culture method for growing tomatoes outdoors.

Later in the Course we will be telling you how to look after the plants while they are growing, as well as giving guidance on problems likely to be encountered and hints on how to ripen up the fruits.

The first section on tomatoes concentrated on sowing the seeds and transplanting, both in the greenhouse and outside in the garden. Now follow their care through to ripening and harvesting.

TOMATOES
growing and ripening

When your tomato plants are growing strongly, your main tasks are weeding, training and watering. The little onion hoe is the best weeding tool to use for the soil of the greenhouse border (and in frames and under cloches), but hoe only lightly or you may damage the roots.

Training and supporting

Keep cordon plants to one stem by nipping out the sideshoots which form in the axils of the leaves (where the leaf joins the stem). Do remember that sideshoots come from the *axils* of the leaves and fruiting trusses from the stem *between* the leaves.

Nip out the sideshoots as soon as they appear; this lessens the danger of damage to the plants. If you are a smoker with nicotine-stained fingers, wash your hands thoroughly before doing this job or else use a pocket knife. Tomatoes are highly susceptible to nicotine virus, and this can be transmitted from your fingers.

As the plants grow, continue to tie them to their stakes at regular intervals to keep them upright, or twist the supporting string gently round them.

Dwarf tomatoes need little or no training. They produce sideshoots naturally, on which the fruit is borne. An easy way of supporting the plants is to fasten each one to a short stake with a single tie; then run a string, in and out of the plants, from stake to stake.

Bush tomato stems also divide naturally, but their sideshoots are more numerous and more pliable. Stakes are not needed, but when the fruits are swelling their weight will pull the sideshoots to soil level. So put down some slug bait and then slide straw, hay, peat or black polythene under the fruits to keep them clear of the soil.

Some bush plants tend to produce more foliage than is required, particularly if they are on good soil. About early autumn (the middle of August) go through them and cut out stems which are just flowering as they will not give sizeable fruits before the end of the season. By removing these surplus stems you give the plants more light and air.

Plenty of water

Watering always poses something of a problem. There are no hard and fast rules, but for greenhouse tomatoes there are broad guidelines. When you transplant, give the plants a good watering; after that water only sparingly until new roots begin to form and new growth is seen. From then on increase the supply as the plants grow. When they are mature it is almost impossible to overwater, and in hot weather it may be necessary to water them twice a day.

With plants in frames or under cloches let nature help. Push down the frame lights, or remove the ventilating panes of the cloches when rain is imminent. Plants under cloches will draw much of the water they need from the sides of the cloches where rain has run down into the soil.

Avoid too dry an atmosphere in the greenhouse. Damp down the path and staging and spray the plants with clear water night and morning to keep the air moist. See that ventilation is adequate; in hot weather leave a ventilator a little way open all through the night.

Heat is more important than sunshine to tomatoes once the fruits start ripening

Setting and feeding

When the plants are flowering, encourage the fruits to set by gently tapping the supporting canes or strings about the middle of the day to help distribute the pollen. With dwarf or bush plants this treatment is not necessary.

Don't start feeding until the first fruits have begun to swell. Use a good, proprietary liquid fertilizer and follow the manufacturer's instructions exactly. If you prepared the tomato bed well, then dwarf and bush tomatoes should not need feeding; bush plants in particular will tend to produce lush foliage at the expense of fruit if given too rich a diet.

Ripening the fruit

As the sun begins to lose strength and the nights turn colder, ripening inevitably slows down. If you have a cool greenhouse, and you have any form of heating, turn it on at night towards mid autumn (late August and September) so that the remaining fruits will ripen. Where you started off the plants in a frame and then grew them on as cordons, cut the strings holding the plants to their supports, remove the canes and then lay the plants down gently onto clean straw or black polythene. Follow the same procedure with plants that outgrew their cloches. Put the frame lights or the cloches back in place, and the fruits will continue to ripen throughout late autumn (October).

Pick all the fruits which have no protection at all by the end of mid autumn (September) and ripen them indoors. Putting the fruit in a sunny window is not the best way of ripening them; neither is it necessary to denude the plants of their leaves in order to expose the fruits to the sun. Leaves should not be taken off unless they have yellowed naturally or are diseased. Both practices spring from the mistaken belief that sunshine is essential for ripening tomatoes; it is not. Providing the temperature is high enough tomatoes will ripen without sunshine. It is quite a common occurrence to find ripe fruit hidden beneath the leafy foliage of a bush tomato plant.

To ripen tomatoes indoors, put them in a basket, cover them with a piece of cloth and keep them in a warm kitchen. Another good way, particularly with the greener fruits, is to put them on layers of cotton wool in a drawer in a warm living room. Any fruits from greenhouse, frames or cloches which have not ripened by the end of autumn (late October) can also be brought in and treated this way.

Below: give fruiting bush plants more light and air by trimming surplus stems

Below: fruits may split if you allow the soil to dry out and then water it heavily

To finish ripening outdoor cordons, lay the plants down on a bed of clean straw

Pests and diseases

The modern tomato is a highly-developed plant and as such is subject to various diseases – most of them occurring in the fruiting stage. However, if you raise and tend your plants carefully, you should be able to harvest a healthy crop without difficulty. The list which follows are the more common troubles that can occur.

Potato blight (so called because it commonly affects potatoes). Affected plants show brownish-black patches on the fruits which quickly go rotten. There is no cure but the disease may be contained if you pick off the leaves and fruits as soon as you see signs appearing. You can help prevent it by spraying with a suitable fungicide towards the end of mid summer (end of June), with a second spraying a fortnight later. Keep potatoes and tomatoes as far apart as possible to avoid contamination. Blight is generally confined to outdoor plants but may appear in frames or under cloches.

Leaf mould This is a serious disease of greenhouse tomatoes. The symptoms are a greyish mould on the underside of the leaves with yellow patches on the upper surface. Remove and burn affected leaves and spray with a systemic fungicide. A stagnant atmosphere, especially at night, is the cause and adequate ventilation is the best safeguard. The disease is more prevalent in some areas than in others; if you know it to be troublesome in your district, spray with the fungicide in mid summer and again in late summer (June and July) as a precautionary measure. The variety Supercross (F.1 hybrid) and some strains of Eurocross are immune to this disease.

Blossom-end rot Generally a greenhouse disease in which the end of the tomato opposite the stalk becomes blackish-brown and shrunken and finally rots. There is no cure. The cause is irregular and faulty watering.

Greenback This is not a disease but a condition. Affected fruits have a hard, yellow patch which refuses to ripen. It may be caused by too much sun, or lack of potash. Eurocross and Alicante are among several modern varieties which are resistant to greenback.

Split fruits Caused by letting the plants get dry and then watering heavily. The fruits cannot absorb the water fast enough and the skin ruptures. It ought not to occur in a greenhouse where watering can be controlled, but it is sometimes difficult to prevent outdoors when periods of drought are followed by heavy rains unless you water regularly during dry spells.

Leaf curl When the leaves curl upwards this is generally a sign that the plants are receiving too much nitrogen. Occasionally it may be caused by minute quantities of spray from a selective weedkiller. Tomatoes are especially vulnerable to these and the greatest care must be taken when using them anywhere near tomato plants.

Red spider mite This tiny creature can be a nuisance under glass, though it is not usually a problem outdoors. It is encouraged by a dry atmosphere. The mites feed on the underside of the leaves which become mottled and may turn yellow. Spray or dust with malathion to control them. The mites dislike water, so regular spraying will discourage them from taking up residence.

TUBERS

POTATOES
preparing to grow

Potatoes are the most important crop in many vegetable gardens. In the first of this three-part section we cover the preparation of soil for growing potatoes, buying seed tubers and sprouting them, and recommend some varieties.

Potatoes fit well into a three-year crop plan, so you can give them one-third of the kitchen garden or allotment. But do not be tempted to exceed this area, for if potatoes are grown too often on the same plot of ground it is liable to suffer from 'potato sickness'. Few vegetables benefit more from crop rotation than the potato.

Types of potato

Potato varieties can be divided roughly into four groups: first-early, second-early, early-maincrop and late – but there are no hard and fast dividing lines between these groups. Some catalogues list only three groups, putting the first-earlies and second-earlies together.

First-early and second-early potatoes are simply those varieties that form their tubers early and so are most suitable for early lifting. These are usually dug up while the haulms are green, but they can also be used when they are ripe and the tops have died. Most early varieties do not crop as heavily as the later ones.

The tubers of early-maincrops or lates can also be used while the haulms are still green, but it is rather wasteful to use them in this way as they will give a much better crop if left to mature.

In a small garden it is generally best to cut out later varieties for storing and concentrate on a few rows of earlies for summer use, because these 'new' potatoes have the best flavour and come at a time when shop prices are high.

Soil requirements

Potatoes will grow in most soils, but the ideal is a medium loam that will not dry out too quickly and is still loose enough for the tubers to grow in. Heavy clays and very light soils are the least suitable, but you can improve these by digging in well-rotted manure or compost so that your soil is in a good, fertile condition.

All potato plots will benefit from adding manure or well-rotted compost during winter digging but, if manure is in short supply, give it to the brassicas (especially brussels sprouts, cauliflowers and broccoli) and follow these with potatoes. Potatoes usually do well after greens.

Some varieties are more suited to certain soils than others. When moving into a new area it is always a good plan to consult local gardeners as to the best varieties to grow.

Above left: potato flowers are followed by small green fruits that are poisonous. The seeds they carry are not worth saving as they do not grow true to type
Left: crop from one root of Arran Pilot

Seed potatoes
Potatoes are propagated by planting selected tubers of the previous year's crop. These are known as seed potatoes, but this is really a misnomer as the tubers are not the seed of the potato. The true seed is contained in the little 'potato apples', about the size of small tomatoes, that form on the haulms. The seed cannot be relied upon to breed true and is not of much use to the gardener, although it is valuable to the plant breeders in their search for new and better varieties. The production of these potato apples varies widely with different varieties and in different seasons.

A tuber, on the other hand, is reliable and always grows true to type. In theory there is nothing to prevent a gardener using his own home-grown tubers year after year, but in practice this does not work because the potato is subject to virus diseases that are spread mainly by greenfly. These diseases cause a rapid deterioration of the stock.

Tubers selected for next year's seed should be put in a shallow box and left outside to harden for two weeks
Right: second-earlies Pentland Beauty
Below right: red-skinned Desirée

Certified stock
In the seed-growing areas of the British Isles (mainly in Scotland and Ireland), potatoes are grown in fields that are too exposed or at too high an altitude for the greenfly to live. These crops are inspected by Ministry of Agriculture officials who certify that the plants are healthy and true to type, and the number of the certificate given is then quoted on all the quantities, however small, that are sold from that particular crop.

Certified seed is generally known as 'new' seed and you should order it as early as possible, although the tubers may not be available until late winter or early spring (January or February).

'Once-grown' seed
New seed is expensive and many gardeners like to make it go as far as possible by growing it on for a second year. The tubers selected for the second crop are then described as 'once-grown'. Where only a few potatoes are grown it is better to buy new seed each year, but a compromise can be made by growing half new seed and half once-grown. This practice is reasonably safe with the earlies, that are dug up before the greenfly can do too much damage, but is more risky with maincrop varieties that are ready later in the year.

Pick out seed tubers as the crop is dug up, taking them from the best roots only. Never save tubers from weak plants. Choose tubers about the size of a hen's egg, or a little smaller, and put them in a shallow box. Leave the box outside until the skins of the tubers have been toughened and greened by the sun; if you suspect the presence of greenfly, spray the tubers with a good insecticide. Store them in a light, cool and frost-proof place until you are ready to chit them up.

Chitting potatoes

Before you plant the tubers in spring, chit them (set them up to sprout). To sprout the tubers, tilt a box (such as a shallow, wooden tomato box) up at one end and stand the tubers upright in it with the rose end uppermost. The rose end of a potato is the end containing the eyes from which the sprouts grow.

Cardboard egg boxes or trays are also excellent for chitting. There is no need to tilt these as the potatoes are held upright in their individual compartments. Fill in any spaces with crumpled newspaper.

This practice of sprouting the tubers has two advantages. By producing sturdy shoots 2–4cm (1–1½ in) long it cuts down on growing time, as sprouted tubers come through the soil much sooner. It also enables dud tubers to be picked out and discarded. Once-grown seed chits earlier than new seed and can be set up by mid to late winter (end of December). New seed should be set up as soon as it is received.

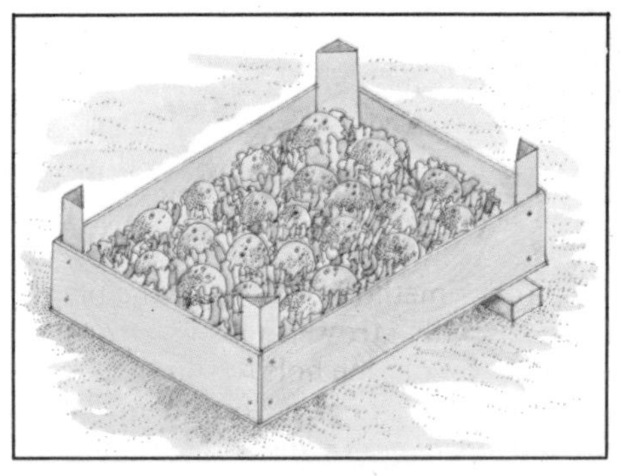

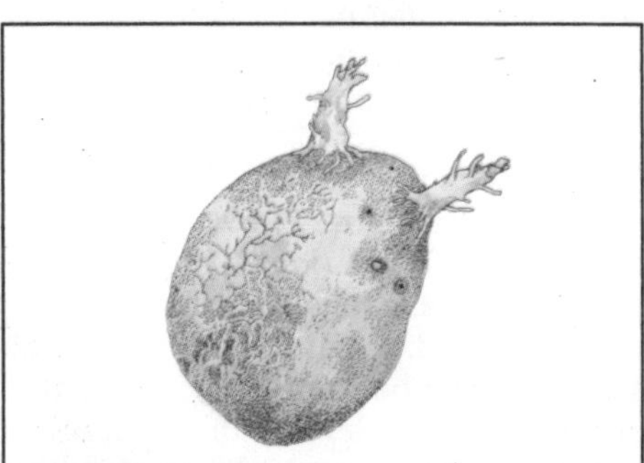

RECOMMENDED VARIETIES

FIRST-EARLIES
Foremost White-skinned and oval.
Pentland Javelin White-fleshed and oval.
Pentland Jewel White and round.
Arran Pilot White and kidney-shaped.

SECOND-EARLIES
Home Guard White and oval.
Pentland Beauty White with pink markings and oval.

EARLY-MAINCROPS
King Edward VII White with pink eyes and kidney-shaped.
Majestic White and kidney-shaped.
Desirée Red-skinned and kidney-shaped.

LATES
Pentland Crown White and oval.
Golden Wonder Russet-skinned and kidney-shaped with white flesh.

Top: to chit up, stand potatoes on end in tilted shallow tray, 'rose' end up, and fill in gaps with crumpled newspaper. When tuber shoots are 2–4cm (1–1½ in) long, they are ready for planting out
Above and left: late variety Pentland Crown is oval-shaped, with white flesh

POTATOES
planting and tending

We have now covered preparation of the soil and buying and sprouting seed tubers. The next stage in the proceedings is to tell you how to plant, hoe and earth-up your potatoes, and also how to cope with frost and pests and diseases. Later on we deal with harvesting and storing your potato crop.

Planting times and distances for potatoes vary with variety. Plant first-early and second-early varieties in mid and late spring (March and April) and early-maincrop and late varieties in late spring and early summer (April and May), or even into mid summer (June). Give earlies 25–30cm (10–12 in) between the tubers and 60cm (24 in) between the rows. Early-maincrop and late potatoes should have 38cm (15 in) between the tubers and 68–75cm (27–30 in) between the rows.

If the seed tubers are new Scottish or Irish stock some of them may be rather large. Provided there is at least one good sprout on each half, these can be cut lengthwise down the centre. Don't cut the tubers until you are ready to plant.

Methods of planting

The trench method is one of the most popular ways of planting potatoes. Put a garden line down across the plot and draw it tight. Keeping the back of the spade up against the line, 'chip' out a trench 10–15cm (4–6 in) deep. Plant the tubers in the bottom of the trench, taking care that the sprouts are not knocked off. Then move the line over the required distance (depending on variety) to mark out the next trench. As the second trench is taken out, throw the soil forward to fill in the first trench, and so on.

Another method is to make the planting holes with a trowel. This way you can vary the size of each hole to suit the size of the tuber. In addition you create minimum disturbance of the soil – an important point if manure or greenstuff has recently been dug in.

In the 'lazy bed' method of planting, place the tubers just below soil level so that they stand upright. Then, using a draw hoe, draw the soil over them from either side to form a ridge. This method is of value on heavy soils where the drainage is not too good, as any surplus water that may lie at the bottom of the ridges will then be below the level of the potatoes.

A more modern method is to plant the tubers just inside the soil and cover them with a sheet of black polythene 60cm (24 in) wide. Slit the polythene just above each tuber so that the sprouts can push through. To keep the polythene in place put stones or soil along the edges. The tubers form under the sheet, or just inside the soil. You can pick out the largest tubers for first use by freeing and lifting each side of the sheet in turn.

There is no saving of time by this method but it does cut out hoeing and earthing-up.

Pots and cold frames

If you have a greenhouse with some heat you can grow pots of potatoes on the greenhouse staging. Half-fill some 20cm (8 in) pots with good soil or compost and plant one tuber in each. Add more soil as the plants grow. When a plant has made a good soil ball and is forming tubers, it is quite easy to tap it out of the pot, pick off the largest tubers and then slip the roots back in the pot again.

You can also plant tubers in a cold frame in early or mid spring (February or early March). Ventilate them freely during the day and replace the light at night until the plants have reached the glass.

Protection from frost

Large barn cloches are good for protecting an early row of potatoes. If there is a ventilating pane, take it out so that the plants are not forced too quickly, but replace it at night if there is any danger of frost. The haulms of potatoes are easily damaged by frost. Shoots that are just emerging from the soil can be covered again by drawing soil over them if frost threatens, but this cannot be done once leaves have formed. Sheets of newspaper, kept in place with clods of earth, serve quite well.

If the young plants are blackened by frost, do not assume that they have died; new shoots will soon form. The crop will be later, of course, and in many cases may not be quite so heavy.

Hoeing and earthing-up

Hoe the plants when the rosettes of leaves have formed, but do it as lightly as possible so that the underground stolons (the shoots on which the tubers form) are not cut off.

Earthing-up takes place when the plants are 15–20cm (6–8 in) tall, and consists of drawing soil from between the

Four ways to plant potatoes. Below left: in trenches 10–15cm (4–6 in) deep; below: in individual holes, causing less soil disturbance; overleaf: by 'lazy bed' method – especially suitable for water-retaining soils; and right: covering with black polythene to save earthing-up

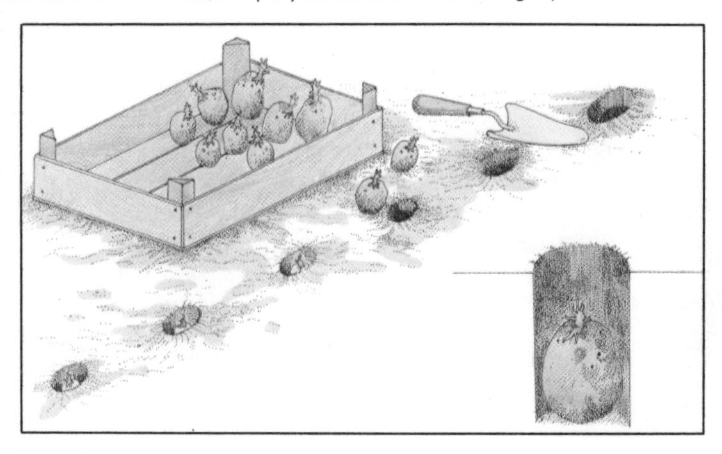

Above: two young plants suffering from potato blight. Right: cover plants with newspaper if there is danger of frost

rows to make a ridge. This prevents the tubers from pushing through into the sunlight. Tubers greened by the sun cannot be eaten.

To earth-up, stand between two rows of potatoes and, with a draw hoe, reach out over the plants and draw the soil up and under the lower leaves with a steady hand. Then turn round the end of a row to earth-up the other side. Repeat until all rows have been earthed-up on both sides. It makes for easier earthing if you first loosen the soil between the rows by forking it over.

Pests and diseases

The most frequently-encountered enemies of the potato are potato blight, common scab and potato eelworm.

Potato blight In mid and late summer (late June and early July) spray the plant with a fungicide such as Bordeaux mixture as a safeguard against potato blight. This is a fungus disease that spreads quickly in damp, humid conditions, and its presence is revealed by dark brown blotches on the leaves and the rapid deterioration of the haulms. Any sudden collapse of the foliage should always be viewed with suspicion. If this happens, cut off the haulms about 30cm (12 in) above the soil, remove them from the plot and burn them. This will prevent the blight spores from getting into the soil and infecting the tubers. The tubers may then be left in the soil for a couple of weeks to ripen off.

Common scab Another trouble that may be encountered is common scab; this is caused by a minute soil organism. The trouble is only skin deep and does not affect the eating or keeping qualities of the tubers. It is usually worse in light, hungry soils. Some good compost or grass mowings, placed in the bottom of the trench at planting time, will help to give clean tubers.

Potato eelworm This pest can be a serious problem. The tiny eelworms, too small to be seen by the naked eye, attack the plant stems and roots. Stunted plants with thin stems are an indication of their presence. The only cure is to starve them out by not growing potatoes on infected ground for several seasons. A three- or four-yearly crop rotation is a good deterrent.

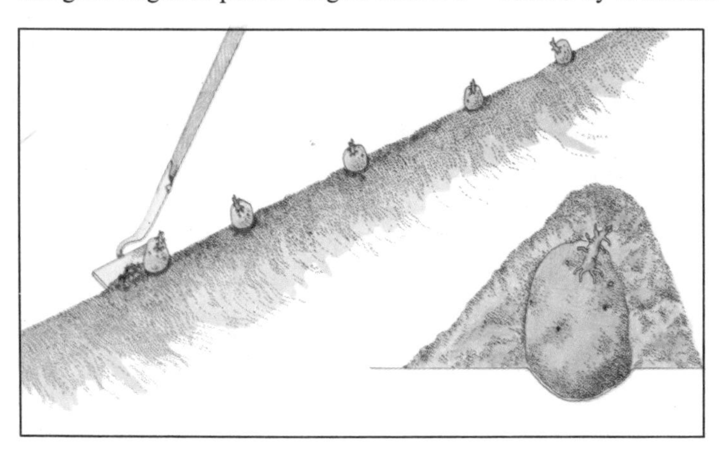

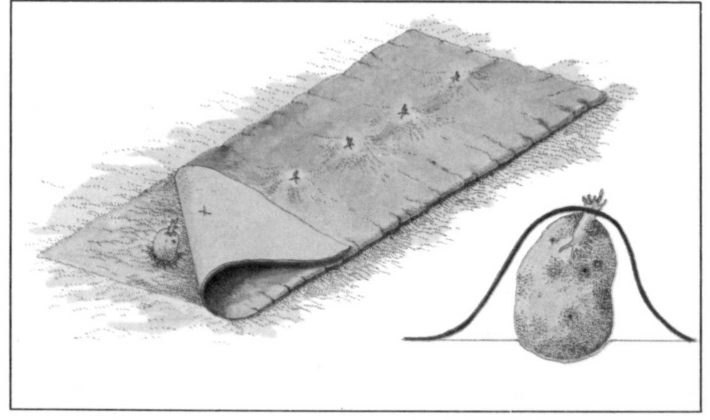

HARVESTING AND STORING POTATOES

The cultivation of the potato has now been described in some detail. Here we explain how to harvest and store this all-important vegetable, to enable you to get the best results.

It is usually the late varieties of potato that are grown for winter use and storage, but if the early ones have not been used up before the haulms have died off there is no reason why these, too, should not be stored. Most earlies, when ripe, will keep until mid winter (late December) at least.

Signs of maturity

The first sign of approaching maturity is a yellow tinge in the lower leaves of the haulms. This is followed by a gradual browning of the leaves and stems, until finally the haulms wither and die.

A change also takes place in the tuber. The skin of a 'new' (that is, immature) potato can be removed easily, whereas that on a ripe tuber is firm; once the skins have 'set', the crop is ready for lifting.

Lifting the tubers

To lift the crop, use either a digging fork (that is, one with square tines) or a potato fork (flat tines). Stand facing the row to be lifted, and thrust the fork in at the *side* of the ridge, not across it, otherwise some of the tubers will be pierced with the tines. Put the fork in at an angle so that when thrust well down, the tines are below the root; then lift the root cleanly and throw it forward. Shake off the dead haulm, and spread the potatoes out so that they are all on the soil surface. Before moving on to the next root, fork carefully through the area to bring up any tubers that remain.

Lift the crop on a dry day, if possible, so that the potatoes can be left out for an hour or two to dry. The soil will then come off them more easily. Rub off as much of it as possible when picking the potatoes up, and sort them into two grades – the eating or 'ware' potatoes, and those too small for use. Never leave the little ones lying about on the soil as they are apt to turn up again later as 'self-sets', producing new potato plants. Any tubers that have been speared by the fork should be placed on one side and used first.

Checking for disease

The ware potatoes can be put into sacks or boxes, or piled up in a heap on the soil. If heaped, they must be covered with the dead haulms or some other litter that will exclude light, to prevent them turning green. Leave the tubers for two or three weeks, before sorting through them all over again.

The purpose of this interim period is to give any diseased tubers a chance to show themselves. If the potatoes were stored away immediately after lifting, and not re-examined, any diseased tubers would continue to go bad, and could spread disease through the bag or heap.

Disease shows as a pinky-brownish patch on the skin. It is not difficult to see on white tubers, but may prove more difficult on coloured ones. If in doubt, scratch the skin with a finger-nail to see whether the discoloration goes right into the tuber.

After lifting, potatoes should be left to dry out for a couple of hours. This makes the removal of soil much easier

How to store

Sound tubers can now be stored for the winter in a cool, dark, frost-proof place. These three conditions are not always easy to meet indoors. A cool pantry, or an unheated spare bedroom or boxroom, would be suitable, or a brick garage –

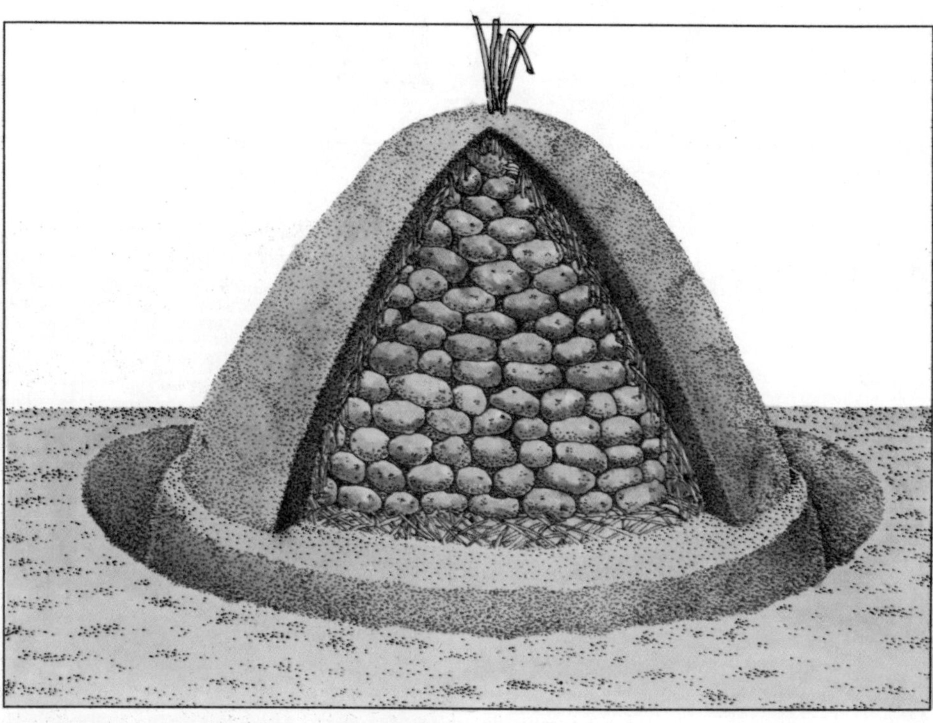

Above: drying off the harvested crop
Right: an outdoor clamp not only saves indoor storage space – the tubers will remain firmer than if in bags
Below right: it is essential to remove any shoots that appear on stored tubers

provided the door is not left open in frosty weather. Wooden sheds are seldom frost-proof, but will serve if extra covering can be put over the tubers during severe frost.

Boxes and sacks If the tubers are stored in boxes, the top of each box must be covered to exclude light. Hessian potato sacks, once so common, are now difficult to obtain and have given way to paper sacks, that can be bought from most large stores. Polythene sacks are not suitable, as a certain amount of light can penetrate and moisture can build up inside.

Outdoor clamp Where the crop consists of more than a couple of sacks, storage space can be saved by making an outdoor clamp (see diagram). This provides ideal conditions, and keeps the potatoes firmer than if they are stored in bags.

To make a clamp, level the soil and tread it firm. Put down a layer of straw to make a bed for the tubers, and pile them up on this. Pack them neatly so that the sides of the clamp are as steep and level as possible. The heap can be round or rectangular, but for average quantities a conical shape is more usual. Then cover the potatoes with a layer of straw (or hay or dried bracken) about 15cm (6 in) in thickness.

The next step is to mark out a circle approximately 25cm (10 in) from the straw. Thrust the spade in all the way round the circle, and dig out the soil beyond it, piling it up on the platform between the mark and the straw. Keep the same depth of soil all the way up. Fill in cracks and hollows with loose soil from the bottom of the trench, and finish by patting the soil smooth with the back of the spade. Subsoil should not be used, so if necessary extend the trench outwards.

To begin with, leave a wisp of straw sticking out at the top of the clamp. With the onset of colder weather, pull this out and fill in the hole. During spells of severe frost, straw or litter spread over the clamp will give added protection; the most vulnerable parts, of course, are those facing north and east.

Inspect the clamp at intervals to make sure that rats or mice have not found it. If there are tell-tale holes, fill them in and set traps for the culprits, making sure that these are safe for domestic pets.

If it is necessary to open the clamp during the winter months, make sure that it is adequately sealed up again, and never try to open it while frost is about.

Towards late spring (end of March), get the potatoes out of the clamp and rub off the sprouts. Any tubers that have been stored indoors should also be de-sprouted in the same way.

CARE AND CULTIVATION

INTENSIVE CULTIVATION OF VEGETABLES

Most gardeners would like to get a 'quart into a pint pot' – particularly where the vegetable plot is concerned. Generally speaking, the smaller the plot the more important it is to obtain the maximum yield from it. To do this, there are certain guide-lines and methods to be kept in mind.

One of the most important factors in intensive cultivation of vegetables is the fertility of the soil. To crop a strip of ground intensively year after year it must be built up to, and maintained in, a high state of fertility. The other main ingredient of intensive cultivation is careful planning. There is no need for an elaborate crop plan, but you should know, well in advance, what you want to plant, and when.

Maintaining soil fertility

When any part of the soil becomes vacant in autumn or winter, dig and manure it as soon as possible. Put all suitable waste material into a compost heap so that it can be returned to the soil. Mulch with peat or compost during the summer months, not only to conserve moisture but so as to add to the humus content of the soil when the mulch is dug in. In the spring, or when follow-on crops are planted during the summer, apply a general fertilizer at the rate of 70g per sq m (2 oz per sq yd).

Aim to get a quick turnaround of crops whenever possible so that valuable space is not left lying idle any longer than is necessary. This is particularly important during the summer months. Do not dig deeply during this period; keep the moist soil down below where it will do most good, and simply prick the topsoil over with a fork to a depth of 8–10cm (3–4 in). Rake the soil down again at once before it has time to dry out.

Choosing vegetables and varieties

Care is needed in the choice of crops to be grown and the selection of varieties. While the choice will depend, to some extent, on what each household likes, it is wise to go for those crops that are expensive to buy and those that soon lose their freshness when gathered (often the two are synonymous).

Sweet corn, tomatoes, salad crops, French beans, peas and young roots of beetroot and carrots are all good choices for intensive cropping. Late potatoes take up too much room, but a row of first-earlies is always worthwhile, especially when they are really early and ready when shop prices are still high. When choosing brassicas avoid the larger cabbages and grow smaller ones like Greyhound (pointed) and Vienna Babyhead (round). Brussels sprouts take up too much room, unless you pick a dwarf variety; you may prefer to grow a row of sprouting broccoli or its delicious autumn counterpart, calabrese.

Choose early varieties for the first sowings and then use them again in late summer when the growing time is short. Let the accent be on varieties that mature quickly, even though they may be smaller, and do not hesitate to sacrifice the tail-end of one crop if, by so doing, there will be time to plant another.

Intercropping and double-cropping

There are two practices that are of special value to the holder of a smaller vegetable plot – intercropping and double-cropping.

Intercropping is the growing of a quick-maturing crop between the rows of a slower one. A good example is spinach between rows of dwarf peas and lettuces planted between rows of French beans. Radishes, that need only three or four weeks in which to mature, can always be grown as an intercrop. Another method of intercropping, often overlooked, involves sowing or planting the intercrop first. If, for example, you sow lettuces or carrots in rows 45cm (18 in) apart instead of the customary 30cm (12 in), you can then plant a row of dwarf cabbages between them in mid summer (June). Provided you keep the basic principles of intercropping in mind – that the intercrop should be harvested before the second crop needs all the room – you can devise many variations on this theme.

In double-cropping the second crop is not sown or planted until you have gathered the first. Examples of this method are brassicas or leeks after early potatoes, or lettuces or roots after a first sowing of peas.

Cutting down on spacing

A further point to consider in intensive cultivation is the amount of room to be given between plants and rows. Every plant should have enough room in which to mature, but no more. Carrots 5cm (2 in) in diameter and beetroot 8cm (3in) in diameter are large enough for general use. Lettuces, that are normally given 30cm (12 in), can be restricted to 25cm (10 in) without any harm being done, while smaller varieties will head at 15cm (6 in). Thinning should be done early so that unwanted seedlings are not competing for food and air.

In recent years the 'block' system has become quite popular; several rows are sown quite close together. A wider space between one block and the next serves as a path. Five rows of carrots, for example, with 15cm (6 in) between rows, followed by a path 45cm (18 in) wide, take up less room than five rows at the customary spacing of 30cm (12 in), and weed growth is also less.

Using cloches

In any system of intensive cultivation cloches are a great help. Try to acquire enough to cover at least one row of vegetables. The value of cloches in warming up the soil in spring and bringing on early crops is well known; less appreciated is their worth in extending the season into autumn and winter. They often make it possible to harvest two crops in a season, and can give partial protection to three or more. As an example, you can sow lettuces in early spring (February) in soil pre-warmed by the cloches. These can be de-cloched in late spring (April); the cloches are then moved to cover a row of early French beans. After the risk of frost has gone in mid summer (early June) you can put tomatoes out under cloches. At the end of the year use them to finish off lettuces sown in late summer to early autumn (July to August).

Right: suggested cropping plan for a plot 9×4·5m (30×15 ft). Row spacing is drawn to scale but not row length, so the plot appears elongated. Some inter-crops are sown before the main crops; for instance, kohlrabi, turnips and carrots go in before late peas. Space has been left for two courgette plants, started in warmth, at the end of the sweet corn rows, lending added interest to the plot

Intensive cultivation of vegetables

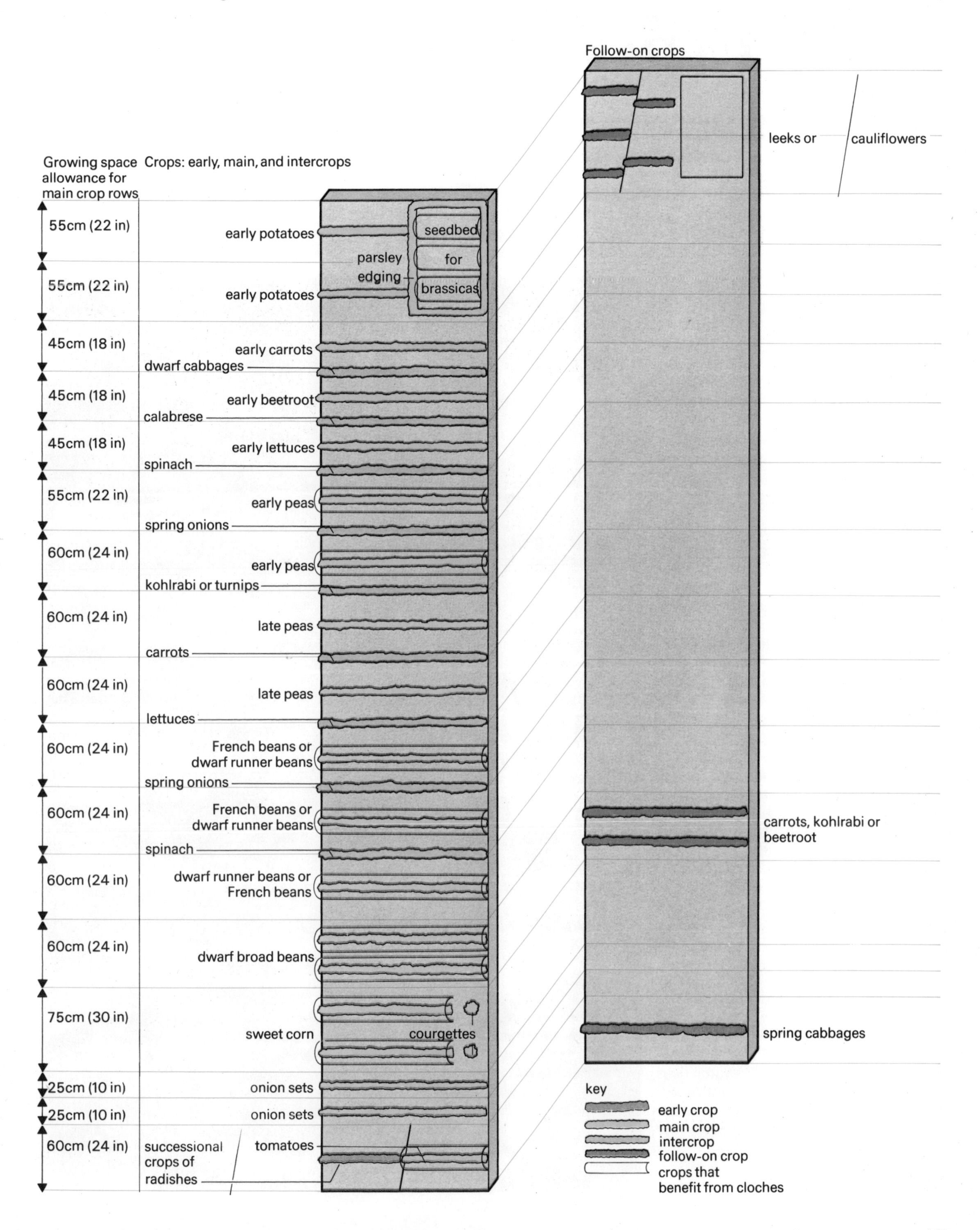

SMALL-SPACE VEGETABLE CROPPING

A small garden need not be a barrier to the growing of vegetable crops. Methods of crop-spacing, involving calculation of the exact amount of room required for vegetables to mature to eatable size, mean that you can grow enough to supply the kitchen throughout the year.

Old gardening manuals indicate that gardeners of bygone days had an enviable amount of space at their disposal. Carrots, for instance, could be thinned to 15cm (6 in), beetroot to 20cm (8 in), parnsips to 25cm (10 in) and swedes to 30cm (12 in). Today, with gardens becoming ever smaller, it is important to make the fullest use of vegetable space. Crops must have enough room to mature, but no more. The problem is to decide exactly how much is enough.

Determining correct spacing

There are several points that must be taken into account in finding a successful solution to this problem. The first one is that you must not fall into the trap of giving the plants insufficient room.

Space is always needed for adequate cleaning and cultivation of a crop; weeds rob the plants of food, light and air, and it is also difficult for the gardener to move freely among rows of plants that are less than 25–30cm (10–12 in) apart, except in the case of the strip method of cultivation that is explained later. Some crops require special methods of cultivation; potatoes, for example, need earthing-up and it is difficult to do this with a row spacing less than 60cm (24 in). This distance can be reduced to 55cm (22 in) with early varieties, where large tubers are not so important and the ridges need not be so well formed. Leeks also come into this category since they can be grown in rows 30cm (12 in) apart, but actually need a minimum of 38cm (15 in) if they are to be earthed-up a little to obtain a greater length of blanched stem.

Give some thought as well to the size of vegetables you require. Those for exhibition will naturally need more room than those for the kitchen. This is not to say that exhibition specimens cannot be eaten – they can – but a housewife needing a medium-sized onion for a stew will not look kindly on one weighing a few kilograms. It is now accepted that small roots have a better flavour than large ones. Generally speaking, the larger a root becomes the more likely it is to coarsen in texture. This size is something that can be controlled by spacing. Carrots for pulling young need be more than 4cm ($1\frac{1}{2}$ in) in diameter, and can therefore be thinned to that distance, while main-crop ones for storing will be large enough at 8–10cm (3–4 in). A beetroot or turnip 10cm (4 in) in diameter is big enough for most needs, while the massive parsnip of former years can be replaced by a couple of roots at half the space – 13cm (5 in). Swedes will be large enough if thinned to 15–20cm (6–8 in).

The size of your family is yet another point that needs to be considered. Today families are generally smaller, and it would seem that the era of the giant marrow and the outsize cabbage has gone. The trend in the newer varieties of cabbage, for instance, is towards smaller, compact ones with few outer leaves, that are more suitable for smaller families; while larger cabbages may serve for several meals they soon lose their freshness when cut open.

Below: summer cabbage Primata, a small ball-headed variety

Left: vegetable plot at Wisley showing maximum use of available space

Particular spacings

The size of cauliflowers is governed largely by the richness of the soil and the amount of space they are given. If you want 'mini' cauliflowers for a small family, the answer is to plant them closer together so that smaller curds will form. For this purpose the usual spacing of 60cm (24 in) between plants and rows can safely be reduced to 45cm (18 in).

With peas the general rule is that the distance between the rows should approximate to the height of the peas. Dwarf varieties 45–60cm (18–24 in) high do well enough with a row spacing of 45cm (18 in). Another method worth trying is to sow three rows, spacing them only 30cm (12 in) apart. They will fill the space and help to hold each other up, and you can pick them by reaching over the rows from either side.

Below: dwarf broad bean The Sutton grows to a height of 30cm (12 in)

Below: strip cultivation of carrots can more than double your yield

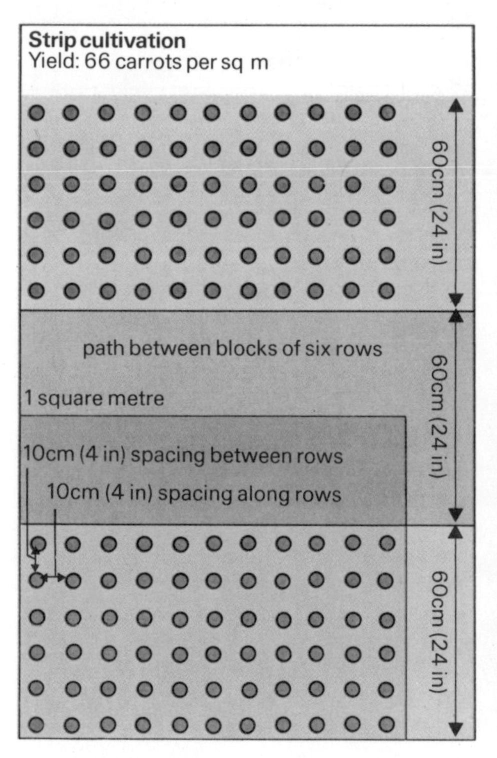

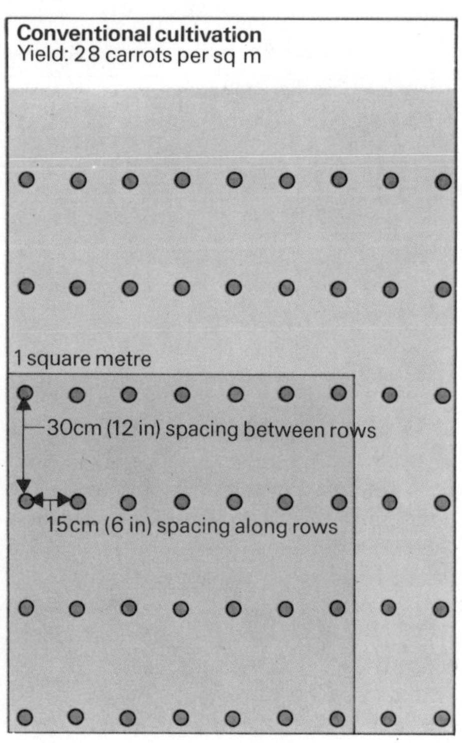

Not much can be done to reduce the normal area for runner beans, especially if they are climbing, but you can grow French beans in a double row, this being a particularly good method if you need only two rows. Space the seeds at 15cm (6 in) with 30cm (12 in) between the rows.

The dwarf broad bean is a most useful vegetable, needing a spacing of 25–30cm (10–12 in) between plants and 30cm (12 in) between rows. Three rows, as suggested for peas, gives a worthwhile sowing, resulting in a crop that can be picked over for several weeks.

The new varieties of brussels sprouts tend to produce tight, medium-sized sprouts suitable for freezing. The older varieties have always been a problem in the small garden as they need 60–75cm (2–2½ ft) of space all round. The varieties Early Half Tall and Peer Gynt (F.1 hybrid) are only of medium height and will crop at 53cm (21 in) between plants and rows.

Strip cultivation

Some research has already been done on this problem of vegetable spacings, and the work is continuing. One method to come out of the research is the strip system of cultivation, that is of particular value for the growing of carrots, but can also be adapted for other roots and for onions.

Briefly, the system is to sow a number of rows close together, with 45–60cm (18–24 in) paths between the strips. For example, six rows of carrots can be given only 10cm (4 in) between the rows, instead of the customary 30cm (12 in). Hoeing with a small onion hoe and weeding can be done from the paths on either side of the strip. One advantage of this method is that after the seedling stage the foliage forms an even carpet that effectively cuts out weeds.

Within the limits of your own soil and site there are minimum distances at which each vegetable will produce a satisfactory crop. To get full production it is worthwhile trying to find these distances, there being plenty of scope for every gardener to experiment for himself. Careful planning in the initial stages and the right choice of varieties are the first steps towards success.

THE IMPORTANCE OF TYPE AND VARIETY

The importance of a good working knowledge of the types and varieties of vegetables available cannot be stressed too much. If you are to make full use of the area you have set aside for food growing, it is essential that you choose wisely.

Fortunately knowledge of which types and varieties of vegetables to choose can be obtained through the pages of an up-to-date seed catalogue. The modern seed catalogue may justly be described as the seedsman's shop window, and nowadays it is an extensive window. Moreover even in these days of increasing costs, the catalogue is free and any seed firm of repute will be pleased to send you one.

Careful study of a good seed catalogue always repays the time involved and will prove of absorbing interest. It also helps to avoid mistakes in selection and planning. As it can be done in an armchair, in front of a glowing fire, there can be few more pleasurable forms of gardening.

Using a seed catalogue

'But why' you may be thinking 'should one go to the trouble of ordering direct from a seed firm when so many shops and stores sell seeds during the spring months?' One answer to this is that the seeds displayed in shops and stores are usually the most popular varieties of standard vegetables. New introductions and unusual vegetables are not generally found there. Another point is that this is purely a serve-yourself service and the assistant at the cash desk will not be an expert on seeds.

If you need help in assessing the merits of different varieties it is better to study a good seed catalogue and then send in an order, or buy from a recognized seed-shop or garden centre where you can seek expert help. It is worth remembering, too, that a good seed catalogue does not only describe the different varieties; it often gives useful tips on sowing and growing them as well.

Seed catalogue terminology

Gardeners are accustomed to talking, rather loosely, about types and kinds of vegetable, and about varieties, strains and hybrids. A newcomer to vegetable gardening often finds these terms rather confusing. 'Types' and 'kinds' really mean the same thing. The broad bean is a type or kind of vegetable; so is a lettuce or carrot. Varieties are selections within the kinds or types; Bunyard's Exhibition is a variety of broad bean, Webb's Wonderful is a variety of lettuce and Early Nantes is a variety of carrot.

A strain is a particular selection of seeds within a variety. When we speak of a good strain or a pure strain we mean that the seeds will always produce plants that are true to the characteristics of that variety. A poor strain, on the other hand, means that those characteristics are less evident than they should be.

You will notice, when reading your catalogue, that some varieties have 'F.1' after the varietal name. This is the accepted symbol for an F.1 hybrid. To produce these, two parent plants with desirable characteristics are selected. These are then inbred (fertilized with their own pollen) until the special qualities are fixed. The two varieties are then crossed and their progeny becomes a first cross (F.1) hybrid. The special qualities of these hybrids are usually increased vigour, better quality, improved colouring and a marked uniformity of size. As the production of these hybrids is more expensive than that of ordinary seeds, they naturally cost more, but they are well worth the expense.

Breeding varieties

Plant breeding and plant selection is going on all the time. Plant breeders do not make their crossings haphazardly (hoping for something to turn up) but with a definite goal in mind. Their main objectives are: first, to breed plants for a particular purpose; second, to breed plants for a particular season; third, to breed plants for a particular micro-climate, site or type of soil.

One of the main groups of vegetables bred for a particular purpose are those that are grown for freezing. For instance the newer varieties of brussels sprouts give sprouts that are tight, of good colour and of medium size. This is what the commercial grower needs in order to satisfy the demands of the frozen food firms. Acres of sprouts, and other greens are now grown for this purpose alone. Similarly, slim carrots that can be tinned whole are now being produced for the canning firms.

Plants bred for a particular season include the early and late varieties. By reducing the time taken for some vegetables to mature, the plant breeder has produced some varieties that will crop earlier than others. There are also varieties with special characteristics of hardiness, resistance to frost or mildew, or with some degree of self-protection (as with cauliflowers) that are suitable for late use. Incidentally, the reason why early varieties of some vegetables are often recommended for follow-on crops that will mature late in the season is because, with their shorter growing period, they are eminently suitable for use when the days are getting shorter.

Above left: Early Nantes carrots are ideal for early or maincrop sowings
Above: Exhibition Longpod, a broad bean that may win you show prizes
Right: if you want a cut-and-come-again lettuce, try Salad Bowl

The third group includes plants for warm areas and for frames and cloches, plants for the colder parts of the country, dwarf varieties for exposed sites and roots suitable for shallow soils – such as stump-rooted carrots and globe beetroot.

Making your selection
It is true, of course, that most of the new or improved varieties are designed for the commercial grower, but indirectly they also help the home gardener, for many of them will appear in the retail catalogues.

You can now see why the selection of your vegetables should not just be a matter of picking up the odd packet of seeds here and there, but the result of a carefully thought-out appraisal of your needs. You must know what your soil is like and what it is capable of producing. You will also need to assess your available time and materials: for instance, whether you have the time and the staking materials for the taller peas and the tallest runner beans. Again, is your garden very exposed? If so, the dwarf varieties of peas, beans and sprouts will merit your attention. If your aim is to grow early crops you will have to make sure that you have the right varieties.

All this may seem to be just commonsense, and to a large extent it is, but it is surprising how often these points are overlooked.

A good seed catalogue classifies early and late varieties, tall and dwarf, hardy or not so hardy. Most of them now show, with an asterisk or similar symbol, the varieties that are suitable for freezing.

Planning succession of crops
All of us, space permitting, want to keep up a steady supply of vegetables. On paper it is not difficult to work out a succession of, say, lettuces that will last throughout the summer months; in practice it will prove much more difficult as the vagaries of climate can play havoc with the most carefully thought-out plan. A cold start in the spring, followed by a sudden spell of hot weather, will sometimes run two sowings into one.

There are two methods of trying to obtain a succession; one is to use different varieties that mature at different times, and the other is to make successional sowings of the same variety (about three weeks should be allowed between sowings). This second method is the cheaper one, especially if you buy a large packet of seeds in the first place.

As an illustration of the first method take the two peas Early Onward and Onward. The first is an early cropper and the second a maincrop variety. By sowing them at the same time, or within a week of each other, a succession will be assured. The same thing applies if the lettuce Hilde (early) and Webb's Wonderful (maincrop) are sown together. The alternative, using the second method, would be to make successional sowings of Early Onward and Hilde.

With some vegetables it is a definite advantage to make small, successional sowings. It is easy to get too many radishes or too many lettuces at one time. Sowing single rows at intervals is much better than sowing several rows together and ending up with a glut. With cabbages and cauliflowers it is a good plan to sow the seeds in two batches. This will give at least two plantings–more if larger plants are put out first– with a corresponding staggering of the harvest period.

Selections for other purposes
Where the vegetables are required for a particular season or purpose (for example, late cauliflowers, spring cabbages or plants to stand through the winter) it is essential to choose the right varieties. The catalogue will state plainly which are the late cauliflowers, which cabbages should be sown in autumn for cutting in the spring, and which varieties are best for surviving the rigours of winter. Many catalogues also have some kind of symbol to indicate the varieties most suitable for frame and cloche use.

EASY-CARE VEGETABLES

There must be many people who, for one reason or another, are prevented from giving as much time to their gardens as they would like. Growing vegetables may seem to need a great deal of time, but there is a good range of basic vegetables that can be grown without too much attention.

One way that you can save some time is to sow as many crops as possible *in situ* and so cut out transplanting. This will mean some loss of the earliest crops, but that cannot be helped. Lettuces, for example, are hardier than is generally supposed and can be sown outdoors from mid spring (March) onwards. Courgettes can be sown in early summer (May) where they are to fruit.

Small cabbages of the pointed or ball-headed types can be sown *in situ*. Simply sow a few seeds at intervals of 30cm (12 in) along the drill, and then thin the seedlings to the strongest plant. Kales can also be sown in this way.

This practice of station sowing can be used for other crops and does cut down the time needed for thinning and weeding as a little onion hoe can be used between the plants. Most root vegetables can be grown in this way, and so can lettuces. Pelleted seeds are useful for this type of sowing.

In the case of lettuce and radishes the packets of mixed seeds now offered by most seedsmen are labour saving, giving longer cropping periods per sowing.

Early potatoes

Save time and energy when growing early potatoes by cutting out earthing-up. Earthing is done to prevent the tubers from pushing through the soil into the sunlight, which makes them green and inedible. However, as earlies are dug up in an immature state and before the tubers have reached full size, earthing-up is not as essential as it is for the later varieties.

Easy peas and beans

Staking is a time-consuming business; avoid it by growing only dwarf varieties. The dwarf pea has been with us for many years and there are some good varieties that only need 45–60cm (18–24 in) in height. Dwarf varieties of broad beans need very little support – a few twiggy sticks pushed in among them will keep them from falling over. French beans, too, need only a few twiggy sticks to keep them upright.

The easiest way of growing runner beans is to sow the variety Kelvedon Marvel in drills 5cm (2 in) deep and 90cm (3 ft) apart, allowing 23cm (9 in) between the seeds. The plants will run along the ground to form a continuous row. Any runners that seem likely to stray across into the next row should be pinched back. To pick the beans, simply lift up first one side of the row and then the other. Some gardeners disapprove of this method, pointing out that pods that touch the soil may be mud-splashed in heavy rains and will not be straight. But as the pods have to be washed and cut up before they are eaten, neither point is of much importance. Slug damage of the lowest pods may occur, but slug bait can be put down to keep these pests at bay.

Tomatoes and celery

Because of the time needed to tie them in and pinch out sideshoots, outdoor tomatoes may not seem feasible. The answer is to grow only the bush varieties, which break naturally and need no tying, unless it is one tie to a central cane. When the weight of the fruits begins to pull the stems down, slip black polythene or short litter under the fruits to keep them clear of the soil.

Trench celery is labour-intensive and has to be ruled out, but the self-blanching varieties are a good substitute. Planted in blocks 20cm (8 in) between the plants they soon fill up the space allotted to them and weeds are crowded out. Boards, pegged round the outside of the block, will exclude light from the plants on the edges, or soil may be drawn up to them.

Bush tomatoes like Pixie don't need to have their lateral shoots pinched out

Simple substitutes

Instead of celery you could grow celeriac. This turnip-rooted form of celery is planted out in flat ground and does not need earthing-up.

Another good 'substitute' vegetable is spinach beet. The true spinach has a comparatively short life and successional sowings are needed to keep up a supply. Two sowings of spinach beet – in the spring for summer use and in early autumn (August) for winter use – will give pickings over a long period.

Other 'easy-care' vegetables

There are other crops worth mentioning in this labour-saving context. Rhubarb, apart from the initial effort of making the bed, does not require much attention. A clean-up of the old leaves each autumn, followed by a dressing of good compost or manure, will keep it going for years.

Onion sets and shallots, once planted, need only regular hoeing along the rows to keep the crop weed-free. Leeks make a good follow-on crop to early vegetables and can stay in the ground all winter; for the gardener too busy to raise his own plants from seed, there is usually no difficulty in buying plants from a reputable nursery or garden centre at the appropriate time.

Kohl rabi is easy to grow and stands drought better than turnips. It can be station-sown *in situ*. In appearance it is rather like a sprouting broccoli and the root – which is really the swollen stem – is formed above ground. The swede may also be station-sown and does not ask for any special treatment. All these vegetables have already been described in depth in their respective sections.

Whether or not to water

One question that can be a real problem is whether to water or not. Watering is a tedious and time-consuming chore, especially in drought periods when hosepipes are banned. It is some consolation to know that, in general, dwarf varieties of vegetables suffer less from lack of water than the taller ones. The best advice that can be given is that if watering cannot be kept going, it should never be started. Leaving the plants to forage for themselves will do them less harm, in the long run, than starting to water and then having to stop.

COMMON VEGETABLE DISEASES

The vegetable grower, taking time off to peruse his favourite gardening books, can suddenly encounter in their pages a horrific array of plant diseases. But the reality is less dreadful. Many gardeners meet few, if any, of these diseases and most of them can, if the right steps are taken, be cured, controlled or prevented, provided they are caught in time.

One of the most important factors in preventing the spread or recurrence of diseases of vegetables is the practice of good crop rotation. Many diseases, in particular virus ones, have resting bodies that lie dormant in the soil until the next growing season. If the same vegetable, or a close relative, is being grown again then the disease will launch a fresh attack. Hence the importance of crop rotation: diseases 'resting' in the soil are encouraged to die out rather than build up strength.

There is another gardening 'rule' that is vital to the checking of disease spread: never compost diseased material. Just because a plant is dead does not mean that the disease is also dead. So destroy all diseased plants – preferably by burning them – to prevent contamination.

Plant-disease organisms are, in general, very specific in their activity, each tending to be restricted to a small group of closely-related plants. Cucumber mildew, for instance, only attacks cucumbers, marrows and other members of the cucurbit family. Consequently, although there are exceptions to this rule, it is helpful to discuss vegetable diseases on a crop basis.

Potatoes

The best-known disease of this crop is potato blight, that blackens the leaves and can lead to rotting of the tubers. To control this disease, spray at the first sign of attack with a copper fungicide and follow this with two or three repeat treatments at 14-day intervals. Finally cut off, remove and burn the haulm 7–10 days before lifting the crop in order to prevent infection of the tubers.

Virus diseases are another major cause of crop reduction. These infections are detected by the yellow mottling, rolling or crinkling of the foliage. Much the best insurance against virus diseases is to buy fresh certified seed potatoes each year.

Common scab is another widely-spread disease. This produces blemishes on the surface of the tubers but otherwise has no ill effects. Incorporating plenty of bulky organic matter into the drill at planting time reduces the incidence of common scab. It is also important not to lime the soil before planting potatoes as lime favours the disease.

Tomatoes

Potato blight is a major disease of outdoor tomatoes; it not only damages the leaves but also causes a black rot of the fruits. Here again the use of regular sprays with a copper fungicide is recommended to prevent this.

Various soil-borne fungi can cause damping off of seedlings and foot rots of older plants. Foot rot is a very general term used to describe various diseases, all due to fungi of one sort or another, that reveal themselves as a blackening and rotting of the plants.

One of these soil-borne fungi, *Phytophthora parasitica*, is also responsible for buck-eye rot of the fruits. This takes the form of dark patches, with darker concentric rings, at the end of the fruit opposite to the stalk. Watering the soil with Cheshunt compound or captan fungicide is the best way of guarding against these diseases. Another fruit blemish, that is similar to buck-eye rot but has no concentric rings, is called blossom-end rot. This trouble, however, is not caused by disease but is produced by water shortages at an earlier stage of development.

As with potatoes, tomatoes can also be infected by a variety of virus diseases that cause leaf discoloration and growth distortion. There is no cure for these diseases, but they can often be prevented by controlling the aphides that frequently transmit the infection.

In a hot dry summer, leaf mould disease may be a nuisance. The leaves develop yellow patches on the upper surface and a brownish mould beneath. The best remedy is to spray at regular 10–14 day intervals with a copper fungicide, used according to manufacturer's instructions.

Peas

Garden peas are subject to attack by various soil organisms, both at the time of germination and in the later growth

Below, far left: potato tuber rotted with blight disease
Below left: tomato with buck-eye rot
Below: yellow and brown discoloration of tomato foliage indicates leaf mould

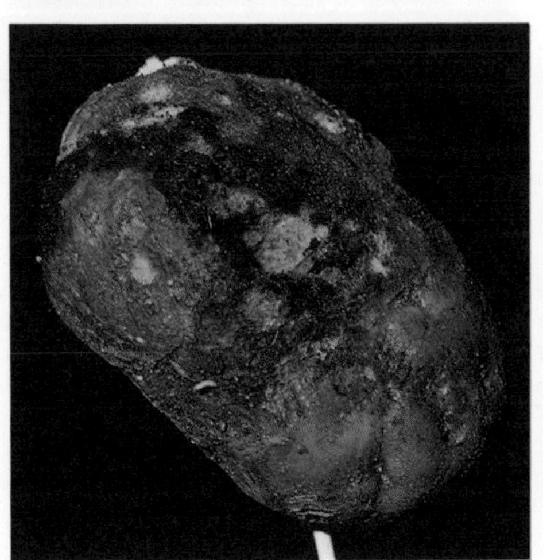

stages. Some protection against these diseases can be obtained by the use of captan-based seed dressings, but it is still necessary to practise crop rotation.

Attacks by powdery mildew (that appears as a white powdery covering on leaves and stems) are common in dry summers, particularly on late crops. Anti-mildew sprays (like dinocap) will help to combat this disease; you should also pull out and burn infected plants as soon as they have finished cropping, otherwise they act as sources of infection for later-planted rows.

Broad beans

Chocolate spot is the commonest disease of this crop. It shows up as chocolate-coloured spots on the leaves and pods and as dark stripes on the stems. At the first sign of attack the plants should be sprayed with copper fungicide and then repeat sprays given at intervals of 14 days. Broad beans are most susceptible to attack when grown in waterlogged conditions, so getting the soil into good condition before sowing the seed reduces the risk of infection.

Runner beans and French beans

These are other crops in which root and foot rots can be troublesome. So here again the use of seed dressings, coupled with crop rotation, is to be recommended.

Brassicas

Club root, which causes thickening and distortion of the roots, is the commonest and most serious disease of brassicas. The soil-borne organism responsible for club root thrives on acid conditions, so the first step is to apply a heavy dressing of lime. Crop rotation should also be practised. Finally it is essential to apply 4 per cent calomel (mercurous chloride) dust to the seed drill and to the planting holes. Indeed, seedlings should not be raised in infected soil. Instead they should be grown in sterile growing compost.

Grey mould (botrytis), downy mildew (that shows as white fungal growth under the leaves, although its disease-carrying bodies rest in the soil), white blister (white pustules with a silvery sheen appearing on leaves and stems) and various leaf-spotting diseases occur from time to time, but these diseases generally do not have serious effects on cropping. The best approach here is to remove and destroy all infected leaves.

Swedes and turnips

Swedes and turnips can be attacked by the diseases listed under brassicas. They may also be attacked by powdery mildew, but this disease does not usually have very serious effects. In addition the roots can be attacked by various root rots. Dry rot shows itself by sunken, cankerous areas appearing on the side of the root. Soft rot may enter through these wounds or where mechanical damage has taken place. This turns the roots to a slimy mass, often leaving the skin almost intact. Black rot turns the flesh of the root dark brown or black. There are no specific control measures for these root diseases, but any infected plants that are discovered should be removed and destroyed.

Parsnips

Parsnips are remarkably free from disease. They may, however, be attacked by downy mildew, powdery mildew and leaf spot. Fortunately these diseases have little effect on the crop.

Canker (sometimes called 'rust') can, however, be very damaging to the roots. This disease first appears as reddish-brown marks on the top of the root. Later it can lead to a general rot. The easy answer in this case is to sow canker-resistant varieties such as Avonresister.

Carrots

Disease is not usually a problem with growing carrots, but serious rots can develop in storage. So it is essential to select only sound roots for storage and to avoid storing the carrots in excessively wet conditions. One disease that is easily recognized at lifting is violet root rot, that shows as a web of violet-coloured fungal threads on the outside of the root.

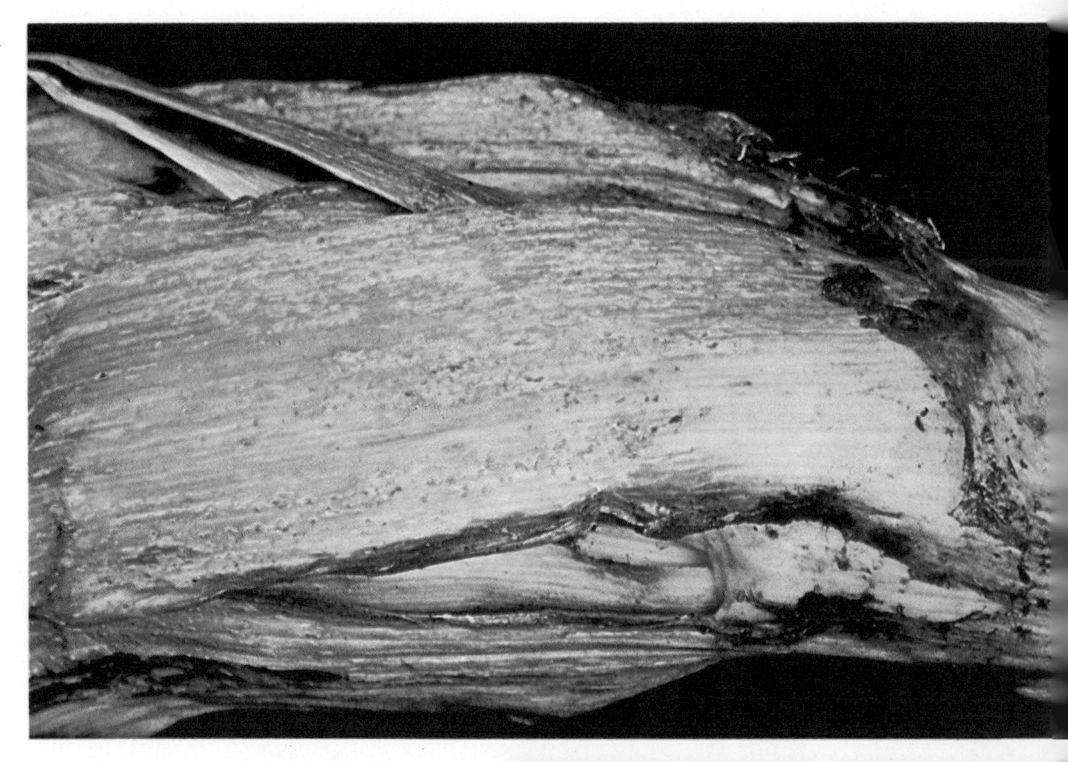

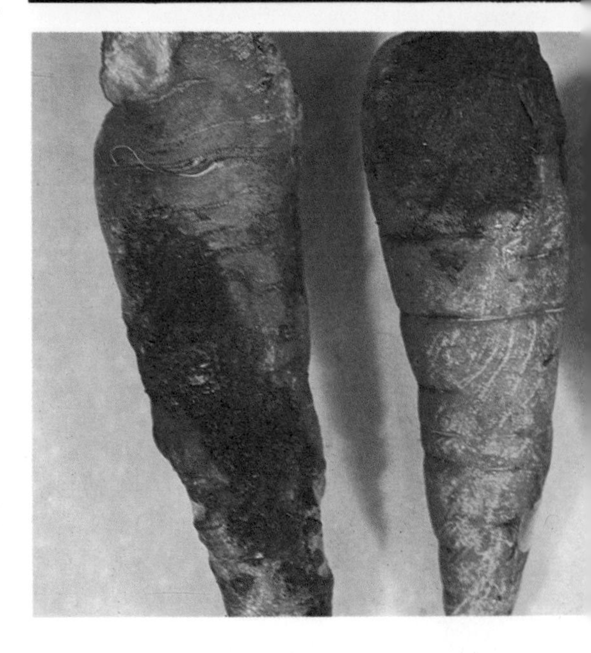

Freshly-lifted infected roots are edible peeled, but liable to rot when stored.

Onions

Downy mildew of onions can be a serious problem in wet seasons. The first sign of attack is the appearance of light-coloured spots on the leaves. These then enlarge and the affected leaves topple over and shrivel. This disease can have serious effects on the crop yield, so the plant should be sprayed with a general fungicide (such as zineb) at the first sign of attack and repeat treatments given at 7–10 day intervals. It is also important to collect and burn any infected leaves in order to reduce the carry-over of disease.

Another common disease of onions is white rot, that is generally favoured by cool conditions. This disease can be detected by the leaves yellowing and wilting even when there is plenty of soil moisture. If affected plants are closely examined it will be seen that there is a white fluffy fungal growth at the base of the bulbs. This cottony growth later gives rise to small, black, dot-like sclerotia that are the resting bodies of the fungus. These sclerotia fall off into the soil and are then spread around by subsequent cultivations to provide a source of infection in later years. At present there is no cure for infected plants nor is it easy to disinfect the soil. So, once the disease has appeared in an onion bed, the only answer is to practise long-term crop rotation.

Leeks

Leeks can be attacked by the onion diseases already mentioned. In addition they are subject to attacks by rust disease, which appears as yellow or orange spots. Any leaves showing infection spots should be removed immediately and burned. A programme of regular sprays with a general fungicide should be initiated to protect the plants from further attacks.

Another important disease of leeks is white tip, caused by the fungus *Phytophthora porri.* Normally this disease is restricted to the tips of the leaves, which die and turn white, but it can also affect the edges of the leaves.

At the first sign of the disease the plants should be sprayed with a copper fungicide and repeat applications given at intervals of 14 days during the winter.

Above left: leek attacked by rust disease
Left: roots of brassica thickened and distorted by club root
Below left: carrots suffering from violet root rot
Below: onions infected with white rot
Below right: lettuce stem rotted by grey mould
Right: lettuce leaf infected with mildew

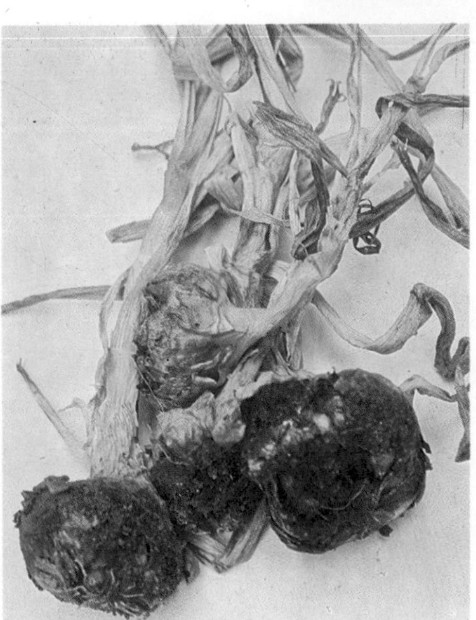

Shallots

Shallots are normally very free from disease though they can, on occasion, be attacked by diseases that affect onions.

Lettuce

Outdoor lettuce is normally fairly resistant to disease attack. In overcrowded beds, however, the plants can become infected with a downy mildew. Affected leaves turn patchy yellow and the fungus can be seen on the underside as mealy-looking spots. Since this disease is usually confined to the outer leaves it does little real damage, though heavy infections can spoil the look of the heads. The answer to this disease on outdoor lettuce is to use wide spacings to ensure free air movements around the plants.

Sclerotina disease, which is also called drop, may develop on lettuce in warm weather. The attack begins at ground level, producing a white, fluffy fungal growth that then spreads over the plant, causing it to collapse. Later the fungus produces its small, black, resting bodies (sclerotia) that contaminate the soil. It is therefore important to remove and burn any infected plants as quickly as possible.

Grey mould (botrytis), only occasionally encountered outdoors although very prevalent in the greenhouse, can cause the plants to wilt completely and the leaves to become covered with grey furry mould; spraying regularly with benomyl or thiram will assist in preventing and controlling the disease.

Marrows and cucumbers

Marrows, cucumbers and other cucurbits are all liable to attack by a powdery mildew (cucumber mildew) that can seriously check their growth. This disease can be controlled by spraying with an anti-mildew fungicide. Infection by mosaic virus is also a common problem with cucurbits. This type of virus is readily recognized by the presence of small, puckered leaves showing yellow mottling. Any young plants with these symptoms should be dug up and burnt as they will not produce worthwhile crops. Established plants that become infected in the later growth stages can, however, be left to grow on, but destroy them after the crop is harvested.

COMMON VEGETABLE PESTS

Success in vegetable growing is measured by the yield of healthy, succulent produce. Crops that are ravaged by insects not only yield less but are also much less appetizing. Sensible and effective pest control, therefore, plays an important role in vegetable gardening.

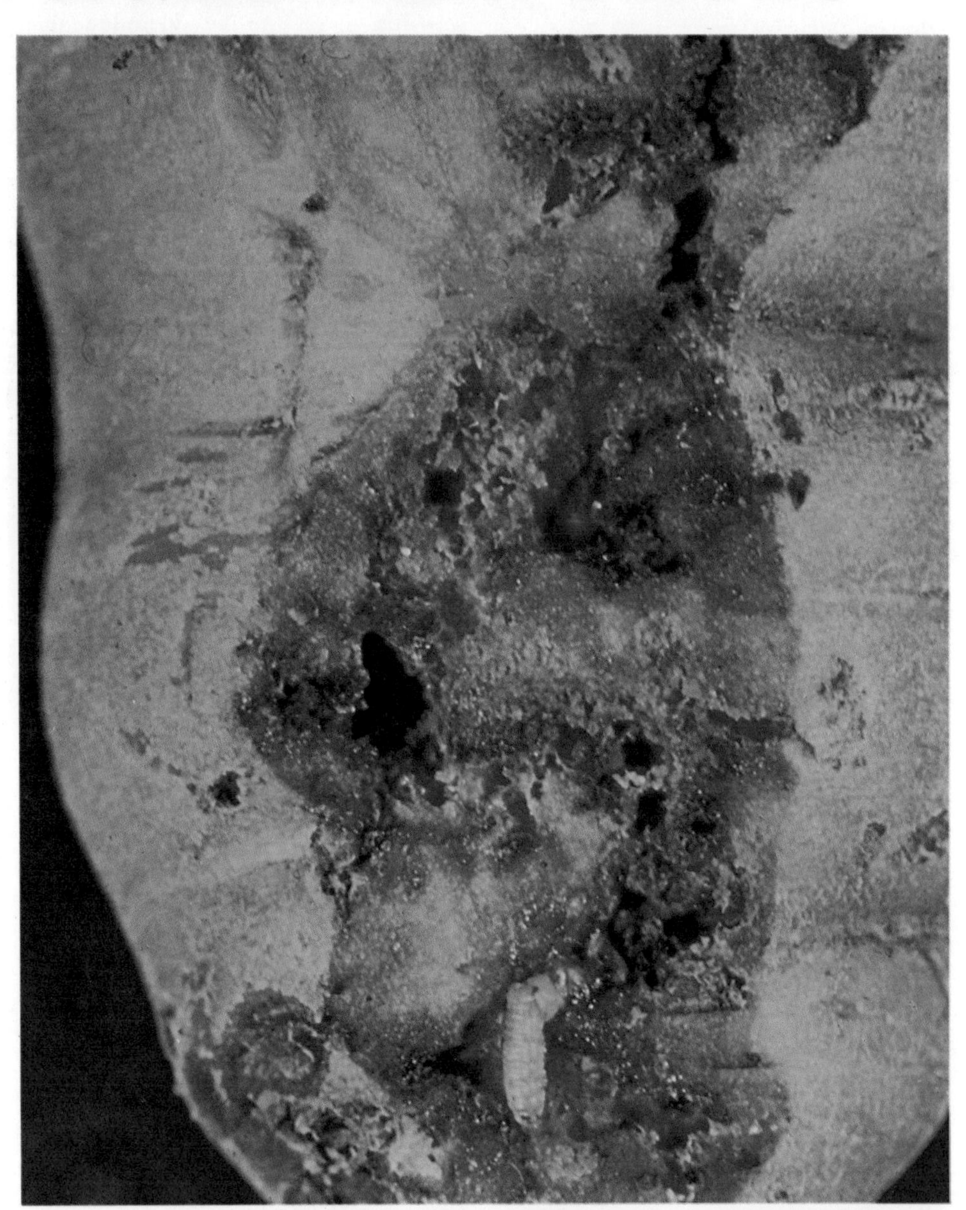

Pests can, and do, attack vegetables at all stages of growth – from seed germination right through to cropping time. Constant vigilance is needed to guard against this type of damage, and some understanding of the nature of plant pests and the timing of their attacks is helpful in planning effective countermeasures.

Seedling pests

Seedlings are liable to attack by soil-borne pests from the moment germination begins. These are the unseen killers that are the main cause of gaps in seed rows or even total failure of the sowing. Insurance against these pests is cheaply and easily obtained by the use of a combined insecticide/fungicide seed dressing. Alternatively, HCH (formerly known as BHC), diazinon or bromophos powders can be dusted into the open seed drills at sowing time.

Root flies

The larvae of cabbage-root fly and carrot fly are common and damaging pests. The female lays her eggs on the soil surface close to the developing seedling and the grubs then burrow down to feed on the root or bulb. In the early stages there are no obvious signs of damage and it is only when the plants are beyond recovery that the extent of the attack becomes apparent. So here again it is important to take preventative action by applying bromophos, diazinon or HCH around the bases of the young plants. As a wise precaution, make a second application about three weeks after the first, to insure against repeat attacks. Carrot fly can also attack parsnips so this crop, too, should be treated in the same way.

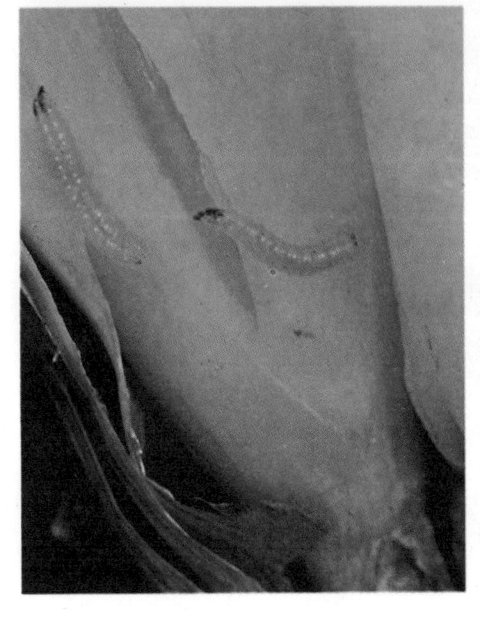

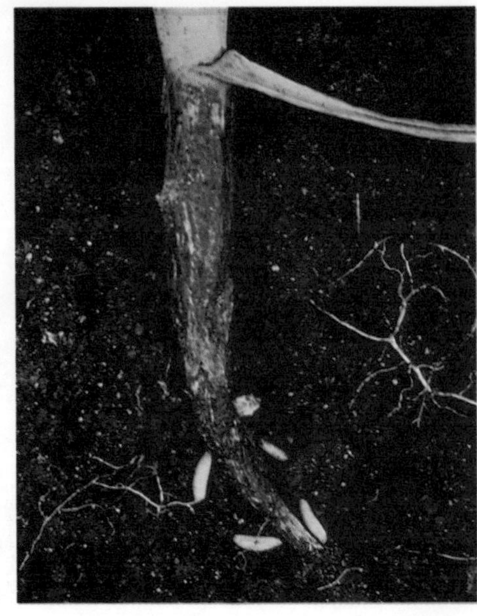

Flea beetles

These tiny beetles live in the soil and are most active at night. Consequently they are not too easily spotted. The damage they cause is, however, only too obvious as the young leaves of the seedlings become pitted with small, round holes. This damage greatly reduces seedling vigour and can lead to the death of the

Left: three examples of plants suffering attack from root-fly larvae – (top) carrot root fly, (bottom left) onion fly and (bottom right) cabbage-root fly
Right: pea moth maggots can quickly bore their way into developing pods
Below: radishes and turnips are especially susceptible to the ravages of flea beetles
Bottom: pea and bean weevils bite tell-tale semi-circular notches out of the leaf margins

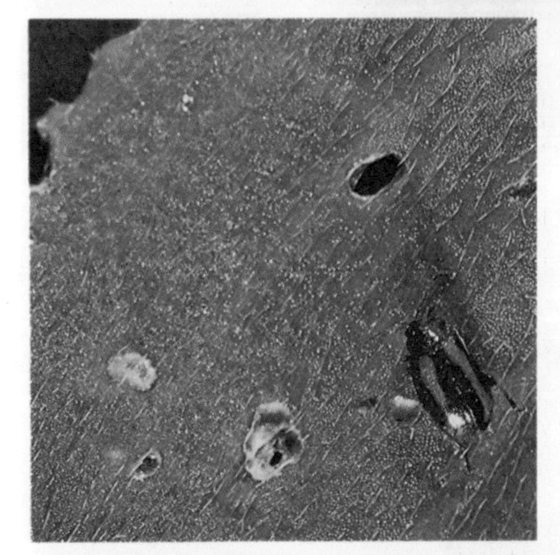

plants. Luckily these pests are readily controlled with an HCH dust. Radishes, turnips, cabbages and other brassicas are vulnerable to attack.

Pea and bean weevils

These small, beetle-like insects live in the soil and commonly feed at night on the foliage of peas and broad beans, biting semi-circular notches out of the leaf margins. Plants damaged by these pests are not killed, but their cropping potential is reduced. So it is well worthwhile to spray both the plants and the surrounding soil with a general garden insecticide at the first sign of attack.

Slugs

Slugs and snails can do enormous damage in the vegetable garden to both seedlings and mature plants. Not only do they gnaw at the stems at soil level but they can also climb and eat the foliage. Most species of slugs and snails are readily killed by spreading slug pellets on the soil around the threatened plants. This treatment, however, is not effective against the keeled slug that is so damaging to potato tubers. This small, dark-coloured slug spends all its life in the soil and is not attracted to the poisoned bait. The only way of reducing crop damage from this pest is to restrict potato plantings to early varieties that are less prone to attack.

Caterpillars and maggots

If these larval forms of butterflies, moths and flies are not controlled they can cause a lot of damage to vegetable crops. Leaf-eating caterpillars of the cabbage white butterfly and other species rapidly make all kinds of brassica crops inedible. Not only do they eat their way into the heads of the vegetables but they also foul the leaves with their green excrement. So it is important to deal with these pests at the first sign of attack. Make regular checks on the undersides of the leaves for clusters of yellow or orange eggs. Any clusters that are found should be rubbed off and the plants given a thorough spraying with a general insecticide. This will deal with any eggs that have been missed and will also give short-term protection against further attacks. Since attacks by these pests can go on over a fairly long period, be vigilant throughout the summer.

Large drab-coloured caterpillars, called cutworms, that live in the surface layer of the soil, can be very damaging to lettuce and other salad crops. Cutworms eat through the plant stems at soil level and the first indication of their presence is when the stems are completely severed and the attacked plants wilt. Cutworms can be controlled by using a spray-strength solution of HCH, diazinon or pirimiphos-methyl as a heavy soil drench along the crop rows.

The young grubs of the pea moth bore their way into the developing pods, infesting the peas and making them inedible. These pests can only be controlled in the short period between the eggs being laid and the entry of the grub into the pod. So spray the plants at early blossoming and then give a repeat spray about a fortnight later.

White blisters on the leaves of celery plants indicate an attack by celery fly. The adult females lay eggs on the underside of the leaves and the young grubs quickly tunnel into the leaf tissue. They then continue to feed inside the leaf, thus producing the characteristic white blisters. Protective spraying with a general insecticide is one way of dealing with these pests. Established infections, however, can only be eliminated by the use of chemicals such as pirimiphos-methyl that can penetrate the leaf tissue and kill off the grubs within the blisters.

Aphides

Aphides can be very troublesome pests since they not only weaken the plants by sucking the sap but can also transmit virus diseases. Blackfly, for instance, are major pests on all types of beans since they damage the flowers and reduce the set of pods. The traditional method of dealing with blackfly of broad beans is to pinch out the growing tips at the first sign of infestation. A more modern approach is to spray with a systemic aphicide such as menazon. Greenfly and blackfly sprays should also be used on runner beans and on French beans where it is not practicable to pinch out the growing tips.

Greenfly can attack most vegetable crops but are particularly damaging on lettuce and carrots. Here again the application of a good greenfly killer should be made at the first sign of attack. Brassica crops are subject to attack by grey aphides that quickly build up into massive infestations. So regular inspections coupled with prompt and thorough spray treatments are necessary to ensure clean, healthy crops.

Most types of aphides are readily seen and easily recognized. Root aphides, however, which live in the soil and attack plant roots (lettuce are particularly vulnerable), are generally not noticed till infested plants wilt and die. When these are lifted it will be seen that the roots are covered with a greyish, 'cottony' mass of aphides. Should this type of infestation be observed then it is a good idea to apply a heavy solid drench with a general insecticide before making further sowings.

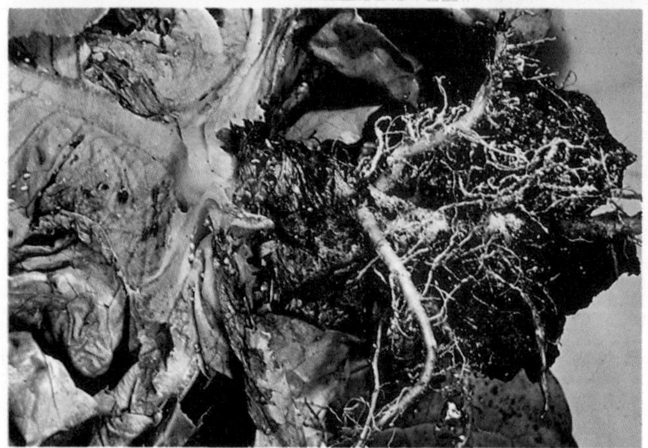

Above: bean that has become heavily infested by blackfly, the bean's major adversary
Left: lettuce root aphides are not often spotted until plants wilt and die

Whitefly

In recent years, cabbage whitefly has become a major pest of all types of brassicas. Like aphides, whitefly weaken the plants by sucking the sap. They also foul the plants with sticky excretions of honeydew that favours the development of disfiguring sooty moulds. Unfortunately whitefly are rather difficult to control because of their complicated life cycle. Crawling larvae hatch out of eggs that are laid on the leaves. These larvae pass through several growth stages before changing into pupae from which new adults hatch out. Only the winged adults are susceptible to most general insecticides, so a minimum of three sprays at 3–4 day intervals is necessary in order to deal with emerging adults that continue to develop from the resistant larval stages. Bioresmethrin, resmethrin and pirimiphos-methyl, however, do have some effect on the larval stages and so products containing these insecticides are to be preferred for whitefly control.

Use of pesticides

Some gardeners are afraid to use pesticides on edible crops because they consider that these treatments may leave harmful residues. But in the development of garden chemicals, several years of intensive research are carried out to ensure their safety in use. For instance, it must be firmly established that the chemicals quickly break down into harmless substances following their application to plants. The speed with which this happens varies with different chemicals so it is important to read the directions for use on the product label. These clearly state what interval must be left between the last spray application and the harvesting of the crop. Provided that this instruction is obeyed there is no risk of the crop being contaminated.

A GLOSSARY OF KITCHEN GARDEN TERMS

Like most other specialists, gardeners have their own words and phrases to describe certain things. Here we list the most common kitchen garden terms, giving a simple explanation in each case.

The following selection of terms is given in alphabetical order for easy reference.

Acid and alkaline An acid soil is one that is deficient in lime, and an alkaline soil one that has enough lime. The degree of acidity or alkalinity is measured by something known as the pH scale – below pH 7 being acid and above it, alkaline. Most vegetables do well in a soil that is slightly alkaline.

Aphides A general term embracing greenfly, blackfly, whitefly and the grey cabbage aphid.

Blanching The practice of excluding light from the stems and/or leaves of a vegetable, usually to improve the flavour. Celery, chicory, leeks and endive all need blanching in this way.

Blind A 'blind' plant is one without a growing point, sometimes the case among the brassicas. As these plants will never make anything except outside leaves, they should be thrown away as soon as you find them.

Bolting Vegetables that run up to seed before their time are said to 'bolt'. This sometimes happens with lettuce, particularly after transplanting in a dry period, and also affects beetroot and carrots, especially when beetroot are sown early. The most common cause is a check to growth.

Brassicas The generic term for greens and brussels sprouts. Swedes, turnips, kohl rabi and radishes are also members of the brassica family.

Buttoning A term applied to cauliflowers when the curd begins to open out while it is still quite small. It is usually caused by the growth of the plant being checked in some way.

Catch-crop Another word for intercrop. Any crop that can be grown quickly between the rows of a slower crop.

Clamp A heap of potatoes or roots covered with straw and then a layer of soil, for winter storage.

Clove A segment of a bulb, often used in connection with shallots or garlic.

Compost Manure made by the rotting of waste vegetable matter. The word is also used to describe a particular medium for seed sowing or potting – for example, the John Innes composts.

Cordon A method of training fruit, especially apples and pears, that keeps plants to a single stem. A cordon-grown tomato, for example, is one that has the sideshoots pinched out as they form.

Curd The head of a cauliflower.

Dibber A steel-pointed stick, about 30cm (12 in) long, with a box- or T-handle, used for making holes for plants when they are transplanted.

Drawn A plant is said to be 'drawn' when it has been brought on too quickly. The result is a spindly, pale-coloured plant. Avoid these when buying young tomato, celery or brassica plants.

Drill A narrow furrow, made with the corner of a hoe, into which seeds are scattered or sown at intervals.

Earthing-up Drawing soil up to a plant, as with potatoes to prevent greening of the tubers, or with celery and leeks for blanching. Earthing-up may also be done to stabilize plants and give them a better root hold.

Eye The growth bud of a potato tuber.

F.1 hybrid A first cross of two plants that have been inbred to 'fix' certain desirable characteristics. In vegetables, F.1 hybrids are usually of better colour and shape than non-hybrids, and are also more uniform in size.

Foliar feed Feeding a plant through the leaves by spraying or watering with a proprietary solution. This is of value for leafy crops such as brussels sprouts or sweet corn.

Green manuring Growing a crop such as rape or mustard to dig into the soil to improve the humus content.

Haulm The top growth of plants, particularly when used in connection with potatoes or peas.

Humus The dark, residual material of decayed vegetable matter or animal manures. It is of particular value in all soils as it improves both the structure and water-holding properties.

'In good heart' A gardener speaks of a soil being 'in good heart' when it is a rich, fertile loam, well supplied with humus. The opposite terms are 'poor' or 'hungry'.

In situ Sowing seeds where the plants are to remain, as distinct from sowing in a box or nursery bed (for transplanting).
Intercrop Same as catch crop.
Light The sliding lid of a garden frame.
Liquid manure This can be made by putting some manure in a hessian bag and suspending it in a tub of water. Leave for several days, and then stir it well, diluting it until it is the colour of weak tea. Proprietary liquid manures may also be bought and should be used according to the instructions on the bottle.
Loam Ideal garden soil – neither too clayey nor too sandy.
Mulch A layer of compost, lawn-mowings, peat, sawdust, well-rotted manure or black polythene put down between rows of vegetables. The objects are to conserve moisture and to smother weeds. Always water soil thoroughly before putting down a mulch, and do not push it right up to the plants – leave a slight gap so that rain can get in.
Root run The area taken up by the roots of a plant.
Set A small, immature bulb – an onion, for example – that is planted to grow on.

Previous page: lettuce that have bolted
Right: spraying a foliar feed over the leaves of a crop of sweet corn
Below: humus content of soil is improved if green manure is dug in during autumn

Spit A spade's depth of soil. To dig 'one spit deep' is to turn the soil over to the depth of the spade.
Stopping Halting the growth of a plant by pinching out the growing point. This is done with tomatoes when the plants have set as many trusses of fruit as are likely to ripen, and also with marrow, cucumber and melon to make the plants produce flowering sideshoots on which fruits will form in due course.
Strain A particular selection of a variety, often referred to as a 'good strain' or a 're-selected strain'.

Tilth Soil worked down to receive a crop. 'A fine tilth' is a soil that has been raked down fine and even.
Tine The prong of a fork, rake or cultivator.
Top dressing An application of well-rotted compost, or a fertilizer that is spread on the soil surface, either before or after planting. This may be lightly pricked into the soil with a fork, or can be hoed in during normal cultivation.
Variety A selection – produced either naturally, or more often by breeding – of any kind of fruit or vegetable.

BIBLIOGRAPHY

Furner, Brian. *The Kitchen Garden* (Pan Books, London 1971)
Genders, Roy. *Simple Fruit Growing* (Ward Lock, London 1973)
Genders, Roy. *Simple Vegetable Growing* (Ward Lock, London 1976)
Hall, Martyn T. *Easy Vegetable Growing* (David & Charles, Newton Abbot 1978)
Hessayon, Dr. D. G. *Be Your Own Vegetable Doctor* (PBI Ltd., London 1978)
Hills, Lawrence D. *Grow Your Own Fruit and Vegetables* (Faber, London 1973)
Potter, Fred, and Shackel, Frank. *Suttons Encyclopaedia of Vegetables* (Pelham Books, London 1977)
Seddon, George. *Your Kitchen Garden* (Mitchell Beazley, London 1978)
Shewell Cooper, W. E. *Basic Book of Vegetable Growing* (Barrie & Jenkins, London 1977)
Simmons, Alan. *Simmons Manual of Fruit* (David & Charles, London 1978)
Simons, A. J. *The New Vegetable Grower's Handbook* (Penguin Books 1962)
Wood, Denis, and Crosby, Kate. *Grow It and Cook It* (Faber, London 1975)
The Fruit Garden Displayed (Royal Horticultural Society, London 1977)
The Vegetable Garden Displayed (Royal Horticultural Society, London 1975)

INDEX

Page numbers in italic refer to illustrations